GROWING
A BUSINESS

RUPERT MERSON is adjunct associate professor of strategy and entrepreneurship at London Business School, where he teaches a range of courses around entrepreneurship and business growth. In 2015 he won prizes as best teacher at both LBS and INSEAD. Formerly a partner at BDO, he now runs his own consultancy advising firms on how to manage growth. He is also the author of *Rules Are Not Enough.*

GROWING A BUSINESS

STRATEGIES FOR LEADERS & ENTREPRENEURS

Rupert Merson

The
Economist | Books

THE ECONOMIST IN ASSOCIATION WITH PROFILE BOOKS LTD

First published in Great Britain in 2016 by
Profile Books
3 Holford Yard
Bevin Way
London WC1X 9HD
www.profilebooks.com

This is an extensively revised and updated version of *The Economist Guide to Managing Growth* by Rupert Merson, first published by Profile Books in 2011.

Typeset in EcoType by MacGuru Ltd
info@macguru.org.uk

Printed in Great Britain by Clays, Elcograf S.p.A

A CIP catalogue record for this book is available from the British Library

ISBN 978 1 78125 242 0
eISBN 978 1 78283 047 4

Contents

List of figures and tables   ix

1   **Introduction: the trouble with growth**   1

2   **Stages of growth**   6
    From leadership to management   6
    Modelling growth   10
    The problem of the final stage: re-creation   26
    Rethinking the dimensions of growth   29
    Growth models: problems and practice   31

3   **Growth enablers and drivers**   37
    A must or a maybe?   37
    Different ambitions and attitudes   42
    The expectations of financiers: potential tensions   43
    New products and services   47
    Markets and industries   60
    The economic environment   69

4   **Growth barriers**   80
    Internal barriers   80
    External barriers   97

5   **Measuring and describing growth**   102
    Revenue, turnover and sales   102

Market share 104
Profit/income: gross and net 105
Headcount and asset capacity 110
Growth: the shareholders' perspective 112
Range and depth 119
Other measures 119
Difficulties of assessment and interpretation 120
Pace and capacity 123

6 **Financing growth** 127
Generating and managing cash 127
Managing the investment in growth 131
Growing too fast 132
External sources of finance 133
Equity finance 138
Exit 146
Going public 147

7 **People and growth** 156
Recruitment 156
Getting the best from people 157
Remuneration 162
Making it a team effort 167
Intangible strengths and vulnerabilities 172

8 **Different types of growth** 177
Hypergrowth 177
Organic growth 179
Inorganic growth by acquisition 183
Inorganic growth by merger 190
Other types of inorganic growth 192
Replication: franchising and licensing 195
Organic *and* inorganic growth 198

9   **Planning for growth**   199
    Accounting for growth drivers and barriers   199

10 **The future of growth**   208
    Bigger is better   209
    Technology and the size of the firm   211
    Small is beautiful   212

    Glossary: an A–Z of growth   215
    Acknowledgements   256
    Notes and further reading   257
    Index   263

Figures and tables

Figures

1.1 US business registrations: number of employees 4
2.1 The leadership/management matrix 7
2.2 Greiner's five-phase model 12
2.3 The Adizes model 20
2.4 The DIAMOND model 22
2.5 Overlapping stages on the DIAMOND model 24
2.6 The Bhidé model 30
3.1 The BCG matrix 52
3.2 Crossing the chasm 54
3.3 Ansoff's two-by-two matrix 58
3.4 Porter's five forces 64
4.1 A matrix structure 93
5.1 The business risk exposure calculator 125
8.1 Process drivers: the best and worst transactions 187
9.1 Internal strengths and weaknesses matrix 201
9.2 Force-field analysis 203

Tables

2.1 The DIAMOND framework 34
7.1 Belbin's role types 169
9.1 Business plan contents 205

1

Introduction: the trouble with growth

THE FOUR FOUNDERS of a software resale and implementation business receive an offer to buy their company. They did not know that it was for sale. As they think things through, it occurs to at least one of them that they had not intended to found a business in the first place. They had all been made redundant by the same company at the same time, and as part of their redundancy package they had been allowed to see some projects through to completion; but a few projects had turned into a few more, and soon they were winning new clients, providing new services, recruiting more staff and finding offices.

The offer to buy the business forces these accidental entrepreneurs to think hard about the business and what they want to do with it. It also forces them to think about themselves. One founder argues that accepting the offer is the obvious thing to do: they had not intended to found a business and now someone is offering a decent sum of money for it; surely they should take the money and get on with the rest of their lives. Another thinks differently: the business has only just started; imagine how much more could be done with it over the next few years. The other two do not know what to think, but they do know that since the offer letter arrived they have gone from building the business to arguing about whether to sell it, and in so doing they have ceased to pay attention to the business itself.

Not having been in this situation before, the four founders do not know that the decisions the offer to buy the business is forcing on them are typical of the decisions asked of countless other managers in successful growing businesses. Selling the business is the easy thing to do: the problems of growth will be passed on to another set of stakeholders and the founders can go their separate ways. The implications of not selling the business are much more complex. For example, what will they do with the business? Should they invest in more service lines and products? Should they sell into different industries? Should they sell overseas? Do they need more office space? Rather than sell the company, should they look to buy someone else's? Is one type of growth better than another? What led them to contemplate accepting the offer to buy? Are they worried about things changing? How much does a business change as it grows, or does it just get bigger? If it does change, how? To what extent could and should they control the rate of growth in the business? What are the real costs of growth: not just the financial costs but the personal costs, particularly to those inside the organisation? What are the enablers of next year's growth, and are there levers they could pull that would help the business grow further and faster? What are the barriers to future growth? Is growth necessary? Is growth desirable?

Part of the problem is the unstable nature of the subject; managers, particularly those ambitious for growth, have to get used to thinking about organisations as transient, in a permanent state of flux. Too much business thinking implies a future state when the business will have "arrived"; more than just achieving stability, it will have reached a stage where the principal management challenge will be to keep it going. But this sort of stasis, even in a successful company, is illusory. Many experienced managers will remember their younger, ambitious selves walking into a new organisation and quickly forming a view of what is wrong with it. "When I'm in charge I'll sort out this and correct that and fire him and promote her – and everything will then be fine." But with the benefit of experience and hindsight these individuals realise that management is not that simple; that problems change even as you attempt to solve them; and that next year's problem is complicated by rather than resolved by the solution to last year's problem. Even if growth is a consequence of success, it brings organisational challenges that threaten the success that caused it. Conversely, to sustain growth it is important to realise that what worked last year will not necessarily work next year; an organisation that wants to manage growth successfully needs to change things that are not yet broken.

The problems brought by change inside an organisation are compounded by changes outside it. Indeed, growth in a business itself often triggers change in a market and industry, which in turn demands further change in the business. Growth may attract competitors, competing technologies and regulators, as well as customers from different markets with different expectations.

Growth gives rise to problems for businesses of all sizes. Different divisions in a big business evolve at different speeds and may therefore be at different stages of evolution, each with its own problems, presenting additional challenges to the organisation as a whole: how to reconcile the competing and contradictory plans of one division with another is a particular growth challenge for the bigger business. Mergers, joint ventures and acquisitions – inorganic rather than organic growth options – present even more challenges, not least with integration. Small businesses have their own particular sort of growth challenge as they seek to establish credibility as well as culture, brand and identity; develop secure lines of supply and sustainable relationships with customers, suppliers and financiers; and manage the changing relationship between owners and managers. An established business in one country investing in a small venture in another needs to acknowledge not just the legal and cultural differences between the two countries, but also the differences between managing a large, corporate business and a small entrepreneurial firm.

Businesses that fail to manage growth become its victims. Some businesses go bust, not for lack of potential, but because they fail to manage the consequences of the growth they have

FIG 1.1 **US business registrations: number of employees, 2008**

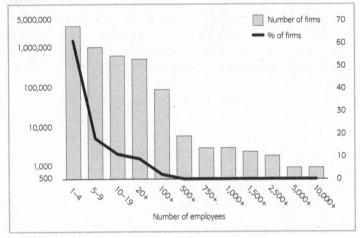

Source: US Census Bureau

achieved. Not least of the problems created by growth is the financial pressure it causes.

Summarised like this it is amazing that any business bothers growing at all. Many cannot or just do not. Figure 1.1 shows that of some 5.9 million businesses registered in the US as having any employees during 2008, over 3.6 million (61%) had fewer than five. As a percentage of all businesses, those with more than 500 employees scarcely register on the graph.

Of course, there are thousands of small businesses around the world, many of which no doubt provide satisfactory returns to those who run them, who have no wish for the business to grow. However, for every business that is content with its current size, there are many with ambitions to grow which struggle with the issues that growth presents.

This book is for them. It draws on the thinking of academics and business people as well as the experience of those working in business in its aim to help managers in their pursuit of growth. It covers a variety of subjects – strategy, performance measurement and management, people management, sales and marketing, finance – and takes into account differences in business size, sector and location. Above all, this book argues that managers and owners who anticipate and manage the challenges of growth give themselves the best chance of ensuring that growth is secure and sustainable.

The four individuals described at the beginning of this chapter took advice and evaluated the offer to buy the business. The amount seemed large, but in reality it significantly undervalued the business. They all agreed that the best option was to grow the business themselves, but in a disciplined and structured manner. They drew up a plan for growth for the next three years; they identified market opportunities open to them and selected the most promising, thus ensuring their efforts were focused; they estimated how fast they could realistically expect to grow funding from internally generated cash flow, thus obviating the need to take external finance; they identified key resource constraints and drew up short- and medium-term plans, including recruitment plans, for addressing these.

They also considered their own ambitions. The founder who had initially argued in favour of the sale decided that he was happiest as a project leader and client-facing manager. He did not want to pay the personal price that growth would have demanded of him, so he stepped back from the senior team, keeping his equity but taking less in pay and bonuses. The other three allocated specific senior roles and responsibilities among themselves and recruited to fill any gaps. They monitored progress against their plan at six-monthly intervals. Some three years after the initial offer to buy the company they sold it, but to a different acquirer. This time the decision to sell was theirs, and the amount they got for the company was many times that originally offered. Two of the four founders stayed with the company after the sale and looked forward to a new set of growth challenges.

Stages of growth

WHEN BUSINESSES GROW they do not just get bigger. Growth delivers qualitative as well as quantitative change. A changing business makes changing demands of its managers. Is it possible to generalise about these changes? If so, might it be possible to anticipate the problems that growth will bring in the future and thus reduce the risks associated with it?

From leadership to management

A good place to start considering the changes caused by growth is to look at the changing role of the founder.

Abraham Zaleznik, then on the faculty of Harvard Business School, was, in 1977, one of the earliest management writers to draw a distinction between creative, inspirational and enthusiastic types, and organised, disciplined, sensible managerial types, using the labels "leader" for the former and "manager" for the latter. Figure 2.1 shows this distinction using the leadership/management matrix from John Kotter's book, Leading Change.[1] It is a distinction that has also been used to contrast entrepreneurs in new businesses and other members of the management team in growing businesses.

Most businesses start high on leadership and low on management. If businesses are to stand a chance of developing into something sustainable, they will need even more of these leadership qualities – energy, inspiration and creativity. A business in its early stages will thus move from 1 to 2 if it is to evolve, dominated

FIG 2.1 **The leadership/management matrix**

by individuals with these foundational qualities of leadership. Organisation, discipline and governance in these early stages are often closely associated with the force of personality of the founder. Indeed, the organisation hardly exists as a separate entity at all, and the business is wholly identified with its founders and owners.

But things have to change as the business grows. In 1997 Jeremy Newman, former CEO of BDO International, wrote:[2]

> *New businesses are started by entrepreneurs who, through some combination of wisdom and luck, create and implement a successful business strategy. The business expands and profits grow and with this comes the need to hire professional managers. So people are recruited and promoted to manage, to cope with the growing bureaucracy and to prevent things getting out of control. And so the organisation grows and management grows to cope with it.*

The introduction of "management" heralds reporting timetables, appraisal schemes, formal agendas and other manifestations of the way to run a "proper" business. From an organisation that thrives on the high octane of entrepreneurship and the excitement of chasing after the next sale, the new business has to evolve into one in which the disciplines of management have far more influence. On the matrix, the business moves from 2 to 3, where leadership and management are in balance; where there is enough business discipline and governance to sustain the business, but not so much that the qualities of entrepreneurship and leadership are threatened or damaged.

For many businesses, staying in 3 sounds good in theory but is difficult to achieve in practice. Some entrepreneurs ("leaders") feel obliged to turn themselves into managers, or at least develop management capability, acknowledging both a fundamental change in role and the need to acquire and utilise new skills. But although people can change and develop, it is rare to find an individual who can operate comfortably at both ends of the leadership/management spectrum.

Rather than take on the managerial role themselves, entrepreneurs often best serve their own and their business's interests by seeking to recruit the necessary management expertise. But in doing this, entrepreneurs should realise that their own role is still likely to need to change. Entrepreneurs and their new managers may not see eye-to-eye, and entrepreneurs who do not adapt to their new organisational circumstances are heading for conflict with their new management teams. This often results in damage to the business and the acrimonious departure of either the manager or the entrepreneur. Too often, a reluctance to face up to the consequences of what is an inevitable tension leads some businesses to duck the problem in the first place by deferring the necessary change until a crisis forces it on them. But businesses serious about sustainable growth must introduce a management infrastructure. Family businesses can be particularly prone to deferring this kind of management professionalisation.

Many people with a managerial bent assume that the management force is more important than the entrepreneurial one. Indeed, this is a tendency in much business thinking. As Newman says:

> This in turn stifles leadership and encourages management and because the business is successful, managers begin to believe that they are the best and their idiosyncrasies become part of the culture of the organisation.

Although it is true that a business without decent management will not survive for long, a business in which the management impulse takes over and the entrepreneurial spirit is squeezed out will become yet another over-managed, under-inspired, middle-aged business on a glide-path to history. Premature ageing in an organisation is almost as worrying as a refusal to let it mature. This is often a characteristic of start-ups established by large companies, as a result of the mistaken assumption that the start-up is just a small version of the big one. In the case of a stand-alone joint venture established by two UK listed companies (one a retailer, the other a broadcaster), the new chief executive was keen to "establish an entrepreneurial culture" but said that his first priority was to discuss implementing a pension scheme for himself and his team. Such a worry about retirement might be prudent but is a sure sign of a business on its way to being old before its time. That it is common for the finance director to succeed the entrepreneur as chief executive in a growing business would seem to illustrate how managers take over from leaders and how the sober discipline of accountancy is likely to supersede the energy, creativity and propensity to take risk of the founder. According to a survey reported on by Grant Thornton in December 2014, some 85% of those in US *Fortune* 1000 corporations believe the chief finance officer would be the most appropriate choice for succeeding the chief executive.

As well as highlighting a contrast between the entrepreneur and the more managerially and governance-minded members of a team, the tension between leadership and management might be turned into a model outlining what is for many businesses a key transformation in their growth and development. The model is primarily about different types of people, but indirectly it hints at different stages of development that all businesses have to pass through as they grow, and suggests how the managerial, organisational, strategic and operational imperatives differ significantly from one stage to the next. In short, as well as growing, businesses have to grow up.

Modelling growth

When those who study business growth have attempted to generalise about its implications, their thinking has often taken the form of a growth model, an analytic framework that describes the stages that businesses pass through as they evolve, the characteristics of each stage, and the changes necessary to facilitate the move of the company from one stage to the next. The remainder of this chapter outlines some of the best-known growth models and explores how useful they are for those trying to grow their businesses or deal with the consequences of growth.

Evolution and revolution: the Greiner model

Larry E. Greiner, professor of management and organisation at Marshall School of Business at the University of Southern California, published his article "Evolution and Revolution as Organisations Grow" in 1972.[3] It is not the first growth model, but it is the earliest one still in common use in the classroom and in the business strategist's office. Greiner initially proposed five phases of growth through which businesses pass, adding a sixth stage in 1998.

Although each of Greiner's phases starts with a period of evolution, it ends in revolution, a period of "substantial organisational turmoil and change". How each revolutionary period is resolved determines whether or not the organisation will develop further.

The periods of revolution are at the heart of the model. Greiner's notion of revolution draws attention to the difficulty as well as the inevitability of change in the development of an organisation. The "critical task" for management in each revolutionary period is to find the new set of practices that will become the basis of managing the next period of evolutionary growth. But in so doing managers "experience the irony of seeing a major solution in one period become a major problem in a later period".

The five phases are shown in Figure 2.2 and are as follows:

- **Creativity.** In the phase of creativity, the founder's energies are consumed by doing rather than managing and decisions are taken quickly and reactively. It ends in a crisis of leadership, in which the business addresses the question of who will establish some necessary order in the chaos. Resolution of the crisis might well involve the recruitment of a "capable business manager".

- **Direction.** The first revolution will be followed by a phase of direction, in which management systems and processes are introduced and developed and communication and management become more formal. As the organisation grows, however, such systems, designed initially to support growth, end up constricting it. There is a crisis of autonomy, in which middle managers are "torn between following procedures and taking initiative on their own".

- **Delegation.** The second revolution is resolved by the establishment and development of a more decentralised structure in a phase of delegation, during which senior executives manage by exception and junior managers have budget and profit responsibility for divisions and departments. But the revolution, a "crisis of control", occurs when senior executives sense that they are losing control of a business with more and more offshoots. For some a reimposition of central control is the obvious way forward.

FIG 2.2 **Greiner's five-phase model**

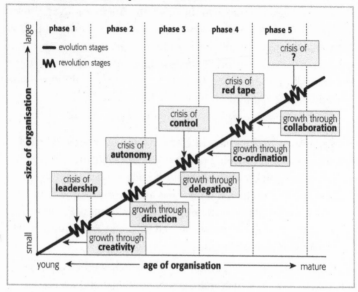

Source: Larry Greiner, "Evolution and Revolution as Organisations Grow", *Harvard Business Review*, 1972

■ **Co-ordination.** However, going backwards is rarely an option for a business with ambition. The third revolution results in a phase in which senior managers use formal systems for achieving co-ordination. Some functions are centralised, capital expenditure is carefully controlled, formal planning processes are established, and share options and company-wide bonus schemes may be used to "encourage employees to identify with the organisation as a whole". But this focus on systems and co-ordination ends in a crisis of red tape, in which "procedures take precedence over problem solving".

■ **Collaboration.** The fourth revolution results in a phase of collaboration in which teamwork, social control and self-discipline replace "formal control". The focus shifts

from process to problem solving, and from headquarters
to interdisciplinary teams. Matrix structures (see Chapter
4, Figure 4.1) are established to balance and resolve the
competing thinking of different interest groups. Above all,
there is a shift from individuals and systems to the collective.

Greiner, in his first article on the subject, said that he did
not know how phase five would end. He hypothesises that the
revolution "will centre around the psychological saturation of
employees who grow emotionally and physically exhausted from
the intensity of teamwork and the heavy pressure for innovative
solutions". He imagines organisations with structures that allow
employees to "rest, reflect and revitalise themselves", making more
use of sabbaticals, and balancing structured work and reflection.
In so doing, Greiner is attempting to describe not so much the
next phase of growth of businesses in general but the organisation
of the future. Thus he is one of the first to discover what many
writers about growth have subsequently discovered: that the early
phases of growth are a lot easier to describe and analyse than the
later phases.

Greiner is also unusual in being allowed to be his own best
critic. His 1972 piece was reprinted as a *Harvard Business Review*
"classic" in 1998. In his comments on his own work after an
interval of 26 years it is phase five that comes in for the most robust
criticism. He suggests that his "speculation that 'psychological
saturation' is the crisis ending phase five now seems wrong", and
that the crisis is likely to be the realisation that there is no longer
an internal solution. To keep growing the organisation needs to
look outside itself – for partners, or maybe for "opportunities
to sell itself to a bigger company". Indeed, Greiner suggests
that maybe there is a sixth phase of growth dependent on such
"extra-organisational solutions", and gives General Electric as an
example of an organisation in which a group of companies has
been built up around a core.

Greiner's model is presented as a series of hypotheses. He

reminds us that in the original article "the phases outlined ... are merely five in number and are still only approximations". The article always was an invitation to others to test, refine and, in all likelihood, correct if not contradict his work. Though many have worked on growth, Greiner's model still serves as the standard against which all others are judged.

Does Greiner's version of growth have any practical utility for managers? Greiner thinks so, though his explicit "guidelines for managers" are modest. Managers, he argues, benefit from knowing where they are in the development sequence and therefore understanding when the time to act has come. His model implies that they should recognise the limited range of their own solutions, and that their interventions are time- and context-specific. Solutions which work well in any particular year might not be appropriate for a different set of problems associated with a new growth phase. Greiner argues that the problems of one revolution are sown like seeds in the solutions to a previous revolution.

Greiner's analysis has a lot to commend it. Business leaders do indeed find it useful to plot growth against Greiner's model, using it to help understand the problems it survived last year and anticipate what might be around the corner. The focus on revolution and crisis is also useful. In an ambitious, successful business, change is continuous. If nothing appears in need of change, ask yourself whether you are looking in the right place, or whether complacency is beginning to set in. "Revolution" also draws attention to the pain that growth brings. If you are ambitious and choose to grow your business, you need to acknowledge in advance the problems you will encounter.

The model's simplicity is beguiling for many of those attempting to anticipate and prepare for the changes that growth will bring, but some find it frustrating and unnaturally deterministic. Cynics might see the oscillation between revolution and evolution as a reflection of the times in which the model was created (the early 1970s), with the barriers not long down outside the Sorbonne and Marxism taken much more seriously in academic and political circles than at any time since. Greiner writes about the importance of the forces of history and notes that he has "drawn from the legacies of European psychologists who argue that the behaviour of individuals is determined primarily by past events and experiences rather than by what lies ahead". Indeed, he is dismissive of managers who "fix their gaze outward on the environment and toward the future, as if more precise market projections will provide the organisation with a new identity". But context is crucial, and a manager who attempts to manage without paying attention to it is risking much. Besides, Greiner himself took to speculating about the future even while trying to outline the characteristics of the later phases of the model. He is surely right when he suggests that managers should pay attention to the influence of "past decisions", although he is perhaps unfair in suggesting that these matter more than "present events or market dynamics". In the real world business leaders need to plan, and planning involves an understanding of the present as well as some anticipation of what the future holds, both in the market place and in the company. Business plans are discussed in Chapter 9.

Small business growth: the Churchill model

Neil Churchill is emeritus professor of entrepreneurship at INSEAD in France and has been a distinguished member of the faculty of other institutions. His article "Five Stages of Small Business Growth" was first published in 1983, and has been revised several times since.[4] Churchill and co-author Virginia Lewis explicitly built on the work of five previous thinkers, including Greiner, but take the thinking further by testing his original hypotheses against 83 responses to a questionnaire distributed to 110 owners and managers of successful small companies who had participated in a small-company management programme. They had also identified as best they could the stages in Greiner's model that they had passed through.

Churchill and Lewis concluded that growth models can and do help businesses. When looking at the growth of small businesses, "points of similarity can be organised into a framework that increases our understanding of the nature, characteristics and problems of businesses". Such frameworks can help "in anticipating the key requirements at various points", and can provide bases "for evaluating the impact of present and proposed governmental regulations and policies on one's business". Frameworks can also "aid accountants and consultants in diagnosing problems and matching solutions to smaller enterprises".

Churchill has the benefit of testing his hypotheses empirically. He points out that growth can be difficult to pin down – growth of what? Too many business leaders think only in terms of turnover and headcount, but complexity of product line, rate of change in products or production technology, number of locations and so on are also important. Churchill is right, though the challenge of framework and model making is always to strike the right balance between simplification and complexity. Too close to the former will result in the model failing to reflect the messy business that is reality; too close to the latter will render the framework incomprehensible and unusable. Churchill also challenged the "grow-or-fail hypothesis implicit in the [Greiner] model". Businesses "plateaued ... with some marginally profitable and others very profitable over a period of between 5 and 80 years". He noted that several of his research subjects were not start-ups but were companies purchased while in a "steady-state survival or success stage" which were then moved further along the growth model thanks to a new attitude (and capability) on the part of new owners and managers.

Like Greiner, on whose work his is based, Churchill describes five phases. He has little truck with Greiner's crises, however, and his phases are presented as discrete stages of evolution:

- **Existence.** In the first stage the organisation is fighting for customers and meeting customer needs. Businesses cannot stay at this stage; they get to stage two or they fail.

- **Survival.** The business has shown that it works, but its main concern is still to cover its costs. In anthropological terms it is eking out a subsistence living. Many businesses stay at this stage, including, Churchill argues, "Mom and Pop stores ... [and] manufacturing businesses that cannot get their product or process sold as planned".

- **Success.** In the first version of his model Churchill calls the third stage the success stage. The business is established and sustainable, and this success offers the owner alternatives. The success stage comes in two forms. III-G is the "success-growth substage", during which the owner throws the dice again in pursuit of further growth. Such a path is inherently risky; the owner may lose. III-D is the "success-disengagement substage". Rather than throw the dice again, the owner chooses to take a step back and live off the cash generated by the business, trusting management to run the business conservatively. On the assumption that the economic environment is stable, Churchill sees no reason why a business might not stay in the III-D phase for a long time.

- **Take-off.** A business owner who chooses to throw the dice again in stage III-G and succeeds will reach stage four, which Churchill calls take-off. He writes about the owner's ability to delegate; the ability of the business to generate sufficient cash to satisfy growth; and operational and strategic planning. By this stage the founder may have left the business.

- **Resource-maturity.** The prize for the successful negotiation of stage four is stage five, called resource-maturity. This is the phase inhabited by bigger, stable businesses. Businesses in stage five need to "consolidate and control the financial gains brought on by rapid growth" while retaining "the advantages of small size, including flexibility of response and the entrepreneurial spirit". The biggest danger is that the entrepreneurial spirit will be crushed as management expands. Churchill suggests that there might be a sixth phase called ossification but does not develop his thinking.

Although Churchill was hugely influenced by Greiner, his thinking differs significantly. Churchill recognises that businesses have options. For Greiner, businesses are set on a historically predetermined path. The pace of change might vary, but the sequence of stages is almost predestined. Churchill allows more room for choice. Indeed, stage three of his original model presents the alternatives III-G and III-D – growth or disengagement. This may not be considered a choice at all, rather a sensible recognition that many business leaders, like most players of Monopoly, will choose to give up playing the game rather than see it through to its later stages. That many business leaders choose not to throw the dice again does not introduce flexibility into the model. Indeed, in later versions, Churchill replaces the alternatives III-G and III-D with a more conventional stage three leading to stage four.

Although at first glance it may not seem so, Churchill's model is much more complicated than Greiner's. Introducing alternatives and choices will complicate any model. Churchill also discusses management factors identified in his research that change in importance as a business passes from one stage to the next. Four of these are related to the company itself: financial, personnel, systems and business resources. Four others are associated with the owner: personal goals, operational abilities, management abilities and strategic abilities. Churchill attempts to wrestle with many more variables than Greiner does. Greiner makes do with one graphical representation of this thinking; Churchill struggles to illustrate his thinking with several. On the one hand this complexity reflects the diversity of the real businesses that lie behind his thinking; on the other hand it makes the model less easy to use by managers interested in the fates of their own businesses.

As already indicated, Churchill has over the years made revisions to his model, including the radical replacement of the choice between III-G and III-D. That his thinking has evolved shows how difficult it can be to generalise about how businesses change as they grow.

An anthropomorphic approach: the Adizes model

Ichak Adizes takes a very different approach to growth from both Greiner and Churchill. Adizes was a member of the faculty of UCLA until 1982, when he founded the Adizes Institute.

Adizes, who outlines his approach in his book *Managing Corporate Lifecycles*, is unusual in that he envisages a ten-stage corporate life cycle charting the life of a business not just from birth to success, but also from success to death.[5] His stages are as follows (the labels are his but the descriptions in brackets are mine):

1. Courtship (the creation of the organisation)
2. Infancy (the commencement of trading)
3. Go-go (energetic early growth with the chaos that can result)
4. Adolescence (the organisation is established but still evolving fast and has recently established an identity independent of its founders)
5. Prime (the organisation has reached its "prime of life" and is therefore at its fittest, most competitive and profitable)
6. Stability (though still effective, and often still profitable, the signs of decline are beginning to appear even if they are not properly acknowledged)
7. Aristocracy (few doubt that the organisation has a powerful place in the market, but it is viewed as inflexible and conservative; nimble new market entrants are beginning to take market share, and maybe market trends are changing, leaving the organisation behind)
8. Early bureaucracy (called "recrimination" in some versions of the model – even the organisation itself acknowledges that

FIG 2.3 **The Adizes model**

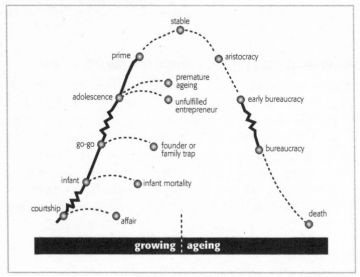

Source: After Ichak Adizes, *Managing Corporate Lifecycles*, Prentice Hall Press, 1999

something is wrong; doubts and internal squabbles distract attention from customer service and the objectives of the organisation)

9. Bureaucracy (attention is focused inwards as the organisation struggles to stay alive; any outward attention is directed at possible exits or the sale of the organisation)

10. Death (or rather the commercial equivalent – one of the various forms of bankruptcy, or protection from bankruptcy – receivership, administration, liquidation – or perhaps sale for break-up)

It is the road to "prime" that matters most to Adizes, and making the changes necessary to keeping your organisation there once you have achieved it.

As Figure 2.3 illustrates, there are several places where Adizes suggests the business can fail. He also uses distinctive language – the language of human development. Adizes is not the only thinker to liken the growth of an organisation to the growth of a human being. Indeed, it can be difficult not to slip into anthropomorphic metaphors when discussing the evolution of the business. Greiner noted the influence on his thinking of the "legacies of European psychologists". But Adizes is distinctive in the extent to which he pushes the analogy.

Undoubtedly, many business founders are comfortable with this sort of thinking, often adopting parent/child-style relationships with the businesses they have created. Their attachment can often seem irrational – for example, when it comes to selling equity in the business, more than one business founder has likened it to selling your children. The risk, of course, when applying the analogy to a growth framework, is one of oversimplification.

The DIAMOND model

The DIAMOND model was created by partners and staff at the London office of BDO Stoy Hayward, now BDO LLP, a global accountancy network. The creators of the model reviewed and critically evaluated the published literature and then tested the resulting hypothetical framework against the experience of the firm's clients. The aim was to synthesise the best of the rest, and produce something business leaders and their advisers could use (see Figure 2.4).

The model envisages seven stages in the growth of a business:

D **Dreaming** up the idea of a new business, developing plans and defining start-up requirements.

I **Initiating** the business plan and inspiring others in order to establish a presence in the market. This is the implementation of the dream.

A **Attacking** the first problems of growth and coping with adolescence. During this stage the business has the ability to survive and it can provide a good living for its owners.

FIG 2.4 **The DIAMOND model**

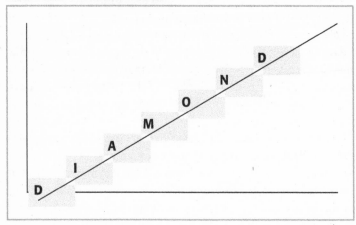

Source: BDO LLP

However, it is not robust enough to sustain a major change in its market or operating environment, and its cash flow and customer base limit its long-term prospects. As a business passes through this stage, the pressures of growth accelerate. Wise and well-advised owners recognise that although the business has succeeded so far, it will not be sustainable for long if it does not anticipate the next stage. For others, failing to recognise and react to the pressure to grow up organisationally can lead to a gradual loss of control, and to accumulating pressures that lead to anxiety rather than action and result in stagnation and even failure.

M **Maturing** the business with an emphasis on establishing controls, systems and methodologies. Management is professionalised to deal with the size and complexity of the customer base or the organisational structure of the business.

O **Overhauling** the organisation with a clear focus on objectives. The business is more competitive and has a strong customer and marketing orientation, but there is a sense that something has been lost after years of going for growth and a consequent yearning to recapture the spirit of the business at start-up – or at least to recapture the essence of entrepreneurship that at times seems threatened by necessary disciplines of control. There has to be, in short, a reaction against the tendency to over-manage and stifle creativity and enterprise if the business is to make it big time.

N Networking the units of the business. Strategic processes have become as important as tactical ones. Maintaining and developing a corporate image are important and, by now, earnings are often being managed for a diverse stakeholder group. The personality of the business – its culture – is now more influential than the personality of the entrepreneur who founded it.

D Diversifying into new products and markets, driving growth through strategic alliances and commercial interdependencies that enable rapid responses to market opportunities. The culture of organisations in this stage is highly focused. The means by which they operate – and the markets in which they choose to do so – are highly flexible. The rate of growth, year on year, often decelerates as a function of the size of the business. This stage also implies a return to the start, the establishment of new businesses within the business in the search for renewal and product development – entrepreneurship reborn as intrapreneurship.

Transitional issues

The use of the DIAMOND mnemonic indicates how far the model has moved from the world of academia and towards that of practical applicability. This is a model to be used, not studied, and other features of the model come from practical experience. Unlike the models discussed so far, the stages, though distinguishable, overlap. There are echoes of Greiner's crises here, but DIAMOND takes them further, turning crises into transitional issues, and

FIG 2.5 **Overlapping stages on the DIAMOND model**

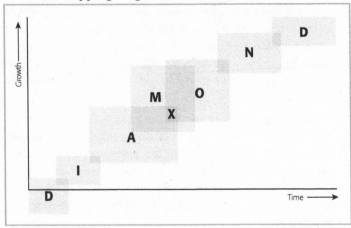

Source: BDO LLP

envisaging that businesses can be in more than one stage of evolution at the same time, and that to presume otherwise is simplistic. Figure 2.5 suggests that growth is not linear. It is possible for a business to exhibit the characteristics of more than one stage of growth at a time.

Greiner's crises in part are a product of the tension between two adjacent stages of evolution, with the problems of the later stage sown in the solutions to the earlier stage. Churchill, when discussing management factors, notes that the skills and qualities required for addressing the problems in one stage of evolution are less relevant to another stage, implying that it is potentially a problem if a business cannot be tidily allocated to one stage of evolution or another.

Some advisers working with real businesses have taken these worries further. A UK clearing bank put together a training programme for managers servicing small and medium-sized businesses with the objective of helping specialist staff appreciate the particular problems their customers faced. The bank also prepared a set of tools, including a diagnostic exercise based on Churchill's model, requiring managers to assess which stage of growth each customer might be in. If a business exhibited characteristics typical of more than one stage, the diagnostic tool invited managers to consider whether that customer might be a credit risk to the bank.

Although the bank is to be commended for acknowledging the distinctive issues that might affect smaller businesses, its interpretation of the implications of a business exhibiting different stages of growth at the same time is surely questionable. Real businesses can use growth models to help them understand challenges and to address them, but invariably real businesses are too complicated to be tidied into one box or another on a model. One firm of real estate agents with an "eat what you kill" culture has sophisticated selling and marketing systems but rudimentary HR processes. The imbalance here is recognised and indeed fostered by its senior managers. This is the sort of business they want to run. Similarly, some companies seeking to innovate establish separate subsidiaries for the purpose of taking the new product or service to market. The subsidiary and its parent are at different stages of evolution; at the same time, both parts of the company need to take advantage of the ties that bind them. Some might argue that each part of the business needs its own model. But this fails to acknowledge the advantages and disadvantages that accrue to the entity in aggregate.

The DIAMOND framework (see Table 2.1 on page 34) has another characteristic that demonstrates its genesis as a management tool rather than an academic framework. In reality, business leaders are rarely interested in plotting the history of their businesses, and the implication of some of the models covered in this chapter is that this is where business managers should start their analysis. Whether their business was in stage three or phase A between 2012 and 2014, or whether the crisis of autonomy took place in 2010 or 2011, are questions of interest to historians and academics rather than managers. Only if the models can shed light on the problems that need to be addressed imminently are they of interest to managers taking today's decisions. Greiner, as has been seen, tries to be useful, encouraging managers to look back into history for insight into today's problems. Even if he is right, managers are rarely persuaded. The DIAMOND framework addresses this by attempting to put more flesh on each of the stages, breaking them down into different dimensions, and inviting managers to consider in more detail the implications of the stage of growth their business happens to be in at present.

Once the present condition of the business is understood, attention can be given to changes necessary to prepare the business for the future. The DIAMOND framework attempts to address this by presenting transitional issues.

The problem of the final stage: re-creation

The models tend to be weakest in their final stages. DIAMOND's networking and diversifying stages echo Greiner's new stage 6, which he speculated about some 16 years after the publication of his first model, but they both seem weak and undefined. Churchill leaves us with a mature business with the threat of ossification on the horizon. Greiner's last stage is still, despite his rethinking, left as a big question mark.

It is as if thinkers believe that although it is possible to generalise about the early phases businesses go through as they grow (not that they can agree among themselves what these early phases look like), thereafter businesses have to find their own and different ways.

Some thinkers, it is true, have attempted to wrestle with the final stages more seriously. Adizes suggests that "prime" is a state to be achieved by big businesses and then sustained through a process of perpetual transformation – from which the only other way is down. One model, outlined in Eric Flamholtz and Yvonne Randle's *Growing Pains*, encourages managers in these later stages to invest time in developing business systems and, particularly, brand and organisational culture, arguing that it is these elements that provide the foundation for sustainable growth.[6] And at least one model, from Denmark, suggests that it is more helpful to think of growth as a wheel and to consider the end of business evolution to be a process of re-creation, with the last stage in a successful business containing the seeds of new businesses which end up demanding their own growth models. In part, re-creation is implied in DIAMOND's overhauling stage, in Churchill's III-G stage and in all Greiner's revolutions. All these models imply a concern about losing sight of the beginnings of the business and the importance of attempting to reconnect with these.

Horizons of growth

One book that considers re-creation in the context of growth in the established business more seriously than most is *The Alchemy of Growth* by Merhdad Baghai, Steve Coley and David White, three McKinsey consultants.[7] Rather than model growth as a series of stages of evolution, they discuss three "horizons" of growth and argue that a business ambitious for growth needs to be active in all three.

- **Horizon one** is the core of the business. It might not be growing particularly fast, but without it the business would not exist. It is where the business started and continues to define its identity. Instead of being run with an eye on aggressive expansion, a horizon one business is run for profit. Efficiency and quality are crucial. In a large accounting firm, horizon one activity might include auditing and tax compliance advice.

- **Horizon two** is less predictable, not least because it is a newer line of business activity. Sometimes the business makes excellent profits out of horizon two activity, but sometimes it makes significant losses. New business is less certain. In horizon one, new business is attracted because of the long-standing reputation of the organisation, but it cannot rely on this for horizon two. In a large accounting firm, horizon two activity might include corporate finance advice.

■ **Horizon three** includes experimentation in new lines of business, few if any of which make money immediately. But this does not mean that horizon three should not be taken seriously. Indeed, Baghai, Coley and White argue that if a mature business is to grow and thrive rather than shrink, it needs to be active in all three horizons, which have a symbiotic relationship with each other. Horizons two and three will help keep horizon one fresh and might turn into new horizon ones in the future. In a large accounting firm, there is always investment in new lines of advice and service, for example in management consultancy and tax planning, of which some will turn into profitable businesses while others wither on the vine.

In a successful business, therefore, the three horizons are not static. Baghai, Coley and White cite, for example, Village Roadshow, an Australian company. Until the 1980s its core horizon one activity was operating local cinemas; the development of a national cinema chain was a horizon two investment along with movie distribution, but the business was already investing in horizon three ideas such as multiplex cinemas and theme parks. By the late 1980s, however, movie distribution had moved into horizon one, theme parks and multiplexes had moved into horizon two, while in horizon three the company was exploring cinemas in Asia as well as TV and film production. By the 1990s, theme parks had moved into horizon one, multiplex cinemas remained in horizon two, and new businesses including entertainment centres and retail stores were being explored in horizon three.

To succeed in all the horizons it is important to recognise that each needs managing in its own way, with different performance measures and different incentives (see Chapter 7). It is unlikely that horizon one people will naturally turn successfully to horizon three activity, or vice versa. Indeed, in a large accounting firm someone who is good at new product development, thinking up new solutions for clients and excited at winning new business, is unlikely to be the best person to lead audit assignments, or would be wasted if given that role. Some of these skills might well be useful in horizon one – hence the importance of the symbiotic relationship of the horizons – but in an increasingly regulated world accountancy firms have needed to think carefully about these links; and where they have not thought, the regulators have thought for them.

Rethinking the dimensions of growth

When defining the stages of growth, the devisers of models tend to assume that the axes against which growth is plotted are time and size. But these assumptions need to be challenged:

- **Time.** Businesses evolve at different speeds. If they pass through the different stages of evolution, they will not do so at the same speed. The time spent in different stages depends on external factors as well as the ambitions and skills of the management team. In businesses that are growing particularly fast, it may be possible to pass through some of the early stages simultaneously, or perhaps for managers to consider missing out some of them out altogether. Businesses that have grown rapidly on the back of technological revolution in particular have experienced rapid growth. Some observers have identified hypergrowth as a different type of growth altogether. (See Chapter 8.)

- **Size.** A question not often asked is "size of what"? Businesses can grow in many dimensions, and which is used on the vertical axis often depends on who is doing the measuring. Many sales managers, particularly those who have grown their businesses from nothing and have successfully attracted new customers and clients, can be seduced into thinking that sales revenue is the obvious measure of size.

FIG 2.6 **The Bhidé model**

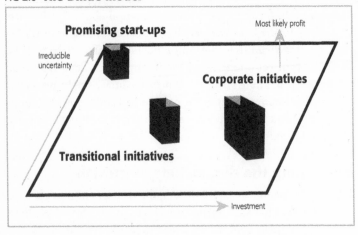

Source: Amar Bhidé, *The Origin and Evolution of New Businesses*, New Oxford University Press, 2000

External shareholders, however, might prefer to measure profit, or returns to investors. Without profit the business will ultimately run out of the capacity to invest; without returns to investors it will run out of capital. There are many examples of businesses that have increased their profits by reducing their turnover. (These financial measures are discussed in Chapter 5.) For general managers the main worry will be the size of the management challenge. For them growth brings complexity. What about employee headcount as a measure of size? Certainly there is a connection between the size of the workforce and the extent of the management challenge. But product range, or number of sites, or geographical spread might also provide appropriate proxies for size.

When considering the evolution of new businesses, Amar Bhidé, a professor at Fletcher School of Law and Diplomacy at Tufts University, focuses less on time and size and pays more attention to risk and irreducible uncertainty, and the relationship of these with profit. In so doing he creates a three-dimensional model of growth (see Figure 2.6).

Bhidé, however, is really drawing attention to a separate factor that changes as organisations evolve from start-up to sustainable business: their appetite for and attitude to risk and the relationship between this and the resources at the disposal of the organisation and planning processes. This is discussed in more detail in Chapters 3 and 4.

Growth models: problems and practice

In recent years the academic community has begun to turn against growth models (see, for example, Jonathan Levie and Benyamin Lichtenstein, "A Terminal Assessment of Stages Theory";[8] and Robert Phelps, Richard Adams and John Bessant, "Life Cycles of Growing Organisations"[9]). Levie and Lichtenstein "conclude that ... growth modeling has hit a dead end and [we] urge our colleagues to abandon efforts to either predict or test a specific set of stages that are meant to describe the growth of business firms". It is easy to understand the reservations of academia. I have myself drawn attention to some of the weaknesses and inherent contradictions in growth-model thinking. Self-evidently, the number, variety and lack of agreement of the models give the lie to any attempt to generalise about the changes that growth brings. Moreover, recent studies have questioned the empirical validity of the claims made by the models when tested with large samples.

Business managers, however, find growth models useful as tools for helping them with their growth challenges. Many better understand the evolution of their own businesses when looking at them through the prism of a growth model; and most have little interest in looking back and considering whether their business histories illustrate the stages the models propose. They are also not particularly concerned about the lack of consistency between the models or the strength of their empirical foundations; they are more interested in the insights to be derived from the models into the problems that their businesses are confronting now, and the sorts of issues that might be round the corner. Identifying a business's position on one or other of the models provokes questions about how it is managed and directed, even if the exercise does not directly propose academically robust solutions.

The models usefully remind all managers that growth means change, and terminology such as "overhauling", "revolution" and "crisis" serves as a timely reminder that change is rarely comfortable. Furthermore, managers worrying about the problems of today and tomorrow need to be reminded that their reputations rest mainly on past successes, and there are strong reasons for their not wanting to accept change that they might intellectually acknowledge is necessary. After all, a growing business is a successful business; if management practice has worked so far, why change something that does not appear to be broken? Business planning in established businesses will unsurprisingly be grounded in existing strategies. Donald Sull, a senior lecturer at the MIT Sloan School of Management, calls this reluctance to move away from the past active inertia.[10] Reconciling this aversion to change with the suggestion that next year's growth might well depend on management's ability to do things differently is difficult. Change asks questions therefore not just about management practice, but also about managers – whether you have the right ones. As you expand the management team you may need to recruit individuals who are very different from those currently in post. And, notwithstanding any need to expand management resources, change will probably mean that some of the current team should go. In drawing attention to the changes that growth demands the models provide a necessary challenge to successful managers.

The growth models also remind us of the particular importance of some of the early stages of growth. Businesses created fully formed may suffer by missing out on the early stages of evolution. Culture and brand – the perquisites of the later stages of growth – can be manufactured, but many of the best brands and organisational cultures grow organically out of the personalities of the people who put the business together in the first place. This has implications for businesses that are growing particularly fast. Companies that enjoy hypergrowth are obviously doing something right – but to what extent in the excitement are they failing to pay attention to some of the fundamentals on which sustainable growth may depend? In the high-tech hypergrowth world companies are as likely to shrink fast as to grow.

Despite their shortcomings, some of the best thinking about growth is contained in the growth models, and they deserve to be taken seriously by managers if not by academics.

TABLE 2.1 **The DIAMOND framework**

Dominant business perspectives	Dreaming	Initiating	Attacking	Maturing	Overhauling	Networking	Diversifying
Owner focus	Do I have what it takes?	Robust corporate structure Shareholder agreements, etc	Giving up some equity	Establishing formal corporate governance	Possible exit MBO/MBI	Diverse stakeholder group	Diverse stakeholder group
Management focus	Business plan Market research Seed funding	Cash flow Winning new business Establishing a presence	Cash flow Establishing stability	Professional, disciplined management control	Addressing balance between leadership and management Refocusing on objectives	Managing corporate image Managing strategy Joint ventures and alliances	Improving brand value Alliances International expansion New products
Finance source	Finding an angel Friends and family	Own equity Angel Clearing bank Cash management	Short-term debt New equity participants Factoring	Structured finance Long-term debt	Structured finance Venture capital	Venture capital Finance markets	Finance markets
Investor focus	What else will they bring other than money?	Meeting their targets Taking advantage of their experience	Sufficient returns	Developing finance strategy	Restricted return for future growth	Retaining stability Maximising returns	Brand equity Shareholder value

Dominant business perspectives	Dreaming	Initiating	Attacking	Maturing	Overhauling	Networking	Diversifying
Employee focus	—	Excitement versus security	Overworked Growing with job	Professional management	Incentive based Emphasis on empowerment Options/equity reward	Career development	Moving around the business for new experience
Marketing and sales focus	Developing contacts Piloting concept	Generating demand Developing distribution channels	Improving customer quality Broadening customer base	Well-established relationships with range of clients Focusing on repeat business	Focus Brand development	Corporate positioning Brand management	Customer relationship management Brand extension
IT focus	Planning basic requirements	Off-the-shelf, simple solutions	Reliable systems	Bespoke systems for competitive advantage	Re-engineering systems to meet business need	E-commerce Intranet	Knowledge management CRM systems
Supply-side focus	Establishing contacts Setting quality/cost standards	Ad hoc, experimental	Negotiating long-term relationships	Multiple supplier management	Rationalising supply Power bargaining	Suppliers as partners	Vertical chain strategies Suppliers in strategic alliances
Community focus	Personal	Local employment	Random charitable, local business associations	Focused charitable and community spending	Focused Reinforcing brand	Focused Reinforcing brand	Political influence

Dominant business perspectives	Dreaming	Initiating	Attacking	Maturing	Overhauling	Networking	Diversifying
Transitional issues	Overcoming gaps in knowledge	Basic systems for income and expenditure	Not robust enough to survive major change	Management surpassing leadership	Business could run away with its own success	Business too large to be responsive to change	—
	Establishing business focus	Basic systems for meeting customer/client promises	Identifying skill deficiencies	Can founders evolve with their business?	Overemphasis on management threatens to destroy leadership spirit	European/economic/export issues	
	Company formation	Lack of focus	Need to introduce professional management apparent	Losing entrepreneurial spirit	Overpromise/under-deliver	Management of overseas subsidiaries	
	Securing finance	Understanding the extent to which growth consumes cash	No contingency planning	Losing touch with the market	Burn out (people and concept)	High turnover of good staff	
	Obtaining premises	Identifying need for and recruiting new members of senior team	Communication lines stretched or inadequate	Increasing lack of organisational flexibility	Lack of corporate governance	Sophisticated management hierarchy	
	Sourcing stock/suppliers	Dealing with the unforeseen – with little experience or skill	Constrained by initial systems selection	Inappropriate performance indicators	Culture still immature – in need of further attention	Pressure from within to start new businesses	
	Improving quality of business plan	Not really understanding the customer	Overdependence on founding team	Executives not incentivised or motivated correctly	Brand management	Development and extension of the brand	
	Developing knowledge of market	Dealing with first reactions from the competition	Failure to analyse and plan scientifically	Innovation dampened			
	Are founders inventors or entrepreneurs?	Ignoring IT					
	Can they do it on their own?						

Growth enablers and drivers

THE NEXT TWO CHAPTERS consider why some businesses grow and some do not. This chapter looks at the forces that trigger, and the circumstances that foster, growth. It starts inside the organisation with things that are within the control of those who run it, moves on to the life cycles of products, markets and industries, and concludes with aspects of the economic and commercial environment that affect the growth of a business.

A must or a maybe?

Is business growth a matter of choice? Or does a business have no choice other than to grow?

With big listed companies the position seems clear. Investors invest in shares in the hope that they will increase in value. CEOs of listed companies receive regular updates on the share price: during the day, after press announcements, on the way home in the car, when the market opens. Analysts assess the success of a business in terms of its performance against plan, its earnings, the credibility of its strategy and the success of management in implementing it, but ultimately what matters is the growth in its share price. Share prices are influenced by many factors, both external and internal, but they also reflect the growth of the business itself in terms of its ability to generate sustainable profit and the value of its underlying assets, intangible as well as tangible. Many directors of listed companies are under no illusion, therefore, that they have no alternative other than to grow their businesses.

In private businesses the position is more complicated. In the early stages of business development few would disagree with the assertion that the business has to grow or die. There is a critical mass that needs to be reached before the business can be considered to be self-sustaining. It will need to be consistently cash positive (generating more cash than it is consuming). To achieve this it will need to have successfully developed a product or service or two for which it has found a sustainable market. And it will need to be led by a team of people that is sufficiently self-sustaining to withstand the occasional resignation.

For many young businesses, however, such a state of critical mass seems curiously elusive. The experience of most who run new businesses is that their existence is fragile: one slip could cause the whole edifice to disintegrate. Owner-managers are left with the nagging feeling that they need just another couple of products, or two or three new accounts, or one more recruit to the management team. But when they get there they do not feel as secure as they had expected. It is as if founding a business is not a matter of reaching a particular position but rather a continuous process of evolution.

In deciding whether or not to continue to grow a private business, once it has reached critical mass, the personal motivation of the founders is often more important than the potential of the business. In the first version of their model of business growth, Neil Churchill and Virginia Lewis acknowledge the issue and argue that the founders of a growing business, once it is past the existence and survival stages, need to choose at stage 3 between success-disengagement and success-growth (see Chapter 2). Owners who choose success-disengagement are opting to step back a little. They might choose to delegate day-to-day management to others, or to take money out of the business rather than invest in it. If they go for success-growth, their agenda and that of the business need to be aligned and personal enrichment needs to be sacrificed for corporate growth.

Of course, stepping back from the business will work only if the business is self-sustaining – otherwise the founders' experience of enjoying the fruits of the business will be short-lived. In reality, for many founders stepping back is likely to be a first stage towards stepping out of the business altogether. The issue is often not that the business no longer needs to grow, but that the owner no longer wants or needs or is able to play a part in it. Those who talk about slowing the pace of growth are really saying that they have had enough, and they should get out before they do the business (their most valuable asset) serious damage. It is perhaps not surprising that in later manifestations of Churchill's model the choice at stage 3 between growth and disengagement has been dropped and replaced by a stage 3 called profitability/stabilisation, which is followed by a new stage 4 called profitability/growth.

For most businesses success depends on further growth, even once critical mass has been achieved – notwithstanding any reluctance on the part of the founders.

The good old days when we were small

A successful architectural practice that had enjoyed spectacular growth looked for help with succession planning, in particular how to replace its founding managing partner. There was a feeling among some of the partners that the firm had grown too big too fast, and that maybe it would benefit by shrinking closer to its previous size. This is not uncommon. Many professional partnerships hang on to management practices that suited them when they were small but no longer work when they become big. Such small-firm mindedness is a typical manifestation of a yearning for the good old days.

The reality, however, for a firm at this stage of its evolution is that reducing its size will not return it to the good old days. When it was young and growing with things to prove to itself and its clients, it would have been an exciting, vibrant firm where ambitious young staff could see developing futures for themselves and their colleagues. For such a firm, becoming small for the second time will be a different experience. It will have become small as a consequence of contraction; it was small the first time as a stage on the path to success. To achieve a reduction in size, staff will have to leave, and despite best efforts to the contrary it is inevitable that the best staff will choose to leave, acknowledging that the firm is no longer prepared to provide a platform for them to satisfy their ambitions. The new small firm will be a tired, jaded business, lacking in ambition. This will rub off on its clients, and before long it will find itself on a slippery downward path.

Living with the growth imperative

In many ways firms have to accept that growth is an important ingredient in what makes the business what it is; it has no alternative other than to grow. This is called the growth imperative, because for organisations with ambition it can seem impossible to escape from its gravitational pull. As argued throughout this book, it can be difficult to live with the implications of the imperative. Growth is a necessary consequence of ambition, but growth demands change, needs investment to support it, and demands sacrifices of time and energy on the part of the stakeholders. No wonder that many of those involved in the most rapidly growing businesses question whether it is all worth it.

Exceptions to the growth imperative

One law firm is perhaps an exception that proves the rule. Founded by a group of lawyers who left one of the so-called magic circle firms of solicitors in London, it developed a niche practice in a particular area of the law. At the outset the partners decided not to increase their number; the firm would always have around half a dozen partners. If one of the partners decided to retire early the others might consider admitting another, but as a matter of strategic intent the firm was to stay the same size. This had considerable implications for management, in particular human resources management. Staff in the firm but outside the partnership knew that there were no prospects for admission to the partnership, so it was inevitable that ambitious staff would leave. Losing good staff was a matter of regret, but was felt not to present insurmountable problems in carrying on business successfully – as has proved the case. More problematic is the longer-term future of the firm. Can it continue to thrive as the founding partners get closer to retirement?

Small professional services firms cannot easily be sold, particularly when all the partners reach retirement at the same time. When partners retire, part of the business retires with them. Big firms get round this by creating a self-renewing wheel in which good staff coming through the firm buy into the partnership and in effect fund the retirement of their seniors. In this case, such succession planning could not happen. To some extent the decision to defy the growth imperative curtailed the life of the firm. In some businesses a decision not to grow need not have such dire consequences, but it is difficult to maintain standards, recruit and retain good staff, and satisfy clients and customers who are prepared to pay good money if a business chooses not to grow.

Instead of concluding that no growth or slowing down growth are preferable options, managers worried about the negative effects of growth might do better to address those that cause them most concern. This may include making sure that:

- the particular characteristics and qualities of an organisation's culture and style can be preserved and managed as it gets bigger (see Chapter 7);

- the management infrastructure keeps pace with growth and does not end up being constrained by the use of techniques that worked when it was smaller but do not now that it is larger;

- enough attention and resources are given to internal communication – this is not a problem in a small business when people see each other every day, but in a bigger business managers need to work on it;

- founders' own roles evolve so that they support and enhance the growth prospects of the business rather than act as a constraint (see Chapter 7).

Managing the negative implications of growth can help strengthen the platform for the next stage of growth.

Different ambitions and attitudes

Just as important as the growth imperative are the personal motivation and ambition of the founders and managers. Regardless of the quality of an opportunity or the appropriateness of a corporate strategy, a business will not grow far or fast if its owners and managers do not want it to. A crucial element in any growth plan – an element that will distinguish a plan focused on growth from a standard business plan – will therefore be some consideration of the ambitions of the owners and managers.

In a classic 1996 *Harvard Business Review* article, Amar Bhidé argues:[1]

> [Successful entrepreneurs] need to keep asking tough questions about where they want to go, and whether the track they're on will take them there.

Successful strategies, he says, provide clear direction, generate sufficient profits and growth, serve the enterprise in the long term and establish the right growth rate. Bhidé encourages entrepreneurs to ask questions about their ability to execute. But above all, he encourages them to ask themselves what they want personally from the business and what sort of business will be required. He also encourages them to consider their appetite for risk.

If there is more than one founder or owner-manager, several sets of questions need to be asked – one for each individual. In an ideal world, owner-managers will want to work as hard as each other, will want the same things from the business, will have the same work–life priorities, will want to retire on the same day and will be happy to sell the business for the same amount of money. None of these things is, of course, likely. But with discussion, negotiation and planning, different sets of personal aspirations can be reconciled with each other, and the same business can satisfy the differing aspirations of different owner-managers. A crucial implication, however, is that owner-managers should attend to their personal planning as well as planning for the business, and, if there is more than one owner-manager, they should maintain an open dialogue with each other. People's priorities change and plans need regular review.

As the business grows, owner-managers should also consider the personal aspirations and concerns of the staff they value and wish to retain. Many founders and entrepreneurs make the mistake of assuming that newly recruited managers have the same aspirations as the founders (see Chapter 7).

The expectations of financiers: potential tensions

Owner-managers responsible for businesses will have other sets of expectations to worry about – in particular the expectations of financial stakeholders. Different types of financial stakeholder will have different expectations. Businesses with angel funding (that is, third-party equity investment from wealthy individuals investing their own money) must acknowledge the personal ambitions of the angels. Angel funding comes with as many different types of ambition as there are business angels, because angel investment is a personal investment and will reflect the interests and prejudices of the angel. Some angels are happy to take relatively passive roles; others are keen to offer their experience and insight in active support of managers. Such support is not always a blessing. In extreme cases, it can seem as though angels are looking for jobs as well as investment opportunities, and can behave as if they are turning themselves into additional owner-managers (see Chapter 6).

Institutional sources of equity finance such as venture capitalists and private equity firms will also have their own agendas, and again it is naive to assume that these will automatically be aligned with the goals and ambitions of the founders of the businesses in which they invest. But in essence the ambitions of an institutional investor will be simpler to understand than the ambitions of an angel. Unlike an angel, an institutional investor is not investing its own money and will therefore have more objective assessment processes and transparent expectations.

The objectives of the financiers, whether individual or institutional, will be implied in the terms on which they provide finance, including the particular returns they are looking for within specific time frames. Invariably the time horizons of venture capitalists are short, often shorter than those of both angels and entrepreneurs. But at the end of their time horizon all financial investors are looking to make a healthy return. Their motivation is financial: they are in business to make money.

In many cases, institutions investing private capital in early-growth businesses will anticipate the need to invest more capital in the business at a later date. In effect, some might be buying an option to participate in a future funding round. This is particularly true of businesses in industries such as pharmaceuticals or businesses dependent for success on phenomena that will take time to develop, such as changes in behaviour on the part of large groups of consumers or big corporate customers, or the turning over of complex regulatory machinery.

The motivation of entrepreneurs and owner-managers is more complex than that of any financial investor, whether individual or institutional, and includes a host of personal considerations. But even in terms of finance a financier's and an entrepreneur's ambitions can be significantly divergent. Financial investors, particularly institutional investors, are typically portfolio managers and will take advantage of their portfolio to mitigate their risks. They will invest only if they can see a reasonable chance of an investment generating a significant return. Obviously, not all their investments will do so – indeed, research shows that the majority of a venture capitalist's investments do not deliver the returns hoped for – but that is the nature of high-risk investment. One venture capitalist warns its potential investors that one-third of investments will fail and another third will not meet expectations. But because financial investors only invest in the hope of having found a big one, they are always pushing the owner-managers of all their investments into decisions that improve the organisation's chances of delivering a big return, even if this also increases the risk of organisational failure.

For the venture capitalist there is always another investment to mitigate the risk, but owner-managers are likely to think differently – even the most entrepreneurial are unlikely to have such aggressive growth ambitions. Owner-managers will not have a portfolio of investments to mitigate their risk; for them the business is likely to be the only ball in play. It is thus inevitable that the ambitions of owner-managers and venture capitalists will be out of alignment. When negotiating a deal, financiers often push entrepreneurs and their advisers to be more aggressive and ambitious when setting targets. Venture capitalist Vinod Khosla is fond of quoting an Indian proverb:[2]

> *If you shoot for the sky, you end up in the tree. If you shoot for the tree, you end up on the ground.*

Tensions between financiers and founders are likely at the negotiation and planning stages – but these are nothing compared with the tensions that will emerge later in the organisation's history when the owner-managers are trying to achieve those targets and are increasingly aware of the implications of failure. Owner-managers in venture capital funded businesses can easily just turn into managers, and a good many end up not even being that.

To be fair, for most new businesses venture capital funding is not an option, since venture capitalists fund only a small proportion of new businesses. As reported by Diane Mulcahy in a 2013 article in *Harvard Business Review*, historically only a tiny percentage (fewer than 1%) of US companies have raised capital from venture capitalists.[3] And the industry is contracting: after peaking in the late 1990s, the number of active venture capitalist firms fell from 744 to 526 in 2001–11; and the amount of venture capital raised was just under $19 billion in 2011, compared with $39 billion in 2001, according to the National Venture Capital Association (NVCA). The combination venture capitalists look for – huge growth potential, a good team, a defensible, scalable business proposition and a clear exit – has always been, and continues to be, rare.

Angel finance is much more common than venture capital finance, but nonetheless most new businesses are obliged to look to their own resources, or to those of contacts, friends and family, and (if they have debt capacity) banks. But there are some entrepreneurs who choose not to take venture capital finance when they can, accepting that they will "bootstrap" their ventures instead. Whereas entrepreneurs with venture capital funding are encouraged to expand their ambitions and their planning horizons, bootstrappers have to focus on other imperatives. "Bootstrapping clears away the clutter and makes you focus single-mindedly on the customer," says Emily Barker in a 2002 article in *Inc. Magazine* about Greg Gianforte, an American software entrepreneur, who has built more than one business as a bootstrapper.[4] In Gianforte's view the rigours of being bootstrapped force the entrepreneur to focus on selling to bring cash into the business. Building a business is all about making a product that people want as fast and cheaply as possible and then selling it. Barker says:

> *I think a lot of entrepreneurs think they need money to build the business faster when they actually haven't figured out the business equation yet.*

Different approaches to funding a business are not mutually exclusive; different styles suit different stages of growth. Even Gianforte accepts that there are times in a business's life cycle when external finance is appropriate. With one of his businesses, RightNow, he looked for external finance only after the business was established and he was seeking to expand overseas. Without the money, Gianforte noted, "we would have executed the same plan, but it would have been a little slower".

For listed businesses it is very different. Shareholders who acquire their shares via a stock exchange do not have the same expectations as private equity investors, either individual or institutional, nor can they hope to have the same access to and influence over management unless they hold sizeable stakes. Managers are accountable to the board, and the board to the shareholders, but the tension between the ambitions of management and the ambitions of shareholders in a listed company is neither as pointed nor as acute as it is in private businesses funded with private equity. The ambitions of management are a more important influence on growth in a listed business than the ambitions of the owners. As Enron, Lehman Brothers, RBS (Royal Bank of Scotland) and others have shown, in listed companies the ambitions of senior managers can sometimes be more aggressive than those of shareholders – even though such managers are often in part rewarded with equity and options in the hope that the ambitions of the two will be aligned.

New products and services

Although business growth is critically influenced by stakeholder ambition, it is evident that business success depends on selling something that customers want to buy. Crucial to growth, therefore, is how successfully a company responds to the changing needs of customers for its products and services.

Discover the need, identify the opportunity

Responding to customer needs requires distinguishing what customers really want from what they say they want, and intuiting what they do not yet know they want. As Anthony Ulwick, a consultant and innovation expert, argued in a 2002 article in *Harvard Business Review*, customer feedback is used properly when it is used to identify what customers value rather than what they say they want.[5] Conversely, the slogan adopted by Ford some years ago – "everything we do is driven by you" – was indeed meant to suggest a product portfolio designed in response to a careful analysis of consumer needs. But many thought that portfolio was dull. Customers want to be surprised, and they will not be surprised if businesses ask them what they want and just give it to them. Customers are not the best people to imagine what they might want, beyond specific changes to products. So be careful when giving customers what they say they want.

When identifying and imagining customer needs it is important not to confuse what the market needs with what you want to supply. Too many entrepreneurs expect customers to be as enthusiastic about their ideas as they are. There is a world of difference between an opportunity and a good idea. John Steinbeck captures the issue nicely in an exchange between Adam and Will in his novel *East of Eden*:[6]

> "I come from a whole goddam family of inventors," said Will. "We had ideas for breakfast. We had ideas instead of breakfast. We had so many ideas we forgot to make the money for groceries ... I'm the only one in the family, except my mother, who didn't have ideas, and I'm the only one who ever made a dime."

Managers interested in sustainable growth should note the following distinctions between ideas and opportunities:

■ Good ideas are timeless and priceless, but good opportunities are defined by more pragmatic qualities. An opportunity is time-specific: it is tied to a particular time and set of circumstances. And it is not priceless: it has a value, and its value is associated with the right time and place. In the world of business, times and circumstances change and opportunities therefore expire. It might be difficult to measure the value of an opportunity in advance, but because the value is tied to its time and circumstance it too is transient. If an opportunity is not pinned down at the right time it will not be worth anything. Good ideas can come too early, before the market is ready for them. The idea Adam was getting excited about in *East of Eden* was to refrigerate lettuces and ship them from California to New York in the winter. He invested a lot of his own money in the idea. The problem was that he attempted to implement it before the first world war; customers would not be accustomed to lettuces in February, Adam's critic, Will, argued. In any case the transport infrastructure was inadequate and the lettuces were rotten when they arrived. But no one today would consider Adam's idea daft. An idea can also come too late, when a company with a competing (and sometimes inferior) idea may have already grasped the opportunity and built a defensible market position. Success can come from taking advantage of the zeitgeist, but the spirit of the times changes. The time has to be right not just for the market but also for the entrepreneur and for whoever is providing the money.

■ Opportunities, compared with ideas, are related to specific market circumstances, particularly customer and client needs. There is often no reason why the market should ever find a need for your idea, no matter how brilliant it is. As if to prove the point some entrepreneurs start not with an idea at all, but with an attempt to identify and isolate a market need. A market need can be quantified and valued. Only after the need has been defined will such entrepreneurs turn their attention to generating the solution, scouring the universities or the design agencies for someone who can come up with a product or service to address the need. Good opportunities are therefore intimately related to customer needs.

■ Ideas are abstractions; opportunities are grounded in reality. Opportunities respond far more to hard work than to inspiration. Understanding the distinction between a good opportunity and a good idea is crucial for managers looking for new ways to grow.

■ Unlike an idea, an opportunity, in and of itself, is not unique.

Uniqueness is created when a team of individuals with a particular blend of experience and expertise successfully takes advantage of an opportunity and turns it into a difficult-to-replicate business.

Execution is all

Just as businesses are built on opportunities not ideas, so successful growth is a matter of execution rather than invention. Inventors are people who dream things up. Entrepreneurs are people who turn dreams into reality. Invention is about creativity and imagination; these qualities are useful for entrepreneurs, but entrepreneurship is far more about implementation. Inventors wrestle with ideas; entrepreneurs convert ideas into businesses.

In a study of entrepreneurship conducted between 1982 and 1989 in the US, only 12% of founders attributed the success of their companies to "an unusual or extraordinary idea"; but some 88% attributed their success to "exceptional execution of an ordinary idea".[7] There are some individuals who have managed to combine both sets of skills, such as James Dyson, inventor of, among other things, the dual cyclone bagless vacuum cleaner. But Dyson is an exception to the rule. Trevor Baylis, inventor of the wind-up radio, is often cited as another, though it was only after an episode of the BBC's *Tomorrow's World* in 1994 and Baylis's subsequent association with accountant Christopher Staines and South African entrepreneur Rory Stear that the invention started on the path to commercial realisation. Even Bill Gates, who is much more in the Dyson than the Baylis mould, relied in the early days on Steve Ballmer, Microsoft's 30th employee and first business manager.

Crazy ideas people are often able to grow a business only when more down-to-earth and pragmatic people work with them. For many inventors, growth happens only after they have walked away. W. H. Hoover knew nothing about hoovers. Several people on both sides of the Atlantic had developed good ideas for using suction to remove dust and debris, and numerous patents had been filed. In 1901 H. Cecil Booth patented a motorised vacuum cleaner. He started the British Vacuum Cleaner Company and his industrial cleaners, powered first by steam and then by oil, were pulled from site to site by horse. Hoover was in the leather harness business, but he had problems as the motor car quickly began to take over from the horse and cart. It was his wife's cousin, James Murray Spangler, who had thought long and hard about vacuum-cleaner technology and had added the all-important brushes to the machine, which was then patented. Spangler did not know how to commercialise the idea, and thought he could not afford to, so he sold the idea and the patents to Hoover. Hoover's Electric Suction Sweeper Company first started selling the Hoover "Model O" in 1908 for the princely sum of $60. Early adopters were enthusiastic, and Hoover became rich. His success was triggered by a structural recession in the industry he knew best, and fostered by his powers of execution in an industry he did not know at all.

For most, growth means recognising that the inventor or the ideas person cannot go it alone. Some ideas people and entrepreneurs remain in touch with their ideas by building up teams of people who know how to commercialise the ideas, and how to execute. Businesses often stand a better chance of getting off the ground in the first place, and grow further and faster, if they are put together by teams of individuals with complementary skills (see Chapter 7).

Stars, dogs and the product life cycle

Markets for products and services evolve, and businesses ambitious for growth need to be aware of the relationship between the maturity of a product and the growth potential of the market into which it is sold.

One of the best-known frameworks for analysing the life cycle of products and services is the matrix devised by the Boston Consulting Group, usually known as the BCG matrix (see Figure 3.1).

FIG 3.1 **The BCG matrix**

Star		**Problem child**	
Revenue	+ + +	Revenue	+
Expenditure	– – –	Expenditure	– – –
Cash flow	neutral	Cash flow	– –
Cash cow		**Dog**	
Revenue	+ + + +	Revenue	+
Expenditure	– –	Expenditure	–
Cash flow	+ +	Cash flow	neutral

High ⟵ Market growth ⟶ Low

High ⟵ Market share ⟶

Source: After Boston Consulting Group

The framework introduced into the vocabulary of managers the terms cash cow, dog, star and problem child. Many product and service portfolio analyses have attempted to categorise products and services using the matrix. The labels in some ways are unfortunate; many managers have assumed that they should be responsible for stars. But as Figure 3.1 shows, stars are products that have lots of potential in terms of market growth and current market share – but it is only potential; in a rapidly growing market there is a lot of uncertainty requiring significant investment. The products that generate cash for the business are older and more established; no longer in a growing market, cash cows benefit nonetheless from high market share and require relatively little expenditure to maintain that position. Stars have potential, but they are risky; cash cows are generating cash now. At least stars are generating revenue. Problem children have low market share in markets with high potential; they are consuming resources but not generating returns. Will they ever? Managers need to consider whether it is worth maintaining the investment in the hope that problem children will turn into stars and then cash cows. The risk is that they might turn into dogs: products achieving low market share in low-growth markets, demanding little investment but generating little return.

The BCG matrix is much used, but it has shortcomings. There are perils associated with focusing too much on markets that are growing, while shrinking markets can offer opportunities for businesses ambitious for growth. Market share is not the only thing that matters and is as much a function of the size of a business as it is a reflection of the success of its strategy. Small businesses entering established markets will never have significant market share, but that does not mean they cannot be successful. In general, the BCG analysis generates the most insight for businesses that are big already, not just because of the focus on market share, but because the model draws attention to the role of product portfolios when developing business strategy. As with many frameworks, this one works less well when applied to younger, smaller businesses, not least because small businesses are unlikely to have much of a portfolio of products to offer. A crucial subtext here for a younger business is the importance of thinking in terms of portfolio when seeking to achieve sustainability – a portfolio of products and services provided to a portfolio of customers and clients in a portfolio of market segments.

Geoffrey Moore has another take on new products and the way they and the markets for them evolve in his book *Crossing the Chasm*.[8] His chief interest is the market for high-technology products, but his observations shed light on how to market any new product or service.

Building on the earlier work of sociologist Everett Rogers, Moore writes most interestingly about the "chasm", the gulf between the geeky enthusiasts that he, following Rogers, calls "early adopters" and the mainstream of the market (see Figure 3.2). A new company providing a new product may find it relatively easy to excite some early adopters, who might be prepared to pay a lot for an as yet unproven and unreliable product. But early

FIG 3.2 **Crossing the chasm**

Source: Geoffrey Moore, *Crossing the Chasm*, Harper Business, 1991

adopters are always likely to be few in number, and their attitudes and enthusiasms are rarely typical of the market as a whole. The mainstream is often a lot more difficult to persuade. An ambitious company in a new market with a new product will have to find ways of crossing the chasm or its growth ambitions will not be satisfied. The mainstream will be more price-conscious and more interested in utility than in novelty and technology. In parallel with the change in customer perceptions will be a change in the competitive environment, with new and larger competitors entering the market to drive down price and improve quality and reliability. A business ambitious for growth will have to change its marketing strategy if it wants to capture mainstream customers. It will also have to look long and hard at its operating model for efficiencies if it is to maintain its margins under pressure from new competition.

Growth outside the portfolio: focus versus diversification

Crucial to business success and growth is being able to recognise and capitalise on your competitive advantage. When doing this a business ambitious for growth may look for opportunities not just with its current portfolio of products and within its current customer and client relationships. In considering diversification it needs to think carefully about the competitive advantage that has delivered growth to date. Either single-focus or diversification-based strategies can provide platforms for growth, and both have their champions:

- **Focus.** A company sticks to what it knows best, thus giving itself the best chance of developing an expertise that can be defended against other market entrants. Focus enthusiasts argue that any attempt to widen a company's range of activities runs the risk of diluting its competitive advantage and spreading its resources too thin. In other words, it is better to do something really well than a variety of things less well.

- **Diversification.** A company ambitious for growth adds different products and services to its portfolio because it is only by broadening its range that it will extend its reach and increase its size. Furthermore, it is simply too risky to have all your eggs in one basket. Diversification enthusiasts argue that well-diversified product, service and customer portfolios are inherently less risky and more sustainable than businesses with a narrow focus.

Supporters of the focus line often argue that core competence should be the cornerstone of an effective strategy. But C. K. Prahalad and Gary Hamel, who came up with the concept in a 1990 *Harvard Business Review* article, did not argue in favour of a single core competence but rather a plurality of core competencies around which a strategy, product or service and organisation is built.[9]

More aligned with focus as a keystone of growth is the thinking of Chris Zook, an American academic, in *Profit from the Core*.[10] Basing their ten-year study on more than 2,000 technology, service and product companies in a variety of industries, Zook and his co-author, James Allen, argue that most growth strategies fail to deliver value – and even destroy it – primarily because they diversify inappropriately from their core business. Zook and Allen argue that three factors differentiate businesses with growth strategies that succeed from those that fail:

- they achieve full potential in their core business;
- they recognise that successful expansion has to be into logical adjacent businesses surrounding that core;
- they acknowledge that their core will need to continuously evolve in response to market turbulence and changes of circumstance.

Zook and Allen draw attention to some telling paradoxes at the heart of many growth stories:

> It is almost as if most growth strategies harbour a dark, destructive force that causes companies to reduce their focus on their core business and thereby to depart from the basis of their real differentiation.

Entrepreneurs who have founded a successful business too often believe that they can walk on water and repeat the trick. So-called serial entrepreneurs are often people who have been lucky enough to make their money on a venture and then for the rest of their careers spend it on other less successful ventures. Being entrepreneurial in many big businesses is a matter of rushing around after the next new thing rather than applying an entrepreneurial mindset to the part of the enterprise responsible for its success in the first place. As Zook and Allen say:

> The better performing of your businesses units are likely to be those operating the furthest below their full potential.

Why? Because those parts of your business that performed well in the past have provided management with an excuse for not paying them the attention that would ensure they perform even better in the present and future. It is only too tempting for managers not to invest in the business they understand the best. However, Zook and Allen add:

> *The stronger your core business, the more opportunities you have both to move into profitable adjacencies and to lose focus.*

A strong core provides the resources but is also an excuse for management to explore other initiatives, at the expense of attending to the heart of the business. For the perils of one manifestation of the temptation to expand at the expense of your core – mergers and acquisitions – see Chapter 8.

Zook and Allen concede that, although the core is important, growth will eventually depend on moves beyond it. In a later book, *Beyond the Core*, Zook makes the case for successful diversification rather than no diversification at all, while arguing that the further you step away from the reasons for your success the riskier it will be.[11]

Many others have written about the risks of diversification. Igor Ansoff's two-by-two matrix (a version of which is illustrated in Figure 3.3) features in many business plans focusing on growing the top line.[12] Box 2 is about finding new products to take to existing markets, and box 3 is about finding new markets for existing products. Both these strategies are inherently riskier than trying to increase penetration in existing markets with the current product portfolio, though as a growth strategy this will be constrained by the size and growth potential of the overall market. Both 3 and 2 are less risky than a diversification strategy (box 4): seeking to develop new products for entirely new markets, where the risks are compounded. But both 3 and 2 are also, in the long term at least, inherently less risky than the version of box 1 that involves doing nothing at all and watching the competitive environment evolve around you.

FIG 3.3 **Ansoff's two-by-two matrix**

	Existing **MARKETS** New	
Existing P R O D U C T S / S E R V I C E S **New**	**1** Do nothing Consolidate Market penetration Withdraw	**3** Market development
	2 Product/service development	**4** Diversification – related – unrelated

Source: Based on Igor Ansoff, "Strategies for Diversification", *Harvard Business Review*, 1957

Of course, a business that is already successfully diversified can take advantage of the portfolio effect to mitigate its risks, and play in all four of Ansoff's boxes, with different products or businesses in each one.

Intangibles: intellectual property and brand as growth levers

As noted earlier, a successful business that has satisfied a market opportunity with a product or service and that is successfully winning profitable new business will find itself attracting the attention of powerful competition. An important way for a business to defend what it has achieved, and to provide a platform for further growth, is through the effective management of its intangible assets.

In some industries, intellectual property – patents, copyrights and trademarks – is critical. Big companies in the pharmaceutical industry can justify their enormous research and development expenditure only because they know they can protect the pharmacological compounds they develop from copycats for a significant period of time. Intellectual property is also an important element in other high-tech industries.

But many businesses invest too much time and effort in protecting their intellectual property. A patent has real value only if the company owning it is prepared to spend money defending it. Defending patents is an expensive business – even more expensive than obtaining one in the first place – and is often beyond the means of many smaller businesses. As well as high-tech firms, big, wealthy companies with deep pockets play the patent game and invest a lot of time (and money) in suing and defending themselves against lawsuits. A patent is worth obtaining and fighting for only if there is a good chance it will secure commercial advantage and value for a significant period of time. In many industries the next, superior product is only just around the corner, and it may use an alternative mechanism or formula or programme that will enable its owner to sidestep the patent you have spent so much time and money on – resources that might have been better spent on marketing or product development.

Some companies, however, argue that time and money spent on patents is time and money spent on marketing. They invest in patents not because of the property rights they bring but because they help reinforce their owners' credibility as cutting-edge players in the industry. For such companies the management of intellectual property has become an element of brand management.

Brand is another intangible asset, the development of which can help defend a hard-won market position and provide a platform for further growth. A brand is not just the name and logo protected by law and called a trademark. It is the indefinable essence or promise of a product or service, comprising many elements and characteristics of the product and the business that produced it. Because a brand is difficult to define, it can be more difficult to copy than the product or service itself.

Chapter 7 considers the role other intangible elements – culture and values – play in the management of the growing business.

Markets and industries

When planning for growth it is important to understand the dynamics of both the industry (the collection of producers and suppliers making and supplying similar products and services) and the market (the collection of customers interested in an industry's products or services) a business operates in. When understanding the industry a company needs to consider its competition; when understanding its market a company needs to understand its customers.

Life cycles

Industries and markets, like companies and products, have life cycles. A new industry will be dominated by entrepreneurs looking not just to shape their businesses but also to dominate the industry, to define its standards and protocols, and in some instances to become the industry – for years a vacuum cleaner was a Hoover, for example – and, arguably, it is now a Dyson. Younger markets and industries tend to be shaped by smaller, entrepreneurial companies rather than bigger companies. Smaller businesses are better at taking advantage of the uncertainty that is inherent in a new market than big businesses, which in turn are far better at allocating resources to the well-defined opportunities that are more likely to characterise mature markets.

Part of the allure of a new market is the myth of first-mover advantage. If you can be there at the start, what is to stop you getting big within the industry that develops to serve the market? Quite a lot, actually. Firms like Hoover are the exceptions that prove the rule that most new businesses do not turn into big ones simply by inventing an industry and then sticking with it. New businesses that invent industries attract competition. Many small businesses argue that they do not have competition, but what they really mean is that the competition has not yet discovered them or the opportunity. When the competition does arrive it is likely to be better resourced than the small businesses that have successfully identified and developed the opportunity. Too often small, innovative start-ups find that they have done R&D for big companies free of charge.

R&D: small companies pave the way for big ones

Title Research, a company specialising in probate research, virtually invented online genealogy for amateurs in the UK when it launched findmypast. co.uk, putting birth, marriage and death records online and charging customers to access them. The website generated more profit in its first year of trading than the company that founded it did in that same year. To sustain momentum, Title Research needed to invest in more data sets, such as census records. But once it had validated the market in the UK, an established US player, ancestry.com, appeared, equipped with census records ready to launch, and offering birth, marriage and death records to customers for free. Suddenly, findmypast.co.uk went from being a success to being a business under siege with a precarious future. Within two years Title Research had sold it. This is not an unusual story. Big businesses often leave the opening up of new industries to small upstarts, preferring to step in only when the potential has been confirmed. Thus smaller businesses rarely turn into big businesses as an industry matures, but rather are replaced by them.

Most importantly, as the Title Research example illustrates, a company seeking to grow needs to understand not just its current competitors and customers, but also its next competitors and customers.

Opportunities of size

Big and small businesses do coexist in the same industry, and the symbiotic nature of their relationship can provide other routes to growth – certainly for the smaller industry players. When times are good, money is plentiful, the economy is growing, chief executives are congratulating themselves for growing with it and big business is out with its chequebook looking for acquisitions. Conversely, at other times in the cycle big companies will be looking to sell businesses either because they are underperforming or because they do not fit with a new corporate strategy. Both instances provide potential opportunities for entrepreneurs. When big companies are acquiring a big competitor might well turn into a potential exit route for a founding team – as the founders of Innocent Smoothies discovered when Coca-Cola bought their company in 2013.

Are you buying or selling?

In economically sunny 1999, with the markets fuelled by the start of the dotcom boom and work generated by the millennium bug, Ford Motor Company wrote a cheque for just over £1 billion ($1.65 billion) for Kwik-Fit, a UK auto-spares business, paying a 33% premium over the market price. Kwik-Fit's founding entrepreneur, Sir Tom Farmer, made £75 million ($124 million) from selling his 8% share in the business, and took a senior role at Ford. Ford's president and chief executive officer, Jacques Nasser, was reported by BBC news as saying:

> *[The acquisition] is an important step towards Ford's goal to become the world's leading consumer company that provides automotive products and services through world-class brands.*

Less than three years later the economic environment was much shakier following the bursting of the dotcom bubble. Kwik-Fit was back on the market. Ford's new boss, keen to roll out a new strategy in difficult times, sold it in August 2002 for £330 million ($545 million), less than one-third of the price paid for the business back in 1999. A Ford spokesman was reported by BBC news as having observed:

> *The sale of Kwik-Fit is a positive outcome for Ford. As we have said since the beginning of the year, we want to divest non-core assets and this gets us very close towards our goal for the year.*

Had Ford paid too much for Kwik-Fit in 1999? Had it sold the business too cheaply in 2002? Perhaps these are the wrong questions to ask. What is more interesting is that an entrepreneur did well in getting a good price when selling the company in 1999, and a private equity firm, CVC Capital Partners, did well in buying it below value in 2002. The wheels of big business move at a different speed and often in a different direction from the nimble feet of the entrepreneurially minded. Entrepreneurs need to remember this, particularly when the business news, which is almost always dominated by noise from big business, is full of doom and gloom.

Another example is that of Lloyd Dorfman, the founder of Travelex, a foreign-exchange business, who recalled that at the launch of the euro on January 1st 2002 many people thought he "should have been in mourning" at the elimination of most of Europe's national currencies. He looked at it differently. The introduction of the euro certainly accelerated the exit from the industry of banks and other large competitors, several of which sold their foreign-exchange businesses to Travelex. However, in the longer term, the market would benefit from an increase in international travel and cross-border trade. Market contraction in the short term gave Travelex the opportunity to consolidate so that it could take advantage of long-term exponential growth.

Assessing the forces at work

A common way of analysing an industry is through the five forces outlined by Michael Porter in his book *Competitive Strategy*.[13] Five-forces analysis attempts to assess the health of the competitive environment in an industry. A company can then consider its own strategy in the context of the industry in which it operates. The five forces are as follows:

- The threat of substitute products and the ability of customers to switch to them.

- The threat posed by new entrants to the industry – and the extent to which there are barriers to entry.

- The power of customers – their ability to dictate terms to you. If there are relatively few customers for your product, each customer will have more power.

FIG 3.4 **Porter's five forces**

Source: Michael Porter, *Competitive Advantage*, 1985

■ The power of suppliers – their ability to dictate terms to you. Again, a monopolistic supplier will be able to dictate price and influence quality.

■ Competitive rivalry between industry players.

A company can consider the strength of the forces in its particular industry and the extent to which the forces are favourable or unfavourable before assessing its response.

An analysis of the industry using five-forces analysis is just a start. Companies planning for growth need to understand how their competitors operate individually and what advantage they might obtain within the industry from the strategic and operational choices available to them. Decisions are taken by managers responsible for companies not industries, and it is possible therefore to achieve competitive advantage and to grow a business in an industry that is exhibiting negative characteristics. Managers interested in growth also need to understand how the industry might change, particularly how competitors are likely to respond to any initiatives included within the growth plan. A growing business might find itself operating in several industries as well as influencing the characteristics of the industries in which it is an increasingly influential player. Growing companies operate in changing industries. Five-forces analysis has been criticised for presuming that industries are more stable than they actually are.

Understanding the complexities

It is easy sometimes to oversimplify the business environment. A company has suppliers and customers with whom it strikes up a relationship. It also has competitors on which it keeps a wary eye, but which by and large it sees as the enemy. As has been suggested, analytical tools such as Porter's five forces can encourage business leaders to think too simplistically about their competitive environments. But the biggest opportunities are available only to those able to think the thoughts that others do not think. Everyone doing five-forces analysis on the same industry will come to similar conclusions. Businesses serious about growth need to think differently. They should start by understanding the subtleties that exist even in the simplest of industries and markets.

In agency businesses, such as estate agents and recruitment agents, customers and suppliers can get confused. A house seller "supplies" the product that an estate agent sells. But it is the house seller who pays the estate agent's fee, not the customer who looks at the estate agent's inventory in its shop window. In a recruitment agency, it is the business doing the recruiting that pays the agency's fee, but the relationship between the agency and the person being placed has many of the characteristics of the company–customer relationship. In complicated markets the definitions of other market players can change. Competitors can turn into collaborators as well as, on some occasions, customers.

Some writers have turned to distant frames of reference when trying to identify and explain subtleties not just in complicated markets and industries, but in simple ones too. Drawing on mathematics' game theory, American academics Adam Brandenburger and Barry Nalebuff conceive of the market as a place where "complementors" as well as competitors, customers and suppliers do business.[14] Complementors, who can operate on the supply side or the customer side, are market participants whose existence improves the position of another company without necessarily being a customer or a supplier. A player is your supply-side complementor if it is more attractive for a supplier to provide you with resources when it is also supplying the other player than when supplying you alone. Conversely, a player is your supply-side competitor if it is less attractive for a supplier to provide you with resources when it is also supplying the other player than when it is supplying you alone. A player is your customer-side complementor if customers value your product more when they have the other player's product than when they have your product alone. Conversely, a player is your customer-side competitor if customers value your product less when they have the other player's product than when they have your product alone.

For example, Microsoft and Intel found they had a complementary relationship – they could work to each other's mutual advantage. Similarly, independent component manufacturers in, say, the car industry, who are accustomed to outsourcing significant elements of the manufacturing process, find themselves in complementary relationships, not just with the car manufacturer but with each other. Again, understanding the nuances of the market, the motives of the players and the rules of the game will help a business identify fresh opportunities and grow faster.

An analysis of complementors adds a layer of subtlety to the black-and-white categories that underlie Porter's five-forces industry analysis. Indeed, Brandenburger calls complementors "the sixth force".

Expanding horizons

Sooner or later a company ambitious for growth, as well as looking to new products and new customers, will look for new business internationally. Companies in small economies will feel the temptation sooner than those in big ones. The US has an economy big enough to satisfy the growth aspirations of many ambitious local companies until they become very large. Conversely, companies in the UK and the Netherlands, for example, have had to turn to overseas markets to satisfy their growth ambitions much earlier in their evolution.

Many companies' first moves overseas are at the request of customers who are happy with a supplier's services in one country and want to use them in another. This helps reduce some of the risks inherent in international expansion, but even so new types of risks will need to be mastered for such expansion to prove an effective growth enabler. These include control risk in a business operation that is likely to be geographically distant, and management risk in understanding cultural differences, which will affect both how the business is to be run internally and how the industry and market in which it hopes to operate work.

These risks are often underestimated, particularly by companies that have experienced success only in their domestic markets and often assume that what works at home will also work abroad. The US is a famous graveyard for the ambitions of UK companies seeking to expand overseas; and Western companies have too often presumed that the Chinese would welcome them with open arms and learn how to do things properly, only to find themselves taken advantage of by canny and ruthless new partners and competitors. Some important considerations are as follows:

■ **Local market differences.** Markets behave very differently in different countries at both the macro and micro levels. Routes to market are therefore different. Big supermarket chains dominate the UK groceries market in a way that is not seen in euro-zone countries. Once a route to market has been agreed, a company must understand that customers and clients in other countries behave differently and have different expectations. "We've had mayonnaise issues," noted Andrew Rolfe, then CEO of UK sandwich chain Pret a Manger, when opening in New York. "Mayonnaise is quite popular in Britain, but Americans aren't so receptive." Pret a Manger experimented with "drier" sandwiches with some success, though the egg Florentine that replaced the egg mayonnaise was described by one critic as having the "colour of neon".

- **Local industry differences.** There will be different competitors in different countries. Industries will be structured differently, so a company's competitive advantage may well differ from country to country. Supply-chain issues will need serious consideration. Can you take advantage of and extend existing supply chains to your new overseas businesses? Or will the cost of exporting dictate the need to source materials and conduct assembly, manufacturing or service delivery remotely? What are the control implications?

- **People management.** This is the issue most likely to be underestimated. Employment and regulation regimes differ significantly from one country to another, with implications for recruitment, performance management, training, health and safety, and redundancy. It is highly unlikely that staff management systems can be imported from head office to a new overseas subsidiary. Cultural differences will also need to be accounted for – different attitudes to authority and control, the work ethic, customer service. A crucial issue when expanding overseas is the appointment of senior managers. Should a company recruit local people or send over expatriates? Expatriates will understand the company best and are more likely to be trusted by headquarters, but locals will understand the local industry and market.

■ **Entry strategy.** This will need careful thought, particularly with regard to how it affects organisational structure. In some countries companies must have a local "partner"; but even when this is not a legal requirement, most companies attempt to minimise the risks through some form of local tie-up, perhaps a joint venture with a local company. Franchising (see Chapter 7) is a common route to international expansion. A local presence helps reinforce credibility as well as secure local knowledge. When Owlstone, a high-tech gas-sensor business originally spun out of Cambridge University by its founders, sought to exploit opportunities with the US military, it decided to establish a new US company, Owlstone Inc, which took ownership of the original UK company. Only by having formal and legal ownership established in the US did Owlstone believe it could secure the contracts it was after.

The economic environment

Having discussed growth levers at the level of the founder, the company, the market and the industry, the last thing to consider is the influence of the general economic environment. Generally, it is easier to grow a business when the economic environment is favourable. Money for investment is more easily obtained; customers and clients are more inclined to increase orders. Conversely, once a recession becomes established, planning assumptions in big companies change: budgets for the next year are reduced, discretionary expenditure is cut, acquisitions are postponed, recruitment is frozen and staff numbers are cut. Actions such as these by firms that dominate their markets and industries in turn fuel the economic malaise they were intended to address. Small businesses, particularly those further down the supply chain, feel the consequences of these actions, with order books cut. As small businesses generally have more restricted portfolios of products and services than big businesses, and often depend on one or two large accounts, a 1–2% cut by a big company can mean a 20–30% reduction in the turnover of a small one. This could be the difference between life and death, unless the small company finds new business or adapts fast.

One company specialising in furniture design and installation is an example. In the boom years up to 2008 the company, which had previously focused on academic, ecclesiastical and other institutions with historically valuable buildings and spaces, expanded its portfolio of services and product lines and began to sell to blue-chip companies that were refitting their corporate headquarters. By 2008, the corporate sector accounted for almost 40% of the company's business, with RBS being its largest client that year. By 2009, the corporate business had evaporated and the company had to embark on a programme of redundancies and other cost-cutting measures in order to survive.

Business planning cycles and economic cycles are rarely aligned. Business planning cycles in big businesses in particular turn slowly: one cycle can take six months; more strategy meetings and more planning meetings are needed before things change significantly again. It is not surprising that big businesses often fall into recessions late, and that they are slow to acknowledge the new dawn. And big companies, particularly ones that spend time benchmarking their performance against their competitors, often behave like sheep, seeking to cut at the same time. They are thus less likely to make the most of the opportunities presented by recessions. Smaller companies, though more likely to be damaged by a recession, can often respond to an upturn more quickly.

Boom-time warning signs

The growth generated when times are good can, however, prove to be illusory or unsustainable. Business leaders determined to establish robust, sustainable growth should watch out for the following symptoms of false, boom-time growth:

- **Unsustainable growth in asset values.** In particular, investments – in recent booms it has been houses, commercial property, stocks and shares; before house ownership was common and before stockmarkets were sophisticated, it was grain, or tulips. The subsequent collapse of every market has always given the lie to the permanence of the growth in values. Business owners need to distinguish between the growth in reported value and real growth in business.

- **Assertions that this time it is different.** Gordon Brown, a former UK prime minister, will never be allowed to forget his claim that he had put an end to boom and bust. Brown is not alone. Herbert Hoover, when accepting the nomination of the Republican Party in 1928, proclaimed:

  > We in America today are nearer to the final triumph over poverty than ever before in the history of any land ... We have not yet reached the goal, but given a chance to go forward with the policies of the last eight years, we shall soon, with the help of God, be in sight of the day when poverty will be banished from this nation.

  Most of the electorate agreed with Hoover, and he won a landslide victory in the presidential election. In 1929 Wall Street crashed, heralding the biggest recession of the century.

- **Risky investments funded by debt.** The rise in asset values characteristic of boom economies is fuelled in part by investors and businesses taking silly risks, and then competing with each other for the right to participate in even riskier investments. Stoking the fire further, money is borrowed to fund flaky strategies. But asset values go down as well as up. Debt remains constant even if the cost of paying interest on it may not, and when the boom is over and asset values have plummeted what is owed may far exceed the value of what is owned.

- **Sensible indicators that do not support a business case being replaced by silly indicators that do.** When money is easy and cheap to obtain, business plans become increasingly unrealistic, and when a boom is rolling reasons are found to sidestep robust checks and controls designed to keep plans conservative. In the boom years running up to 2008, and in the earlier dotcom boom, many business plans were based on the flimsiest of assumptions. At the heart of many were projections of infinitely increasing returns, long before the putative business had generated any cash flow. There was much talk of "a new paradigm", which essentially meant that targets based on profit and cash flow became less important than market share targets, or subjective assessments of future advances in technology, or the size of the customer base. As Chapter 5 makes clear, sustainable growth is all about the quality of cash flow.

- **Determination only to believe the optimists.** Those who say that what goes up must come down are too easily dismissed as doom-mongers when times are good. Even those who are prepared to admit the inevitability of the end of the boom are likely to call it a correction or choose to believe that any slowdown will be gradual and therefore manageable. People argue that the boom will not end not least because they cannot afford for it to end. Even when the numbers begin to turn bad, there is a tendency to remain bullish. Red numbers look black through rose-tinted spectacles. The consequence is that the bust is a nasty surprise and the bigger the boom, the nastier the bust.

- **Growth hides weaknesses.** When times are good the flaws in business models and strategies lie hidden, ready to strike when times turn bad. Growth in good times hides operational and strategic flaws; it does not eliminate them. It takes a dose of bad times to test the robustness of a business model.

Entrepreneurs born in adversity

Just as good economic times can be bad for growth, bad economic times can be good. Indeed, recessions are cradles of entrepreneurship. Many entrepreneurs are neither born nor bred, they are created by force of circumstance. Many small businesses are born when their founders' long-standing employers let them go. The redundancy payments that sweeten the pill have in many instances provided the working capital for the new businesses that have been founded as a result. Most of these new entrepreneurs would not have taken the decision on their own. In a 2009 report for the Kauffman Foundation, Dane Stangler argues:[15]

> Good things do grow out of recessions. Hundreds of thousands of individuals do not wait for others to ease their economic pain – they create jobs for themselves and others.

And those who find themselves jobless when recession hits should heed the advice of Declan Donnellan, a theatre director and writer:[16] "Take your work seriously, but improvise your career."

The sharper the recession the greater the source of opportunity and the longer the list of businesses that are created; indeed, according to the Kauffman Foundation report, well over half of *Fortune* 500 and almost half of the fastest-growing firms in the US were founded in a recession or a bear market:[17]

> Each year new firms steadily recreate the economy, generating jobs and innovations. These companies may be invisible, or they may one day grow into household names. But they constantly come into being as individuals bring forth their economic futures.

In 2003 in the *American Economic Review* Alexander Field argued that the 1930s were the most "technologically progressive" decade of the 20th century.[18] FedEx began operations in April 1973 in the depths of a recession. Its original name, Federal Express, was a sly swipe at the Federal Reserve, with which its founder, Frederick W. Smith, had hoped to get a contract. He did not succeed, but the company that delivered 186 packages to 25 cities on its first night of operations was by 2008 managing more than 7.5 million shipments a day worldwide. General Electric (GE) was founded in 1876 by Thomas Edison, creator of the electric light bulb, in the severe depression following the financial crisis known as the Panic of 1873. Hewlett-Packard Development Company was born in a Palo Alto garage in 1939, towards the end of the Great Depression, supported by an initial investment of $538.

Businesses founded in recessions seem to be better placed for growth when times turn more benign. A 2009 study for Cambridge University's Institute for Manufacturing by Alex Drofiak and Elisabeth Garnsey suggested that high-tech firms were more successful if started in tough times; indeed, high-tech businesses founded in Cambridge in the 1990s recession enjoyed consistently better survival rates than those started in the boom years that followed.[19]

Entrepreneurs have always been peculiarly suited to difficult economic circumstances. William Sahlman, a professor at Harvard Business School, defined entrepreneurship as "the relentless pursuit of opportunity without regard to tangible resources currently controlled" and "the continuous development of intangible resources to pursue opportunity". In other words: "I haven't got the money, the people or indeed any other of the things you might expect of someone looking to put together a new business – but I'm determined to do it anyway." It seems that adversity, whether caused by personal circumstances or the commercial environment, is almost a precondition of entrepreneurship. As Victor Kiam, an American entrepreneur and investor, observed:

> *Entrepreneurs are simply those who understand that there is little difference between obstacle and opportunity and are able to turn both to their advantage.*

Recessionary opportunities

There are undoubtedly some types of opportunity that are more likely than others to turn into growing businesses when times are bad. In bad times people continue to buy food. It is easy to assume that the demand for luxury goods is more likely to suffer, but the purchasing power of the super-rich is relatively unaffected by recessions, though people may decide to be less conspicuous in their consumption. Some corners of the market for ultra-exclusive products seem to be fairly recession proof. While most car manufacturers were reporting year-on-year sales decreases, in autumn 2008 Rolls-Royce was reporting that it was still on track to beat forecasts.

Business managers looking for opportunities when times are bad need to look more carefully at market microclimates. Consumers on fixed incomes – pensioners, for example – are under less pressure than others to change habits; such consumers are more likely to be affected by inflation and the interest they are earning on their savings. For most parents, it will always be a case of "children first" regardless of the economy.

Consumers are only too often prepared to act irrationally when spending their money. The *Financial Times*'s Lex column noted in 2008:

> It pays to be sinful in a downturn. Analysis by Merrill Lynch
> shows that, during the six recessions since 1970, alcohol, tobacco
> and casino stocks have, on average, returned 11% against a
> 1.5% loss for the S&P 500. Incredibly, these sectors not only
> had superior earnings growth but also, in five out of the last
> six recessions, cigarettes, booze and gambling stocks actually
> increased absolute earnings.

People do not forgo other types of luxury either. Häagen-Dazs, a US ice cream-maker, saw sales soar in the recession of the 1990s. People still take holidays, though perhaps they just take them closer to home. Butlins, a UK holiday-camp operator, reported a bookings increase of 15% in summer 2009. In the last quarter of 2008, UK consumers spent 8.1% more on confectionery and sugary snacks. Match.com, an international online dating site, reported a 35% increase in new sign-ups in 2009. In the UK, cinema and theatre attendance and DVD rentals also increased in 2009. In the US, cinema attendance fell by 5% in 2010, but that was while the economy as a whole was recovering. Second-hand bookshops reported a sharp increase in business. Sales at charity shops were 5% higher in 2008 than in 2007.

John Quelch and Katherine Jocz, two Harvard Business School academics, have dug deeper into the ways in which different groups of consumers react to changing circumstances. They report their observations in two 2009 articles, published in *Harvard Business Review*[20] and the *Financial Times*,[21] though they use slightly different terminology in each for describing new segments of consumer generated by the recession:

- Naysayers – "frightened consumers who have stopped buying any discretionary purchases and are trimming their daily purchases".

- Short termers – "younger, urban consumers with few savings who have, therefore, lost little in the financial meltdown". They change little in their purchasing behaviour until fired; then they change overnight.

- Long termers – "consumers who see the reduction in their retirement accounts as an unfortunate bump in the road". They amend their behaviour slightly rather than shutting off altogether, and are sensitive to better value. They are "worried but not panicked".

- Simplifiers – these include "baby boomers who have lost a significant percentage of their savings". They have more to worry about. They are changing their attitude to risk. Quelch and Jocz distinguish between those who are deciding to postpone retirement, and those who are just deciding to make do with less – though this suggests that further segmentation in the model is needed.

- Sympathisers – "savvy consumers who switched into cash ahead of the crash". Generally, they are continuing to spend as before, but perhaps have decided not to buy a new car even though they can afford it because "they do not want to appear ostentatious".

- Permabulls – the "relentlessly optimistic" whose "appetite for consumption remains constrained only by the availability of credit".

When cash is tight it is to be expected that value-for-money segments of the economy do well. In the 1930s, GE, Kellogg and Procter & Gamble all grew out of value-for-money strategies that gave customers more for less. In 2008 and 2009, low-price retailers such as Lidl and Aldi similarly took advantage and have subsequently forced a fundamental restructuring of the supermarket industry in the UK. In 2015 Aldi overtook Waitrose to become the sixth-largest supermarket by market share in the UK. Whichever way consumers are segmented and labelled, the crucial point is that not all consumers will react to a recession in the same way. Thus for entrepreneurs with insight into how different groups of consumers behave, there will always be profitable opportunities to exploit.

What is true of consumers is also true of the business-to-business sector. The demand for some goods and services increases when times are bad. Just as pawnbrokers and loan sharks thrive when consumers are short of cash, any companies that can help cash-starved businesses stay solvent by cutting costs and increasing margins should be in demand. Outsourcing will seem a more attractive proposition if it reduces costs for customers. And because more organisations go bust, in recessions there are more fire sales – opportunities to acquire plant, machinery, people and businesses at a deep discount. All customers give serious thought to change during recessions. No long-standing customer relationship should ever be taken for granted, especially when customers themselves are under pressure. Businesses that fail to recognise this are at risk from those that do – as well as from opportunistic entrepreneurs.

Other external factors

- **Demographic and sociological changes.** The changing age profile of populations in the West has enormous implications for organisations big and small, both as suppliers of products and services to a changing population and as employers. Changing levels of education can improve significantly the supply of human resources, which in turn can facilitate growth. Western universities are full of East Asian students, but universities in China and India are rapidly catching up. At the same time, technology companies in the UK complain of a shortage of appropriately qualified British employees, even in the depths of a recession. Similar claims are made frequently by employers in the US, particularly when seeking to justify increases in the cap on visas for non-US employees – though research suggests that employers are more influenced by the fact that non-US employees are happy to work for less, another important demographic issue. Changing levels of education can also significantly change patterns of demand. Changes in patterns of migration provide opportunities for growing businesses – as the increase in the number of businesses catering for economic migrants from eastern Europe to the UK shows.
- **Technological advances.** These have significant implications for growth. The life cycle of IBM illustrates how an organisation can grow and change as a consequence of technological change. IBM grew as a consequence of following, if not indeed initiating, the rise of the computer and its application in business and commerce. But other organisations, notably Microsoft, were far quicker in

following the trend towards desktop computing, and then from hardware to software, as the principal source of value in the IT industry. While seemingly core components of IBM, such as its personal computer business, have been sold, the company has developed successful advisory and consulting services. Technological changes in one industry frequently have implications for others, as parallel technological changes have a habit of stoking each other and converging. Technological change affects growth in other ways too. The millennium bug, whether founded on fantasy or fact, generated an enormous amount of economic activity around the world in the years leading up to 2000. And the development of the internet and e-commerce has provided growth opportunities for new and old businesses – as well as sounding the death knell for others.

- **Political changes.** These can be as important as cyclical economic changes. More widespread prosperity and the commercial success of businesses in Brazil are largely a result of relative political stability in recent years. Growth in China is certainly a direct consequence of changes in attitude among the political elite and the relative economic stability that followed. Such changes in the West are less radical, but their influence should not be discounted. Politicians can foster a positive climate for entrepreneurship far more directly than economists, or even bankers. For example, regulations governing employment in big companies can act as an incentive for companies to stay small. Planning restrictions may foster an illusion that a city centre looks as it did 100 years ago, but they may also prevent businesses from growing.

Growth barriers

ANYTHING THAT IMPEDES the facilitators and drivers of growth highlighted in the previous chapter is a potential barrier to growth; and even if a business is growing, such barriers may well be present and limiting the growth rate. When times are good, barriers to growth and other organisational weaknesses are often hidden; but when times are harder such barriers may become all too apparent and have a devastating effect. When formulating their growth plans, managers should identify potential as well as self-evident barriers to growth, looking for internal as well as external barriers.

Internal barriers

"More businesses die from indigestion than starvation," David Packard writes in *The HP Way*, suggesting that internal issues rather than an inability to generate new business are the most awkward barriers to growth.[1] Lack of new business is rarely the biggest barrier to growth faced by successful entrepreneurs. This is not to diminish the importance of new sales to a growing business. To qualify for the label "entrepreneur", business founders are usually good salespeople in the first place. Entrepreneurs have to be confident in their ability to keep their businesses well fed. But an entrepreneur too obsessed with the top line will pay insufficient attention to the increasingly sophisticated engine room needed to support growth. A growing top line may make a business appear successful and healthy to outsiders, while management and staff are only too aware that on the inside the organisation is suffering from all sorts of growth pain. Before taking too much pride in top-line growth it is useful to bear in mind the maxim that turnover is vanity, profit is sanity but cash flow is reality in any business, especially a rapidly growing business.

There are several types of internal barrier to growth that a business may have to overcome when seeking a cure for organisational "indigestion" or dysfunctionality. As well as those discussed implicitly in the previous chapter, bear in mind the following:

- personal barriers associated with the founders and their respective roles;
- people-management barriers associated with the function and management of senior and middle management teams, and the remuneration of individual members;
- structural barriers associated with spans of control, reporting lines and communication channels;
- intangible barriers associated with the waning influence of the founders and the need to replace this with business characteristics such as culture, brand and organisational value as the business grows.

It might be observed that all these internal barriers are dependent on the effectiveness of management. Indeed, the most important lesson from this chapter is that the biggest barrier to growth in any business is management, in particular its capacity and capability.

When founders get in the way

If it is accepted that businesses need to change as they grow, it should also be accepted that the roles of those who found businesses need to change too. Indeed, as they will have been around the longest and will have steered the initial activities and set the style of the business, the founders will find that their roles have to change more than any other element of the business as it grows.

Many CEOs and entrepreneurs have commented on the difference between their respective roles. In a 2015 interview for *Entrepreneur* magazine, Nadav Shoval, a young entrepreneur, comments:[2]

> *An entrepreneur can afford to have tunnel vision. Focusing all of their attention on the opportunity they see in front of them is critical for their success. But, to continue the metaphor, a CEO needs to have double vision. They need to be able to see both the opportunities for growth and the obstacles that lie in the way of that growth.*

In a 2013 article in *Inc. Magazine*, Steve Tobak, a former senior executive in and now executive coach to companies in the tech industry, identifies five of the most common pitfalls that entrepreneurs make when attempting to step up to the CEO mark: they're too invested in their own vision; they aren't willing to make the hard choices; they don't have a passion for managing; they don't get marketing; and they usually aren't willing to step down.[3]

In a 2002 *Harvard Business Review* article, John Hamm, a partner at VSP Capital in San Francisco, argues that the qualities that make for successful entrepreneurs often end up being weaknesses in chief executives in established businesses.[4] The single-mindedness and focus that are so important in the early days can turn into the tunnel vision of a chief executive determined to take no notice of the fresh thinking brought by new members of the management team. Loyalty to those who were instrumental in establishing the business can become a liability when the business has outgrown their capabilities. The pragmatism and task-orientation that distinguish entrepreneurs from inventors and dreamers can easily metamorphose into an obsessive attention to detail and a reluctance to delegate when they try to run their business with the help of a professional management team. The informal, can-do, personal style that was instrumental in establishing the flexible culture in a young business may not adapt to the necessarily greater bureaucracy of the larger business.

Business founders also need to acknowledge why they founded the business in the first place, and the extent to which their personal motivation is becoming a business constraint. Those who wanted to escape from a big business to run their own show will find themselves, if successful, running the same sort of venture they wanted to leave.

If business founders do not want to or cannot change, they should acknowledge that it is a question of when rather than whether they should pass the baton to someone else. J. K. Galbraith, an economist, distinguishes between "corporations in which age, size and simplicity of operation still accord power to an individual who has control of capital and those where the technostructure has taken over". It is rare for entrepreneurs to find themselves sitting on top of the latter. Indeed, as Galbraith puts it in his book *The New Industrial State*:[5]

> *The great entrepreneur must, in fact, be compared with the male Apis mellifera [honey bee]. He accomplishes his act of conception at the price of his own extinction.*

Noam Wasserman, a professor at Harvard Business School, reported in 2008 that from his researches into 212 American start-ups in the late 1990s and early 2000s, by the time ventures were three years old 50% of founders were no longer the CEO. By year four only 40% remained. Fewer than 25% of founders led their businesses to IPOs (initial public offerings). Wasserman's comments serve as a warning:[6]

> *There is ... another factor motivating entrepreneurs along with the desire to become wealthy: the drive to create and lead an organisation. The surprising thing is that trying to maximise one imperils achievement of the other. Entrepreneurs face a choice, at every step, between making money and managing their*

ventures. Those who don't figure out which is more important to them often end up neither wealthy nor powerful.

When a business begins to have an existence separate from its founder – when it becomes "the" business rather than "my" business – it has reached a crucial stage in its evolution. A business that is too dependent on its founder usually finds its growth potential capped, regardless of whether the founder is aware of the need to change; the capacity and capability of even the most talented founder are not limitless. Such a business will also be difficult to sell – when such founders walk away from their businesses a significant amount of the value goes with them. Separating founders from businesses, although a necessary component of many growth strategies, is difficult and risky.

Getting the best out of founders as you grow

The founders of sandwich retail chain Pret a Manger, Julian Metcalfe and Sinclair Beecham, recruited an executive with first-class credentials, Andrew Rolfe, to implement their international expansion plan. Metcalfe's first action was to take a three-month holiday, not just to get some well-earned rest but also to give Rolfe space to establish his authority.

A more interesting situation is when founders step back into their businesses if the delegation of authority to incoming management proves unsuccessful. Rolfe left Pret a Manger in 2003 after a couple of years of successful growth, followed by fundamental disagreements about future strategy in the light of subsequent poor business performance. Metcalfe stepped back in as "creative director", a role not found in any governance handbooks. But Metcalfe did not intend to run the business; he appointed another individual, Clive Schlee, to manage the turnaround.

Steve Jobs of Apple is another founder who stepped out (in his case after a row with the board in 1984) only to step back into the role of CEO in 1997, a year after NeXT, the company he had founded in the interim, was bought by Apple, by which time Apple's own position had deteriorated. Unlike Metcalfe, who appointed someone else to the role of CEO, Jobs took the top seat himself, and subsequently led a spectacular turnaround in Apple's fortunes. Interestingly, however, when Jobs took six months' leave for health reasons in 2009 and died in 2011, observers worried about the future of the business, even though Apple was by then one of the biggest listed companies in the world. It is as if Jobs's relationship with Apple had changed little as the business had grown. Commentators noted his obsession with design, and his enthusiasm for the micro-management of parts of the business in ways more often associated with CEOs of much smaller businesses. Two years after Jobs's death the business press was lamenting that Apple had lost 25% of its value. "Two Years After Steve Jobs' Death Is Apple A Different Company?" is the title of one piece.

People – and the management of them

Growth barriers caused by founders can be addressed by refreshing and adding to the capacity and capability of the management team. This is easier said than done.

"If you want a job done properly around here you have to do it yourself" is a sentiment widely expressed by senior management in many businesses. The inference is that good staff are difficult to find; the reality is that the sentiment betrays a reluctance to delegate. Ask to see the organisation chart in many young owner-managed businesses and you will eventually receive, fresh from the drawing board, a diagram showing all members of the team reporting directly to the founder. The first task for those serious about growth is to unplug the top end of many of those reporting lines and plug them into a team of professional managers who can take the business to the next stage of its evolution and thus free the founder to focus on other matters.

Senior managers, rather than working on the assumption that no one else can do the job properly, should accept that doing the job themselves is at best a temporary fix for a short-term problem. They will give themselves the best chance of managing growth if they accept that one of their roles is to make themselves redundant and to recruit people who can do the senior management job better than they can. Unfortunately, even those who think the right thoughts about delegation make the mistake of thinking "what this business needs is someone else like me". This is the essence of the brief given to many headhunters and recruitment consultants by successful senior managers (business founders in particular) anxious to build the senior team fast. Teams that are most likely to be future-proof are built out of differences in personality, constructive disagreement and creative abrasion – individuals that complement each other rather than seek the easy life through complimenting the founder. This means recruiting a team fit for building tomorrow's business rather than running yesterday's business, a team with different sorts of people, not just more of the same.

New people brought in to help manage a business will not relate to it in the same way as the founder, and will need to be motivated and managed in different ways. If this is not done, the team that has been constructed to eliminate one barrier to growth will itself become another barrier. As Jon Katzenbach and Douglas Smith state in their book *The Wisdom of Teams*, the performance of a group of people thrown together will not even add up to the sum of its parts without significant team management effort on the part of the business founder; whereas a well-managed and effective team will give the business the capacity not only to put out the fires that need fighting from time to time but also to pay attention to the bigger picture.[7] Team management is addressed more fully in Chapter 7.

Recruiting complementary team members has implications for the existing team members, who will have to give up some elements of their roles to outsiders. Some find this hard. New team members find it hard as well. New managers will have been brought in for their ability to take the business to the next stage of its evolution, but what they find in the meantime may come as a shock – a step back in their careers. They may have been oversold the role in the first place by founders and managers proud of what they have done so far and keen to boast about it.

As well as having different expectations from existing managers, new managers often feel differently about remuneration. They are more likely to expect a decent salary. First-generation managers may be satisfied by the excitement of founding a business reinforced by options or equity; managers with the experience of building and managing a big business expect to be paid properly, probably more than existing managers. This is a common cause of tension between different generations of management in a growing business.

Remuneration is not the only source of tension. For example, once a firm has grown to a size that warrants the recruitment of its first HR manager, it is often not long before the HR manager has become HR director, and supervises a compensation and benefits manager and a recruitment manager, each with assistants and their own budgets. In parallel, other managers in the business, as they build their own management infrastructures, begin to offload people-management problems to the HR team.

Businesses find that matters that used to be part of the portfolio of general management skills are compartmentalised: for example, good people management is now the responsibility of HR; and sales management is the preserve of the sales department. The infrastructure that has been built to support the needs of the business has given line staff and managers the excuse to retreat from good people management, and from personal interaction with clients and customers. The structure itself has become a barrier, not just to growth but also to good business. This in turn will lead to another reconstruction of senior management, this time one that attempts to reconnect managers with their people and clients. Specialist HR, sales, marketing and operations departments are not closed down – the organisation is now too big to do without them – but their roles are redefined along the lines of internal consultants so as to support line management rather than substitute for it.

People-management barriers exist in big companies just as much as in small ones. Indeed, they are so important in companies with ambitions to grow that they merit a chapter of their own (Chapter 7). But it is important to note that growth means change, and change means changing people – their roles and their behaviour. The reason change in a business can be so difficult is that for it to happen every individual in the business must change too. Everyone is different, approaching change with different preconceptions and experiencing it differently. Individuals who choose not to change will be replaced – including, of course, senior management.

Organisational structure

Organisational structures can be barriers to business growth, and the solutions to many growth problems are often structural.

A new business does not need much of a structure. However, a business will not be able to take advantage of the benefits of scale without structuring itself appropriately. Different structures suit different businesses at different stages of their development, and struggling on for too long with last year's structure will constrain growth.

There are two types of structure to be considered:

■ **Corporate structure** refers to the relation between the various reporting units in the business – divisions, subsidiaries and other group entities.

■ **Management structure** refers to reporting lines between individuals, in particular the composition and functioning of board and board committee members, board committees, management and members of the management team.

Different parts of the business may be set up as separate divisions, which in turn may be set up as separate legal entities owned by a holding company. Or the directors may choose to avoid the additional layers of management a more complex corporate structure would require by managing the whole business through a single corporate structure. There is an unresolvable contradiction here. If a business comprises different disciplines, a single corporate structure may fail to acknowledge the nuances existing in each individual discipline; conversely, if too much management is delegated to the division or the individual discipline, there is the danger that each division will unnecessarily invest in duplicate resources or, worse, pursue initiatives that damage other parts of the business.

It is not possible to eliminate these tensions and contradictions, but they can be managed sensibly. Research and development departments, and parts of the business investing in entrepreneurial activity, may benefit from the relative freedom that a separate division or corporate entity would give them. Such a structure could also facilitate external investment or joint ventures with third parties that might not be possible if business is conducted through a single structure. Of course, reporting lines would need to be established between the various parts of the business, and each part would need to be accommodated within an overall planning structure with allowance made for the specific challenges of each. (See the discussion of the three horizons in Chapter 2.) Creative use of share ownership and remuneration structures could also be used to tie disparate parts of the business together. When Title Research created its online genealogy business it set it up as a separate corporate structure with its own managers who drew on the intellectual capital of the group as a whole and reported to a group board, which retained financial control. Staff throughout the group were given equity and options in the new business regardless of where they worked, which helped to ensure that the new business did not attract too much attention and resources.

Governance is the name given to attempts to structure the relations between stakeholders – managers and owners in particular. Governance is what happens to management structure when the regulators step in. Other than companies in highly specialist sectors, regulators are interested in big businesses rather than small ones, given that in many small businesses the owners and the management are the same. Thus the demands of governance provide an additional impetus for structural change as a business grows.

A key component in any governance structure is the board. The board of directors, appointed by the shareholders, holds management to account. In small businesses owner-managers may be directors of the business according to company law, but there are minimal distinctions between the roles. The evolution of the distinctions is one of the changes growth brings. The greater the separation between owner and manager, particularly once external financial investors take an interest in the business, the more is the need for a board to formally assume supervisory responsibilities over management.

Different countries and regulatory environments have different approaches to governance structures. In the US and the UK, the focus of authority in big corporations is a unitary board, comprising both executive directors (that is, senior members of management) and independent non-executive directors. In the US, an all-powerful chief executive typically has executive authority and is also responsible for chairing the board. In the UK, in big companies at least, the roles of chairman of the board and chief executive (or managing director) are separate, with the former responsible for managing the board and the latter for managing the business. The separation of the role of chairman and CEO is an important principle of UK corporate governance that listed companies must comply with or explain why they have not. There are no such requirements that the top role will be separated in listed companies in the US, but the separation is increasingly common nonetheless.

Big businesses in Germany are obliged to have separate supervisory and management boards. Even though in the UK the unitary board structure is favoured, many companies recreate a supervisory/management board structure by having a management company (directed by one board) owned by a holding company (directed by another board), thus using a corporate vehicle to structure management. Management structure and corporate structure can therefore be interrelated.

Family businesses often adopt a similar dualist approach as they grow. One of the inevitable rites of passage for family businesses is the recruitment of professional non-family managers and the delegation of responsibility to them. This rarely occurs without tension between family and professional management over involvement in if not control of the business. It is the old tension between management and ownership but with a family twist. Some of the largest family businesses have attempted to resolve this with a two-company, dual-board structure, with the family having seats on a holding company board but leaving a subsidiary operating company board to the managers. Which decisions need to be referred from one board to the next is carefully identified and codified in constitutional documentation, giving the board of the operating company the flexibility to do its job while keeping the family sufficiently involved.

Spider plants, spaghetti or hierarchies?

Structure is not just a matter of governance. Businesses have other structural decisions to take as the business grows. Every structure comes with advantages and disadvantages.

A management hierarchy

Turning a simple founder-led business into a complex hierarchy demands the addition of layers of management, thus extending its ability to control its expanding resources. Such an organisation is often highly centralised, with clear chains of command and a strong locus of power in the senior management team. However, an organisation constructed on these lines does not have to grow much before it becomes very different from the one the founders created. The ends of the chains of command will find themselves a long way from the centre. Though disciplined, such organisations can be slow-moving and find it difficult to respond to changes in the market or the economy. Customer-facing parts of the organisation can find their authority restricted. This may not matter in a stable business in which customers have simple expectations, but in many industries customers are not so easily satisfied. More typical is the business that grows from a small one in which customers value dealing with the boss, to a big one in which they feel that customer care has been compromised. Middle managers often find it difficult to exercise authority supposedly delegated to them – colleagues objecting to decisions and lucky enough to have a personal relationship with the founder can easily give them a call and bypass the bureaucracy. Such a structure may also present problems when the founder steps down, particularly if management processes have not been documented.

A decentralised structure

The problems inherent in a multilayer hierarchy usually encourage growing businesses to decentralise management processes and build management and corporate structures that facilitate this. A business may be subdivided by product type or geography, for example, or just broken down into smaller, decentralised units. Each unit is typically granted authority to take decisions on matters that might previously have been the responsibility of the senior management team. Such organisations are flatter than traditional hierarchies. They are also more flexible and more responsive to customer needs, as the decision-takers are closer to customers. This type of structure will generate internal competition, which should help sharpen quality; but competition might degenerate into destructive backstabbing, with bits of the organisation acting in their own interests rather than those of the organisation as a whole – a problem that is particularly likely when managers are ambitious and have strong incentives to achieve personal targets.

The corporate structure may follow the management structure, with each division set up as a company with its own board, and maybe its own back office. However, it is easy to see under this arrangement how management costs can spiral; indeed, a new CEO seeking to turn around such a business might want to strip out pockets of "redundant" management and pull some back-office functions into a central service centre. An opposite reaction might be to sell off divisions, exchanging stand-alone businesses for cash to reinvest in those that remain. A business that grows by building and delegating to divisions is not unlike a spider plant, and one consequence of its flexibility is its ability to deconstruct itself piece by piece. Again this distinguishes it from a more tightly constructed hierarchical business.

Other structures

There are compromise structures that might sit between traditional hierarchies and decentralised, divisional structures. A matrix structure attempts to retain both the discipline of the hierarchy and the flexibility and decentralisation of the divisional structure (see Figure 4.1).

In such a structure a senior finance manager, for example, in a division reports in two directions: to the CEO of the division and to a group head of finance in head office. Divisional CEOs in their turn report to a group CEO. Such organisations can quickly become complicated, and managers may find themselves caught in the middle. On the positive side, the structure itself will force

FIG 4.1 **A matrix structure**

Source: Author

the debates that matter to the surface: debates between the centre and the division, and between those responsible for setting corporate strategy in pursuit of growth and those responsible for implementing decisions from day to day. Such structures also help to expose managers with a tendency for building personal fiefdoms at the expense of corporate objectives.

Some organisations, taking advantage of the connectivity offered by computer systems, have invented even more radical structures: networks of individuals connected to each other virtually; and organisations in which people report to each other variously depending on the project – for example, A might report to B in one project while simultaneously B might be a member of another team led by A. For an increasing number of organisations structure is fluid, continuously adapting to meet current circumstances. Boundaries between different types of staff and different types of activity are losing definition, as are boundaries between work and play, employment and self-employment. Even boundaries between client and service provider are becoming blurred as project teams include client representatives and suppliers; customers up and down the supply chain adopt open-book costing and accounting strategies; and industries adopt lean manufacturing and just-in-time supply chain processes. Organisations are reaching towards stranger metaphors to capture what they are trying to achieve with structure, such as "upside down management" and "the spaghetti organisation".

Structure: discipline and freedom

Nypro, a plastics mouldings business, worked hard to create flexible management and corporate structures that sustained rather than obstructed growth. With headquarters in the US and turnover of more than $1 billion at the time of its acquisition in 2013 by Jabil, a global manufacturing services company, Nypro was a big business. The deal was unusual as Nypro was owned by 2,000 of its own employees. And Nypro was unusual in the way in which it approached the structuring of local management.

Regional businesses were run by boards of directors comprising senior staff drawn from other businesses in the organisation. This fostered a sense of co-operation between businesses across the organisation. Remuneration strategies also encouraged co-operation. Performance-related remuneration was determined by the performance of the team, not the individual. Project teams included client representatives, thus ensuring client interests were recognised.

At the same time, Nypro had a strongly competitive streak. Teams and businesses competed with each other. The organisation's strong flair for innovation was driven in part by its competitive culture. An obsession with client service also played a role, as did the fact that good ideas developed in one part of the business quickly found their way across the business, not because of command and control, but because of the determination to be best and the fact that senior managers found themselves responsible for several teams, if not several companies, within the organisation. Indeed, Nypro's culture was a curious balance between co-operation and competition supported by the way it structured itself and its management.

Why, then, was the business sold to Jabil? Ultimately, its unusual incentive and ownership structure turned from strength to weakness, with its employee ownership inhibiting its ability to raise capital to invest when needed in a changing market. Jabil, as a listed company, did not suffer the same disadvantages. Yet another example, perhaps, of the strengths at one stage of growth turning into disadvantages at the next.

In family businesses the need to deal with family issues adds another layer to an organisational structure that is probably complicated enough already. Well-managed family businesses work hard at identifying and analysing family issues and business issues, determining where they reinforce and undermine each other. Such businesses are often as "businesslike" about family issues as they are about business issues, forming family councils and constitutions to manage such things as remuneration for family members, recruitment and, most important of all, succession planning from one generation to another.

In many ways most family business problems are sophisticated manifestations of a problem that faces all growing businesses: understanding and managing the difference between control and ownership. Sorting out the structure is often an important part of the solution.

Reluctance to change

As the coverage of organisational issues in this chapter and of growth models in Chapter 2 makes clear, a reluctance or, worse, an inability to change is a substantial barrier to growth.

A growing business needs to anticipate the future and prepare for the challenges of the next stage of evolution. This may require changing something that is not yet broken. The faster the business is growing, the more likely it will need to change, but the more difficult it will be to make the case. Much of the reluctance to change, therefore, will be the fault of management responsible for yesterday's success. In his book *The Prince*, published in 1532 (five years after his death), Machiavelli is as pertinent as ever about change:

> *It ought to be remembered that there is nothing more difficult to take in hand, more perilous to conduct, or more uncertain in its success, than to take the lead in the introduction of a new order of things. Because the innovator has for enemies all those who have done well under the old conditions, and lukewarm defenders in those who may do well under the new.*

Much has been written on change management, but for growing businesses the following principles are important:

■ When time is tight or you have a crisis on your hands, a top-down, strongly directed approach is often best. But do not expect the experience to be a happy one.

■ When time pressure is easier or when a business is doing well, a bottom-up, participatory process is better.

■ For a business with ambitions to grow it is as well to keep change permanently on the agenda. Like tai chi, it may not be comfortable but will keep you supple as you get older.

Given that a growing business is a business that is doing well, change is most likely to be successful if it is a bottom-up, participatory process, in which those involved or affected have a sense of ownership of the change initiative, than might be the case if change is imposed. Similarly, a business ambitious for growth should find ways of keeping change on the agenda, ensuring last year's successes do not turn into next year's sacred cows. In a 2010 article in *Harvard Business Review*, Freek Vermeulen and Phanish Puranam of London Business School and Ranjay Gulati of Harvard Business School argue that seemingly healthy well-performing companies can be vulnerable because of a build-up of what they call "corporate cholesterol".[8] Such organisations should make sure that they use more than one type of change to clear it otherwise the process of change may become routine. Growing organisations that do not look for change as a matter of course eventually find themselves cornered in a crisis, and the only way out is a top-down, directed, painful and expensive change programme.

External barriers

It is easy to blame a failure to grow on external barriers, many of which are propped up by internal barriers, the most common involving people. For example, private equity firms and venture capitalists will often note that they invest in management teams not businesses – and so a company wanting to raise money should ensure its team is robust. In many instances the barrier is not the lack of finance but the capability and attitude of the people behind the business – such as a reluctance to take on debt or equity on the part of owner-managers. Conversely, external barriers may be seen as opportunities that will – or could – provide a springboard for further growth.

Nevertheless, there are external barriers to growth that lie beyond management's sphere of influence. In some industries there are institutional and regulatory barriers that prevent organisations growing; and organisations attempting to sell to some markets find that external factors limit their size. External factors include the following.

The personal touch

Markets that demand the "home-made" or "personal" touch present particular growth challenges. Those that succeed in selling into these markets often find themselves dependent on one or two pivotal members of the company. How businesses work at converting personal characteristics such as personality and individual skill into corporate characteristics such as brand and organisational culture is discussed in Chapter 7. Some businesses have worked particularly hard at adjusting automated mass-production processes to replicate the characteristics of hand-made processes. Batch-made premium potato chips are described by some manufacturers as "hand-made" in the UK, while in other parts of the world manufacturers describe them as "kettle-made". In both instances processes will have been developed to continuously rake the chips to prevent them from sticking together. But there will come a point when the fundamental mechanics of production or of just doing business will run out of process innovations. Either growth will falter or essential qualities of the product or service will change. Businesses that revise their product or service in these circumstances risk a lot in the name of growth, particularly when they see other, smaller businesses move into the hand-made, personal-service space they have vacated.

Other businesses look for scale in replication, ensuring that the essential unit of the business itself stays the same size and seeking growth through increasing the number of business units. Pret a Manger makes sure that sandwiches are always made on site. Each shop has its own kitchen, adding significantly to the fixed costs of the business as a whole but enabling it to maintain claims about the freshness of its products and also to cater better for local demand. Most of its major competitors have taken advantage of growth by centralising manufacturing and shipping products to shops daily. Thus they have achieved economies of scale but have sacrificed "made at home" qualities that are difficult to centralise.

Strategic constraints

Michael Porter, a well-known writer and thinker on business strategy, considers the tension between effective strategic positioning and an ambition to grow in an influential 1996 article in *Harvard Business Review*:[9]

> *Too often, efforts to grow blur uniqueness, create compromises, reduce fit, and ultimately undermine competitive advantage. In fact, the growth imperative is hazardous to strategy.*

By implication a converse proposition also has to be true: that some strong strategic propositions impose constraints on growth. Porter argues that competitive strength is derived from a differentiated strategic positioning. For him differentiation is not just about product definition, it reaches deep into a business's "activity system", influencing decisions about how the operations are constructed and aligned behind a market proposition. Too many growth proposals risk diluting differentiation. When looking for growth Porter encourages managers to look to "deepen" rather than "broaden" and "compromise" a strategic position:

> *A company can often grow faster – and far more profitably – by better penetrating needs and varieties where it is distinctive than by slugging it out in potentially higher growth arenas in which the company lacks uniqueness.*

Premium brands are confronted with an obvious subset of the type of growth barrier that Porter worries about. Exclusivity, although it allows a business to charge more, will constrain volume. Ferrari initially planned to build only 444 of the 550

Barchetta (although 448 eventually appeared), largely because of Japanese superstitions about particular numbers. Producing the vehicle in significantly larger quantities would have risked damaging the perceptions of the famous marque – and might not have been any more profitable because of the lower prices that would have been charged for the cars. Indeed, Ferrari on occasions works hard at making the already exclusive even more exclusive. In 2009 it announced that it would produce just five 550 GTZs based on the Barchetta in conjunction with Zapato. All five cars were sold for £1 million ($1.6 million) each before the official announcement. For Ferrari less is more; its most important growth measure is the perceived increase in the brand's prestige. Ferrari will never be a big company by any of the measures of size and growth discussed in this book.

Many differentiated propositions inevitably, therefore, address smaller markets. The size of a prestige market itself is a barrier to significant growth. Product diversification may open up new market segments and therefore appear to provide routes to growth, but in following them managers run the risk of damaging the prestige brand. Conversely, big players in an industry might try to acquire small, niche, prestige businesses, believing they can add resources and investment and bask in the reflected glory. Again, both businesses run the risk of doing each other damage, and the strategy seems to fail more often than it succeeds. Ford has had a long and chequered history of buying exclusive car manufacturers and then regretting it, including Aston Martin and Jaguar. In the 1960s Ford thought it had done a deal to acquire Ferrari, only for the owners of the Italian company to pull out at the last minute. (A consequence of this was the production of the Ford GT40 sports car, designed to beat Ferrari at its own game. The GT40 went on to win at Le Mans for four consecutive years but did not win for Ford a sustainable position as a manufacturer of supercars.) Volkswagen owns Bentley and has won plaudits for its work with the Bugatti brand, though in truth it did little more than buy a defunct name with a glorious history.

The growth problems associated with premium brands do not always stop with small niche companies. Mercedes-Benz has always been much bigger than Ferrari, but it has successfully built a premium brand proposition on a reputation for quality and reliability. Daimler-Benz's 1998 merger with Chrysler was a deal all about growth, but as a strategy it failed. The costs of investment and the management effort required to bring Chrysler up to European standards drew resources and management attention away from the core German business, jeopardising the brand qualities that made Daimler-Benz successful in the first place. Even before customers started questioning the quality of their new Mercedes, market observers were talking about the damage the Chrysler tie-up might do to the Mercedes brand just by association. The CEO of Daimler-Benz admitted the deal had been a failure at the St Gallen Symposium in 2008, a year after selling Chrysler for $1:

> *The reality was that we couldn't actually achieve global integration because it was at odds with the image of our brands, the preferences of our customers, and many other success factors – all of which were far more diverse and fragmented. It's fair to say that we overestimated the potential of passing leading-edge technology from Mercedes-Benz to Chrysler. Unlike premium brand customers, American volume brand customers are far too price-sensitive to absorb its cost ... In the final analysis, we learned a practical lesson about the limits of globalisation.*

The company also learned an important lesson about growth.

Measuring and describing growth

THIS CHAPTER DISCUSSES some of the methods used to measure growth. Managers are more likely to achieve and sustain growth if they have a means of measuring it. But they must first decide what they are seeking to grow and why. Businesses are multi-dimensional and can grow in different ways and directions. When plotted on the same graph the growth of different elements of the business will not necessarily move in parallel.

Companies at different stages of evolution will experience different rates of growth and have different perspectives on it. A successful small company can grow by multiples over a single year but still make little impression on any market-share table. A bigger, mature company may be delighted with double-digit growth, but may be even more interested in its position in the pecking order relative to other big companies.

Revenue, turnover and sales

In the US the terms revenue or gross sales are used, whereas in the UK turnover is commonly used. Revenue appears at the top of a company's income statement (profit and loss account) and has the nickname "the top line". Thus a business whose revenue is growing is exhibiting top-line growth. The number on the top line is easy to spot, and a business ambitious for growth will help substantiate its growth claims if it can show consistent growth in revenue. J. K. Galbraith called revenue growth the "*sine qua non* of growth". Turnover suggests more than sales volume; it also implies a measurement of the rate of activity in a business, the speed with which the engine of a business is turning over. Regardless of its label, however, the revenue/sales/turnover figure in the accounts is a product of price and volume. It is therefore possible to show an increase in revenue by increasing prices while volume stays the same, or even decreases. Furthermore, increases in revenue mean more in relative than in absolute terms. An increase in revenue also needs to be considered in the context of the rate of inflation. Inflation, too many managers mistakenly assume, pushes prices up; it does not – inflation pushes real prices down. It is managers who push prices up, something they need to remember in their growth plans.

Revenue, along with other measures discussed in this chapter, is sensitive to changes in accounting policy, and accounting, particularly management accounting, is more an art than a science. Accountants and regulators and the interpreters of accounts worry about "revenue recognition" in particular. For example, when should a sale be booked as a sale: when the order is placed? Or when the payment deposit is received? Or when the product is delivered? Or when any outstanding money has been paid?

When preparing financial statements for publication companies are required to follow the prescriptions of the accounting regulators, which will often provide industry-specific answers to questions such as these. But it is inevitable that prescribed accounting regulation will occasionally lead to accounting treatments that make less sense when applied to the specific circumstances of a transaction in real life. It is not unusual for a sales team to close a deal that they consider to be commercially secure only to find it cannot yet be included in the published financial statements. Of course, when preparing internal management accounts that are used to run the business, companies all over the world have much more flexibility to come up with a policy that suits their own particular circumstances. The policy selected for management accounts may differ from that demanded by the regulators for published financial statements, which means that a company may report figures in its published accounts that are different from those it uses to run the business.

Notwithstanding prescriptive regulation, companies still have judgments to make when drafting their financial statements for publication. These judgments are codified in a set of accounting policies, which are published in the notes to the financial statements; these should be studied carefully by anyone attempting to use the financial statements to discover a growth story. When companies get entangled with accounting regulations the consequences can be serious. When Morrisons took over Safeway in 2004 it decided to restate the first-half sales figures that Safeway had previously issued to take account of new accountancy guidelines on revenue recognition. The restatement implied a like-for-like sales reduction of 2.5%. Tesco got into all sorts of trouble with revenue recognition in 2014, confessing that it had as a consequence overstated its half-year profits by an estimated £250 million.

Assuming the same accounting policy is applied consistently from year to year and business is fairly consistent, different policies are unlikely to have much impact on published numbers in the long term. But a change from a conservative revenue-recognition policy to a less conservative one might have the effect of increasing reported revenue in one year.

Revenue/turnover/sales is a measure of how much product or service is being sold and at what price, but it says little about the efficiency of the operation, its ability to turn sales into profit and then cash. A business that grows revenue but pays insufficient attention to profit and cash measures is one whose growth is likely to be unsustainable and whose future is uncertain. Revenue is vanity, profit is sanity but cash flow is reality.

Market share

Big businesses that dominate their industries consider market share an important measure, as it indicates the success of the business compared with the competition. For small businesses, or businesses in a fragmented industry in which no company dominates, market share is a less meaningful indicator. In a growing industry it might be argued that it is easier to grow the top line. In reality, however, a growing industry is one that will attract new entrants. A business in such an industry may be able to grow its top line while reducing its market share. Conversely, in a shrinking industry companies may find themselves competing ever more aggressively over a smaller amount of business, putting pressure on sales price as well as volume. However, companies may also be rushing to exit, enabling those choosing to remain to consolidate a strong position by buying market share at a discount – something Travelex succeeded in doing (see Chapter 3).

Profit/income: gross and net

No business can survive in the long term without generating profit or income (as it is often referred to in the US). When assessing an opportunity, entrepreneurs rightly worry about market and industry size, and the ability of the founding team to build a healthy revenue top line. Top-line growth figures, the proportion of invitations to tender converted to real business, and so on, all matter. But the attractions of top-line growth can be dangerous; an understanding of profit – the "bottom line" – and how it relates to revenue, demands an appreciation of the other factors needed to run a business, including pricing and costs, salaries, overheads, raw materials and the cost of finance. Sales people understand sales, but successful business managers need to understand profit if they want to run a successful business. That profit is important may seem obvious, but it is easy to overlook when assessing the growth potential of businesses, particularly high-tech businesses, and particularly when the markets are frothy and the bubble is looking increasingly fragile. In March 2015 Tech Tour released the Tech Tour Growth 50, a list of Europe's fastest-growing, high-tech, pre-exit companies. Its published assessment criteria included 50% sales growth, $100 million valuation, at least $10 million of revenue and at least $20 million of funds raised. There was no mention of profit or income.

On the assumption that all businesses exist to make a profit – or at least have an ability to generate profit – most would argue that profit is an important measure of success. Many would argue that profit is a more important measure than revenue, and that growth in profit is more important than growth in revenue. Growth in profit may come as a consequence of business decisions that lead to decreases in revenue. Businesses wishing to cut costs often seek to cut staff, which might then mean the withdrawal from less profitable or unprofitable lines of business. The organisation might end up much smaller according to some measures than it was, but if its profits have increased, in one important sense the business has still grown.

Types of profit

There are different types of profit.

Gross profit

Gross profit (turnover minus cost of sales – that is, the costs directly attributable to each sale) and gross margin (gross profit as a percentage of sales) indicate the health of the essential engine that underpins the business. Businesses in different industries have different gross profit profiles, so gross profit should best be used to measure the performance of a company's product or service against projections and against similar businesses in similar industries. Different products sold by the same company will have different profit profiles. Wise managers know that they should be wary of favouring high-margin products within their business portfolios just because they are high-margin. High-margin and low-margin products and services often have complementary relationships within the same company. Gillette makes more profit on the refills for its shavers and its shaving accessories than on the shaver itself, but it would be foolish for the company to focus only on refills and accessories. Similarly, printers are cheap because manufacturers make their money on ink cartridges. Service businesses, which have few raw materials costs, are inherently more profitable than manufacturing businesses, and a business that assembles and installs automatic doors will also want to sell the contracts for maintaining the doors. There are instances of companies fighting to secure a position in a market by underpricing and selling products at a loss to obtain the service contracts that might follow.

Gross profit is profit after deducting only the costs directly associated with the sale. It ignores the costs associated with back-office functions: the overheads. Gross profit is a measure of interest to companies in the same industry that may wish to buy the business; they may see much of the back office doubling up resources that they already possess. Deciding which costs to deduct when calculating gross profit is often a matter of judgment.

Net profit

Net profit (and net margin – net profit as a percentage of revenue) is profit after all costs, including back-office costs, have been deducted. Net profit indicates the ability of a business to generate a return. Calculating net profit before deducting tax, interest or depreciation (earnings before interest, tax, depreciation and amortisation or EBITDA) is common, as this focuses attention on the cash-generating capability of the business. Tax is an allocation of profit rather than a cost that is incurred to generate it. Similarly, interest is an appropriation by a financial stakeholder rather than a cost incurred in keeping the wheels spinning. Depreciation is an accounting adjustment to the value of the assets rather than a cash expense.

Managers who focus on profit as well as turnover or market share are acutely aware of the importance of price, perhaps more so than volume. Sales people may be keen to underprice in an attempt to win business. Getting the price right at the outset therefore is critical; it is a lot more difficult to increase it afterwards. One approach to increasing sales volume is to cut prices. But a price cut goes straight to the bottom line, and the operating model of the company will multiply its effect. For example, a business making a 10% margin decides on a 5% price cut to boost sales. It had been making $10 on every $100 of sales; now it makes only $5 on every $95 of sales, assuming volumes stay the same. A 5% reduction in price has led to a 50% reduction in margin. Volumes will have to more than double to make the 5% price reduction worthwhile. Conversely, raising prices – or at least ensuring they keep pace with inflation – is the easiest, cheapest and quickest way of increasing margin.

Rigorous cost control as a route to increasing profit will take longer but can be less risky than increasing prices – at least a business does not have to speculate about the impact of its decision on its customers – unless cost cuts mean a poorer product or service. Some industries have been revolutionised by new entrants that have focused on fundamentally rethinking the cost side of the business. Southwest Airlines was one of the first of many low-cost airlines. It ran only one type of aircraft to minimise the costs associated with maintenance, training and turnaround. It focused on short flights, thus reducing the costs associated with meals. It chose to fly from small airports rather than big international ones with high landing charges, and focused on the segment of the market that was more interested in getting there than in getting there in style.

But cost management can spring surprises. In many businesses, particularly knowledge businesses, the most significant costs are the costs of staff. Keeping down staff salaries might be at the expense of encouraging staff to leave, which in turn will increase recruitment and training costs. Similarly, striking a hard bargain with suppliers may make enemies in the industry that a business could do without, particularly when new competitors enter, or when it is looking for favours. As is often the case, short-term cost control measures can have unanticipated long-term consequences.

Determining profit

Determining profit is even more subjective than determining revenue, as it is influenced by accounting regulation and policy and the choices made by management affect expenditure as well as revenue. Whether or not to capitalise expenditure – that is, enter it on the balance sheet as an asset rather than write it off against revenue as a cost on the income statement – can have a significant impact on reported profit. In some instances, there is not much of a decision to make. If a company buys a freehold property, it will capitalise it; the investment will then sit on the balance sheet and the consequent depreciation charge will hit the company's profit. In many instances, however, the decision to capitalise can be a matter of judgment.

Profit and value

Title Research, when setting up its genealogy search business, findmypast. com, spent approximately £1 million ($1.6 million) digitalising births, marriage and desk records. After discussions with their accountants, the managers decided to write off the investment costs as there were significant uncertainties associated with the new business. This reduced the profit (and tax) for the year. When selling the business several years later, the managers needed to persuade buyers that the book value of assets on the balance sheet significantly undervalued the business because it did not include the digitalised data sets from which the business was still earning money.

Just as an undue focus on revenue can lead to an unsustainable growth path, so can an undue focus on profit to the detriment of other measures damage a business's long-term prospects. Profit in the short term can be increased by cutting costs. Taken too far, cutting costs will compromise the long-term growth of the business. Indeed, some might argue that to an extent growth and profit maximisation are contradictory objectives. In the short term, in many businesses it is possible to increase profit by slowing down the rate of growth. There is no single right answer to the question of how to manage the tension between profit and growth, and getting the tension right involves understanding a complicated tangle of variables both inside and outside the business. Ultimately, achieving the right tension is, once again, an art rather than a science.

When considering profit as a measure in a growing business it is important to consider the concept of break-even. When a company, or a business within the company, breaks even it has reached a size sufficient to cover its fixed costs and make a "contribution". A business's break-even position may be expressed as a formula: fixed costs divided by gross margin.

For example, a business venture has fixed costs of $100,000 a year and a gross margin of 25%. Its break-even position is therefore 100,000 ÷ 0.25 = 400,000. In other words, when sales reach $400,000 a year the business will cover its fixed costs and break even.

The concept of break-even is important in a growing business. Break-even is a crucial moment in the evolution of a business and its relationship with its financial stakeholders. It also highlights the importance of margin or profit. The healthier the margin, the quicker the break-even point will be reached and the easier it will be to sustain subsequent profitability.

Different parts of a company's business (analysed by geography, category or product) will have different characteristics and will generate different profit levels, so getting the mix right and understanding its implications is important when assessing profit.

Headcount and asset capacity

Headcount, the number of staff on the payroll, is one of many measures that gauge the extent of the resources deployed by an organisation. Some businesses may be more interested in measures that reflect the capacity of other assets in the business, for example capital employed, or factory size, or acres under cultivation. Government bodies often use headcount as a proxy indicator of an organisation's size. A bigger business generally employs more people; more people to manage presents management challenges that businesses with fewer people to manage can avoid. Headcount is therefore for many industries a good proxy for the size – and complexity – of an organisation.

Asset-capacity measures and profitability measures can be connected by measuring the return to a particular asset category – for example, by dividing net profit by the cost of fixed assets to assess how much profit fixed assets are generating. The value of employees is not captured on the balance sheet, but annual profit can be divided by annual total employment costs, giving a measure of profit generated per employee dollar. An early indication of the changing fortunes (changing for the worse, that is) of a business ambitious for growth is a declining value added per employee–dollar ratio.

Such measures are good, but by no means perfect. When times are good, businesses often recruit new employees ahead of the growth curve; when times are bad, they often cut back on human resources in anticipation of lost business. Revenue and headcount curves therefore do not move in parallel. Besides, different types of industry have different human resources requirements. A property business can trade in property portfolios worth billions of dollars and generate significant profits with only a handful of staff; other industries are far more people-intensive and generate less profit.

As with revenue, an organisation's wage bill is influenced by price (that is, salary levels) as well as by headcount. Headcount is perhaps the more obvious measure of growth, but total employment cost is an important measure as well. As argued elsewhere, the most important constraint on growth is management capacity and capability. Some of the most frequently used business performance measures assess returns on critical resources. Rather than measure return on equity or return on invested capital, why not measure return on management? Robert Simons, a professor at Harvard Business School, has argued in favour of attempting this, as it would focus management's attention on where it can add most value, but such a measure would need to be qualitative not quantitative, and thus its calculation is fraught with practical difficulties.

Employee turnover, or the rate at which employees are leaving the business, (usually calculated by dividing the number of employees who have left in the year by the number of employees in employment at the end of year, and expressed as a percentage) is also a useful measure in a growing business attempting to increase its headcount. It is not sufficient for a growing business to be good at recruiting new staff; it also has to be good at retaining staff.

Growth: the shareholders' perspective

Revenue, profit, asset and employee measures consider the performance of a business from the inside out. But for those who believe that a business exists to generate returns for the owners or shareholders, the most important measures are those that look at the company from the owners' perspective. Growth for shareholders means an increase in the value of their shares. This essentially is determined by an assessment of the underlying assets together with the dividends and other cash payments expected to be paid to shareholders, which in turn are underpinned by business fundamentals, which will take an analyst back to actual and forecast profits, revenue and headcount. But shareholders and the analysts who advise them are unlikely to stop there.

Assessing shareholder value and shareholder return is a discipline in itself. When assessing the returns that a business generates from the point of view of the shareholder, it is important to consider alternatives. Just as in a big business revenue growth should be considered against the growth in the overall market, so returns to a shareholder should be compared with what those investments might have earned if they had been invested elsewhere. At the very least shareholders should be entitled to expect better returns than they would have got had they invested in risk-free securities, as any investment in shares carries an element of risk. Business valuation methodologies often attempt to take account of the risk inherent in the business and consider the value of the anticipated cash flows likely to accrue to shareholders accordingly.

The share price of a listed business is an obvious indication of its worth, reflecting the value the market puts on future returns to shareholders. But even in a listed business, value is a more slippery concept than the share price might suggest. A listed company wishing to take control of or buy another listed company will often have to pay a premium to persuade enough of the shareholders to give up their shares. If more than one acquirer is interested, the price might go higher still.

Private companies

In private companies valuation is more complicated. As there is no ready market for the shares they are less liquid, which makes them less valuable. There is no real-time external market mechanism for assessing shareholder value. There are consultants who, for a decent fee, will be prepared to value the company, and such valuation exercises are common, particularly when employee equity and share-option schemes are being set up.

Before attempting to value a private business, it is important to determine who wants to know and why. If a company is not expected to continue trading but is to be broken up, any value it might have will be tied up in what can be realised from the resale of its individual assets. Some of these may have been used as security for debt and thus will be of little value to the shareholder. When a company is being valued as a going concern, its value is driven by the future ability of the business to generate cash. Valuers might express this in terms of a price/earnings or P/E ratio. Some might consider the prices paid recently for businesses in the same industry and how these prices compare with the profits made by the same business, and use the formula so derived to calculate a value for your company. Others might attempt to assess the future cash flows of the business directly, and then discount these using a discount factor reflecting the perceived riskiness of the business (the riskier the business, the higher the discount factor and the lower the resulting value – or the higher the cash flows needed to satisfy the investor). But any such calculation is fraught with subjectivity: the valuation is highly sensitive to changes in the discount factor, which itself is determined on the basis of some well-educated guesses about the future of the business and the industry; and then there is the reliability of the business plan from which future cash flows will have been derived. When one successful online business was for sale it received several offers, the highest of which was more than twice the lowest, even though the vendors offering the highest and lowest amounts had used the same valuation methodology. The MBA-educated founder drily notes that "using the technical knowledge I acquired on the valuation courses at business school, I decided to go for the highest offer".

Ultimately, shareholder value in a private business can be determined with certainty only when a price for the business has been determined that is acceptable to a vendor and an acquirer – in other words, when it is sold. At that point two sets of shareholders, the old and the new, have reached an understanding as to what the business is worth (usually leaving both parties feeling slightly hard done by).

People businesses and partnerships

When owner-managers sell a business they withdraw their own contribution to the business, and this may have a significant downward influence on its value. This is seen clearly in professional services firms, which are often structured as partnerships rather than companies. The partnership model suits industries, usually people- rather than asset-intensive, in which the association between the owners and the business is important. In professional services firms, despite the knowledge-management revolution, most of the business's assets are still in the heads of the partners.

A partnership allows individuals to take advantage of scale, and the efficiencies to be derived from working in close proximity with people with complementary skills, but it is still in essence a collection of individuals each with personal relationships with a set of clients. It is significant that many partnerships take their corporate name from the names of the founding partners. The implications of this are often misunderstood, even by partners, and particularly by those in knowledge businesses who have converted their partnerships into incorporated entities, and who thus own share certificates that give their owners the illusion that they own a share of a business that has a value separable from themselves. (Just as there are large partnerships that are in effect run as corporate entities, so there are limited companies that are still partnerships both at heart and as a matter of commercial reality.)

This comes to a head when partners, particularly founding partners, with their names on the door, seek to retire. For many, the prospect of retiring involves a presumption of "selling" their share of the business to the junior partners. Far from being grateful for the opportunity, many junior partners in these circumstances argue that the retiring senior partners are trying to have their cake and eat it. If their personal role has been so considerable, it and its value will leave with them on their retirement. They cannot have it both ways: if they stay, they are of value and will earn well; if they go, they will enjoy their retirement but will not earn, and will not be rewarded for any "value" left behind in the business because there will not be much. In essence, therefore, many people businesses, regardless of their legal form, are mechanisms not for aggregating value but for distributing income. The most significant financial capital that is needed in many people businesses is working capital: capital is not needed to finance assets, and surplus financial capital does not find it easy to earn a return, which again has implications for stakeholders who define their objectives in terms derived from more typical shareholder-company models.

The "consolidator" phenomenon in the accountancy industry illustrates how the partnership model and the relationship between partners, the business and financial stakeholders, work. Accountancy is a profitable industry, and financiers have circled it for years wondering how to get a piece of the action; or rather, imagining that there is some action that it would be interesting to get a piece of without having to worry about the perils of owner-management. Indeed, a partnership that makes money, and that is so inherently scalable (just add more people who are good enough to find new clients), is surely a decent investment proposition.

In the past few years, financiers have been spinning the wheels on just such a model. The thinking has had a defensible logic: create a business vehicle; list it on the stockmarket; and use the money raised to buy up small practices around the country. Smaller practices are constrained by lack of resources. Membership of a bigger, better-financed entity would give them reach and resources that would otherwise be unobtainable. Furthermore, partnership capital is illiquid: you cannot realise it until you retire, and then you have to find someone willing to finance the withdrawal of your capital. This is likely to be the existing partners or individuals promoted to the partnership to fill your chair, but neither might leap at the opportunity. If you are close to retirement, faced with limited alternatives, you might be tempted by the opportunity to exchange your partnership for cash and marketable shares in a listed entity.

But for many, the reality has been very different from the dream. Numerica, with Levy Gee as its largest member firm and "base tenant", raised $40 million in the markets and set about acquiring and consolidating smaller accounting practices. But the wheel turned. After a difficult period of trading, Numerica itself was swallowed up by a bigger spider, Vantis, another of the consolidators, in 2005. Vantis went into administration in 2010.

Why the difficulties, particularly given the undoubted profitability of the industry as a whole? Some partners, now directors or other types of employee in a listed entity, take the view with hindsight that they were sold a pup. The share options that many of them took (rather than free equity or cash) tied them in rather than offered them realisable value. Even those holding real paper were obliged to watch it decline in value as the consolidators failed to make an impression on new investors. The model was troubled for other reasons. Decision-takers in partnerships are often partners who are close to retirement; but the partners on whom future business depends are often younger partners, whose earning potential continues to be tied up with the future of the business. Some consolidator deals were made by older partners who took the money and looked forward to imminent retirement, but the partners who were left to do the work were left also with the prospect of having to share their returns with financial stakeholders.

Some have defined the problem as old partners retiring unfairly at the expense of junior partners. But it goes further than that, as firms seek to recruit junior staff at the bottom of a machine that ultimately depends for its success on its ability to develop senior staff and partners in the future. Why join a practice where the future earnings potential is reduced? As noted above, partnerships of knowledge-management professionals are mechanisms for sharing income, not for appreciating value. Another reason the decision-takers in firms selling to consolidators might have wished to sell was that their income had not been sufficient to support their expectations. For them, the consolidator model was a ticket out; for the consolidator, the model had the effect of attracting firms that had not been successful enough to realise their ambitions on their own. They have ended up with senior staff frustrated at sharing business returns with financial stakeholders.

The real issue is that value in a professional services business is achieved very differently from that in most shareholder-owned businesses. This can be seen in the way that many professional services firms choose not to account for goodwill when measuring equity value. In other words, a partner's equity stake in a business is valued only as the capital introduced into the business by the partner and the partner's share of the profits, which have yet to be taken out. No value is attributed to the partner's share of the business itself. When such a business is acquired, any value placed on the business in excess of this is also attributable to the partners, but the fact that many businesses refuse to account for such value themselves should serve as a warning to any potential acquirer of the dangers of overpaying. What is true for professional partnerships is true to varying extents for many other knowledge-based owner-managed businesses.

External shareholders

From the perspective of external shareholders who are not owner-managers, it is important to distinguish the value of an investment to the shareholder from the value of the company. The two are not necessarily the same. Share values for listed companies go up and down with the market as well as being influenced by turnover, market prospects and profitability. Many shareholders, though technically owners of a slice of the business, behave as if they are owners of their portion of capital, which they have given to the company for a return. Shareholders in this sense are inclined to behave like debt holders rather than equity holders.

In recent years, and particularly since the economic collapse of 2008, there have been calls for recognising the interests of a broader range of stakeholders rather than giving too much priority to the interests of shareholders. There is a lot of sense in this. Too much attention paid to shareholder interests to the detriment of other stakeholders has not been in companies' long-term interests.

When the interests of management become too closely aligned with those of shareholders, usually by way of equity incentives for managers, companies have paradoxically found short-term gain taking priority over long-term sustainability. If you want management to act in the interests of shareholders, some have argued, take away management's shares.

On the other hand, satisfying the goals of a broader group of stakeholders sounds good in theory, but is difficult to achieve in practice and even more difficult to measure. One reason the CEO of a listed company finds it easy to focus on shareholder value rather than stakeholder value is that increases in shareholder value are much easier to measure. Theorists cannot even agree about which of the rest of the stakeholder group they should be worried about, let alone how to measure growth in returns to them.

Range and depth

Many new ventures start with one service product, and often just one client or customer. An important task for a new business team seeking to build a sustainable business proposition is extending the range of the business's products and services and its number of customers and clients. The range and depth of an organisation's business are thus important elements of a successful growth proposition.

As is often the case, the proposition can work in reverse. Many a management team talks about the 80:20 rule: that 80% of its revenues or profits come from 20% of its customers or products. Successful growth comes, therefore, not just from acquiring new business but also from acquiring the right kind of business.

Other measures

There are other measures of growth, many reflecting unusual characteristics of the industry in which the company operates. Oil companies may be interested in the volume of barrels of oil produced, or filling stations opened; a record company or publisher in copies sold, or royalties earned, or prizes won, or titles published. Many organisations work towards certifications of quality.

Some organisations have taken unusual approaches to assessing their success. Skandia, a multinational financial services company based in Sweden, generated a lot of publicity when it attempted to measure elements of its intellectual capital including its "competence base" (defined as employees' professional insights, applied experience and organisational learning) and "performance procedures" (defined as how its customers are handled, and how its operations, processes, business development and logistics are conducted). The Kingdom of Bhutan already claims to measure gross national happiness. Many large companies attempt to measure employee satisfaction and corporate well-being, principally using quantifiable outputs from employee attitude surveys.

In general, any organisation keen to demonstrate how well it has done will choose to highlight some measure by which it can be judged to have done so.

Difficulties of assessment and interpretation

In young businesses, measuring all aspects of performance, including growth, has its own challenges. When preparing management information, it is immediately apparent how much standard accounting relies on the historical record and on policy and practice. New businesses do not have any history. It is difficult to interpret trends in a young business in which good business practice has not been established and therefore cannot be relied on. Young growing businesses change more quickly and more fundamentally than established ones; the assumptions behind an accounting policy are likely to date and therefore the policy will need to change. Whether or not to write off expenditure or to capitalise it is a matter of judgment and policy. There are detailed rules governing how a business should answer this sort of question when drafting public financial statements, particularly in the US. But new businesses have to determine their management accounting practices as the business model evolves.

In owner-managed businesses, regardless of size, the line between the owner-manager and the business becomes blurred, making it difficult to isolate and assess the performance of the underlying business. Whether a private business makes an accounting profit or just breaks even is often a matter for the owner-manager and the tax authorities. Owner-managers might charge to the business expenses that might be disallowed in a big business, not because they are illegal, but because when the business is yours you do what suits you best provided it is legitimate. In young businesses, financial performance as recorded in the accounts is often distorted in the other direction. Business founders often do not take a salary or a return from the business in the early days. Either way, the true costs of doing business are often not reflected in the financial records.

It is naive to assume, particularly when businesses are growing, that it is possible to confine the measurement of growth to a single measure. Companies that focus too intently on one measure run the risk of dysfunctional performance. American academic Chris Zook notes that companies that grow revenue but not profit do not create value in the long term; however, companies that grow profit but not turnover are on an unsustainable growth path. Companies that grow revenue and profit but do not earn their cost of capital run out of investors. Zook's list is not meant to be complete. Growing companies should worry about management capacity and infrastructure, as well as maintaining an asset base sufficient to support sustainable growth. Managers in pursuit of sustained growth should keep their eyes on a range of dials on their dashboards.

An added complication is that some business activities are easier to measure and assess than others, and there is no corollary between ease of measurement and importance. As Einstein noted,

"Not everything that can be counted counts, and not everything that counts can be counted." Items that have human activity at their heart can be particularly difficult to assess. Big numbers like revenue and profit help present a broad-brush picture, but it is the detail that matters.

The complications of change

Another factor is change. In a business that is evolving as well as expanding, new product or service lines can have a significant impact on both performance and the nature of the figures reported. A manufacturing business that introduces customer service and product maintenance will find that the dynamics of the business model changes, so the basis of a new set of numbers showing increasing profit needs careful analysis. Change has implications for accounting policies, which might need to be adjusted to reflect changes in the underlying business model.

It can be difficult therefore to measure growth either side of a change of strategy or accounting policy or the introduction of a new line of business. For example, the performance of some large companies in the years preceding the 2008 credit crunch was buoyed by the profits earned by their financial services divisions. On April Fool's Day 2008, Porsche was reported as having published figures showing that sales had plummeted 27%; but the company reported increased overall profits, notwithstanding the decline in car sales, thanks to the performance of its financial services division.

Furthermore, although managers often project steady and smooth growth, in practice it rarely happens linearly, the reality being a series of steps and lurches. A business investing in the next stage of its development may put pressure on its margins until the investment starts to pay back. Fixed costs and variable costs are never as clearly distinguishable from each other as accountants would like. Fixed costs (overheads) can be cut or increased. Again, adding to overheads usually happens in large steps. Conversely, variable costs are rarely as variable as their label might suggest. Components and resources are often sourced in bulk to achieve economies of scale. Accountants might smooth the reported purchases figure in the accounts by taking account of the movement in stock or inventory, but the underlying reality of the business is anything but smooth.

Then there are the consequences of mergers and acquisitions. Organic growth on its own is difficult enough to measure, but combining two organisations introduces further distortions. Lines of seemingly similar accounting information in two different organisations rarely reflect identical activities. Combining two organisations carries its own integration costs. Expansion overseas brings complications caused by fluctuations in exchange rates, different tax regimes, different ways of doing business – including attitudes to payment and employment – and different attitudes to accounting practice. The net effect is that it can be difficult to measure growth from one period to the next.

Pace and capacity

Another important variable is the pace of growth. Businesses can grow at the wrong speed. Businesses that grow too slowly may lose advantage in the market to competitors. Those that grow too fast may lose control with dangerous consequences across several dimensions. Toyota's rapid expansion up to 2009 has been blamed for the safety issues that led to the recall of at least 8.5 million vehicles. Ahead of an appearance before a US congressional hearing, the company's president, Akio Toyoda, conceded that the firm's growth "may have been too quick". Toyoda suggested that the company's "priorities became confused" as the carmaker grew. Toyota's reputation suffered as a consequence of a sequence of major faults across different types of product, including faulty accelerator pedals and braking systems. A business growing too fast is also one that risks losing the confidence of its staff. Driving an out-of-control business is just as scary as driving an out-of-control train, with every chance of it ending in disaster. Businesses that grow fast put pressure on their cash resources (see Chapter 6) as growth consumes cash, which must be found from internal operations or from external financiers. Businesses go bust, not because they do not make enough profit, but because they run out of cash.

What is an acceptable level of growth? There are three simple tests:

- Growth is financially acceptable if management know in advance how it is going to be financed (see Chapter 6).
- Growth is strategically acceptable if it continues to secure and enhance the company's position in the industry and marketplace.
- Growth is operationally acceptable if management know how it will be controlled and supported.

The first test is about financial capacity. The second test is about management's understanding of the commercial environment. The third test is about management's real understanding of the business.

Understanding your own strategy

Sock Shop was one of the UK retailing sensations of the 1980s, selling socks and hosiery from small outlets in locations with a high footfall such as underground railway stations. Following initially modest growth plans, the business grew rapidly, but when it expanded from the London Underground to the New York subway, and then onto the high street, Sock Shop found itself in difficulty. Trading underground in New York proved far riskier than trading underground in London. And on the high street, where rents were higher and competitors included established high-street retailers, Sock Shop found it had to reinvent its business model. Its customers changed too, with more considered, price-conscious purchasers replacing the business people rushing to buy socks or replace laddered tights before a meeting in the City.

By 1990 Sock Shop had called in the administrators. Thus an essentially sound business that was misunderstood by its owners was sold – only to go bust again in 1996, and again in 2006.

The third test is about management capacity. In a 1999 article in *Harvard Business Review* Robert Simons proposes an interesting framework for assessing the business risk faced by a growing company, which also captures the complexity inherent in the business.[1] The business risk calculator – tested, Simons claims, by "managers from hundreds of different companies" – invites managers to categorise and assess the extent to which their business is exposed to each category (see Figure 5.1).

Questions companies should ask are as follows:

- **Growth.** To what extent are managers and staff under pressure to deliver? How fast is the company growing? To what extent do managers and staff have experience of the situation in which the business finds itself? High scores

FIG 5.1 **The business risk exposure calculator**

Growth	Pressure for performance		Rate of expansion		Inexperience of employees	
	?	+	?	+	?	=
Culture	Rewards for entrepreneurial risk taking		Executive resistance to bad news		Level of internal competition	
	?	+	?	+	?	=
Information management	Transaction complexity and velocity		Gaps in diagnostic performance measures		Degree of decentralised decision making	
	?	+	?	+	?	=

Source: Robert Simons, "How Risky Is Your Company?", *Harvard Business Review*, May 1999 indicate a company that may be growing and changing more quickly than the capability and capacity of management to control it.

- **Culture.** This section assesses some of the softer elements in a governance framework likely to be tested in a growing business. How significant to staff are their potential rewards for risk taking? How resistant are executives to receiving bad news? ("Don't give me problems, bring me solutions.") How competitive is the internal environment? High scores in this row suggest that individuals, in the interest of meeting targets, are likely to take more risks than is good for the company. They are also less likely to draw problems to the attention of management in time for them to be addressed.

- **Information management.** This section covers the complexity that comes with growth. How fast does the business engine that underpins the business turn over, and how many components are in the engine? The more there are the less likely it is that management will be aware of all aspects of the business. To what extent do the indicators chosen to measure performance capture the total activity of the business, or are there fundamental gaps? How decentralised is decision-taking? Have controls been put in place to supervise the managers to whom authority has been delegated, or have senior management in effect confused delegation with abdication?

The three rows in Figure 5.1 and each item within them are interlocking. High scores in all sections suggest a business that is growing fast, is becoming more complicated and is not under the control of management. Simons proposed his model in 1999, but his lessons have not been taken to heart. Evidently no one at Enron or Andersen paid much attention. Nor were there many low scores among firms that came unstuck during the global financial crisis, such as Lehman Brothers and RBS.

6

Financing growth

THE CAPABILITY AND CAPACITY of the management team are the most important barriers to growth, but without the necessary financial resources growth will be impossible to achieve. A crucial capability of a management team is its ability to raise the funds necessary to finance and support growth.

Generating and managing cash

The most discussed sources of finance for a business are external, in the form of debt or equity, but the first place to look for cash is inside the business itself. Every business should be a machine that generates cash. Of course, in its earliest stages a business will consume cash from founders and funders as it seeks to get established, and even after that most managers must expect, and can be forgiven for, the occasional lapse when the business consumes rather than generates cash, but over the longer term its operating model must be able to convert sales opportunities into cash. As well as generating cash, a business must look after it effectively. This requires skilful management of the balance sheet, making sure that cash flows through the business as efficiently as possible and that the balance sheet is not unnecessarily weighed down with assets such as trade debtors and stock or inventory, which might otherwise be converted to cash.

Business managers who are good at managing cash are aware of how much cash is tied up in various parts of the business and how long it sticks there; and they are good at clearing unnecessary blockages. If the nature of a business means it has to keep stock or inventory, this will lengthen the time it takes to convert raw materials or purchases into cash. In some businesses, such as bookshops, stock is slow-moving. In others, such as supermarkets, it moves much faster. Some businesses, notably service businesses, do not need to tie up cash in stock at all, though they may tie it up in unbilled work in progress. If customers and clients of businesses in an industry routinely pay for products up front (as they do for the products of most retail businesses), cash will not be tied up in accounts payable or trade debtors. But businesses (such as most business-to-business ones) that depend for their income on customers who can dictate lengthy payment terms will have to wait for cash to come in.

Businesses that pay their suppliers immediately are at a cash-flow disadvantage to those that pay their creditors on terms. The longer the terms a business can negotiate with its suppliers, the longer the business can keep cash in the business, and the less it has to rely on external sources for the cash to finance the business. The timing of cash flows in and out of a business is never entirely at the discretion of management, but management teams that do not pay attention are just as likely to pay their bills too soon as too late. Big businesses can and often do dictate payment terms to small businesses. When the recession struck, some big businesses told their customers that they expected payment within two weeks rather than 30 days. Most businesses, especially big businesses, find it easier to bully their suppliers than their customers.

Bullied by customers

In autumn 2008 Tesco, the UK's largest retailer, wrote to its non-food suppliers to inform them that it wanted to change its payment terms from 30 to 60 days with effect from December 1st. In a statement, Tesco said:

This is a move to align payment terms for our larger non-food suppliers across the Tesco group which currently vary from country to country and within product categories. We have written to suppliers to seek their agreement to the change and hope to implement it before the end of the year.

Most suppliers, anxious to keep the Tesco account, would not have regarded the letter as an attempt to "seek their agreement". The consequence of the change of terms was to improve Tesco's working capital and cash position at the expense of its suppliers. Tesco is not alone. Frank Garson II, president of The Loveable Company, a supplier to Walmart, said of the latter in a 2003 interview in *Fast Company*:[1]

They have such awesome purchasing power that they write their own ticket. If they don't like your prices they'll go vertical and do it themselves – or they will find someone who will meet their terms.

The Loveable Company had had a contract with Walmart that Walmart had unilaterally revised, forcing Loveable to give up the business. Three years later, Loveable went under. "Walmart chewed us up and spat us out," Garson said.

It is often assumed that cash management is something that small businesses are more likely than big businesses to get wrong. Maybe, but the fundamentals of cash management are as relevant for big businesses as for small businesses, and they can go wrong for big businesses too. When Travelex completed its acquisition of Thomas Cook Global Financial Services for £400 million ($640 million) in March 2001, it established that it could run its new acquisition with £130 million ($208 million) less working capital than the previous management. In effect, £130 million-worth of cash was sitting unnecessarily on the company's balance sheet. This made a significant contribution to Travelex's repayment of the loan needed to buy the business in the first place.

Cash management is closely related to the effective management of margin, which in turn is closely associated with cost control. Early-stage businesses that have plenty of cash are rare, so tight control of costs is crucial. Most start-ups have to make do with less cash, or with none at all. Start-ups are usually advised never to buy up front what can be paid for in instalments or on credit; never to pay on credit for what can be leased or hired at sensible rates; never to lease or hire what can be borrowed for nothing; and not to be afraid of looking a gift horse in the mouth if it appears, swallowing pride and saying "thank you".

Effective cost management requires a ruthless examination of the detail and an ability to distinguish the critical from the merely useful. Companies that are growing quickly are under more pressure than stable companies to protect their margins. A growing company needs to be careful with its prices. A price reduction might increase the rate of growth but put additional pressure on profit, which will be under pressure because of growth in the first place. Big, slow-growing companies might more easily enter the market at a discount. Suppliers of goods or raw materials might put up their prices in order to share in your success. Success might mean a move to more expensive premises in a better location. Big companies that want to strengthen their cash position, however, will work hard at reducing costs as well as adjusting the timing of their cash flows. Whether or not to pay a dividend and how much the dividend should be is a bigger issue for listed businesses than it is for private ones, especially those that are owner-managed, because of its relation to share price, but it is also about cash conservation.

Sometimes margin and cash management pull in different directions. Offering discounts to encourage swift payment on the part of customers may speed up the flow of cash into the business significantly. But such discounting can cut heavily into margins and as with all price cuts will go straight to the bottom line. Too often, customers, particularly big ones, take the discount and still pay late, so their suppliers lose both ways. The converse is also true of purchase discounts. Taking advantage of a purchase discount by paying suppliers quickly may improve margins (though not as much as choosing not to offer a sales discount), but it might put pressure on a business's cash resources as cash will have to leave the business sooner.

Managing the investment in growth

Growth is costly. In the long term it may be the only way to secure a sustainable business, but in the short term it will cost money. A growing business must reinvest in itself and will need increasing amounts of working capital (the amount of resources tied up in the balance sheet in the cash cycle). A manufacturer will need to invest in raw materials, some of which will sit on the balance sheet. It may have to offer payment terms to its customers, in which case trade debtors will sit on the balance sheet as well. To a certain extent working capital pressures from stock and debtors may be lessened by payment terms taken by a company from its suppliers, but for many companies the terms they obtain from their suppliers are less generous than those their customers demand. When a company grows its working capital requirements increase, usually in advance of sales and profits turning into cash. Increases in working capital are at the expense of cash in the business.

Many growing businesses, especially business-to-business ones with reliable customers, take advantage of asset-based finance, borrowing mainly against debtors and occasionally against inventory as well. Borrowing against working capital is a particularly effective form of finance for a growing business as its capacity to borrow effectively grows with the business. But borrowing against working capital is often expensive. Moreover, every business has a debt capacity beyond which, if it is incapable of generating any more cash from its operations, it will be in danger of overtrading – or trading at a level beyond its own financial capacity.

Those who have studied the arithmetical relationship between financing needs, profitability and growth, such as Neil Churchill and John Mullins in a 2001 article in *Harvard Business Review*, noted that in theoretical terms it is possible to calculate to what extent cash constraints determined by cash flows in and out of a business will allow the business to grow.[2] Their essential principles should be taken to heart by the managers of every growing business:

- A business that ties up cash unnecessarily on the balance sheet in the form of excess inventory or uncollected debtors is putting itself under unnecessary cash pressure.
- A business that is paying its suppliers more quickly than necessary is putting itself under unnecessary cash pressure.
- The higher a business's margins, the greater its cash-generating capability is likely to be.
- The faster a business grows, the more pressure it will put on its cash resources.

Growing too fast

A business that is growing too fast is overtrading. As with many growth problems, it is ironic that the problem of overtrading is a product of success. In the simplest terms, a business that is overtrading is attempting to do too much with the cash resources at its disposal. It is buying more raw materials, products or employee time than it can afford to satisfy the customers and clients who have not yet paid for the products or services they have ordered. Such a business has too much of its wealth in non-cash assets, the organisational equivalent of too much cholesterol. A business facing overtrading has three options:

- To generate more cash, faster, from the business itself. This is unlikely to work. In a business that is overtrading every element is already being tested to the utmost.
- To slow growth down, which is also surprisingly difficult to achieve. It may require turning business away, and incurring the risk of disappointing sources of future business and upsetting customers and ambitious staff. One strategy may

be to increase prices. This will have the effect of increasing the cash the business operations are generating as well as choking off some demand from customers who are unwilling to pay the higher price.

■ To seek external financing, probably equity finance, as debt capacity is likely to have been reached.

Managers in successful, fast-growing businesses must look out for signs of overtrading. These include cash balances trending downwards, payment terms to suppliers lengthening and the overdraft facility being used more frequently. When the current ratio (current assets/current liabilities) is less than 1, questions should be asked about the business's ability to pay its short-term creditors; in other words, its ability to keep going.

External sources of finance

External sources of cash are needed to fund a business when internal sources are insufficient. This is generally the case when the business is young. It is a rare new business that requires no capital commitment and instantly generates cash. Government and other types of grants might be available, for example if the opportunity is associated with a technology being developed by a local university, which may be able to offer the support of a local business incubator, providing relatively cheap and flexible accommodation, as well as access to professional expertise and the brainpower in the university itself.

Internal sources of finance will also be stretched when a business, regardless of size, embarks on major strategic change or a significant acquisition. As noted, such a business will need to look for external cash when its activities fail to generate sufficient cash. This might be in times of economic trouble, or when the business is overtrading.

Debt finance

Debt finance – borrowing the money – allows a company to raise cash without giving away any share capital or equity. The company can offset interest payments against tax (assuming it is making enough profit to incur tax), and thus there is good reason to expect debt finance to be relatively cheap. In theory, therefore, debt finance has a lot in its favour. In practice, however, it may not be so easy to obtain – and those made cynical by bitter experience may grumble that banks are happy to give you money when you do not particularly need it; and then when you really do need it, they are only too keen to take away what they have given you so far.

If a business is looking for debt finance, especially when times are hard, it helps to understand how banks think, and thus avoid any unnecessary misunderstanding or disappointment. Banks lend their money in return for interest. A bank will lose a lot more if the company it has lent money to goes bust than it will earn from interest if it does well. If the company does spectacularly well, the bank will be a little better off. But it will need to earn a lot of interest from a lot of clients to recover what it has lost on a client that has gone bust, unless it can protect itself in some way. In many ways the hue and cry against the banks in 2008 and 2009, when debt capital seemed so much more difficult to raise, marked a return to sensible banking – dull, conservative, risk-conscious, but nonetheless sensible.

There are various types of debt finance.

Overdrafts

Overdraft funding (sometimes known as a "revolver") is risky for the bank and for the borrower. In any business, small or large, it should be used only to fund short-term cash flow shortfalls – helping to smooth out the ups and downs of the working capital cycle. An overdraft can be called in at any time, so it is a high-risk strategy for a business to rely on it for longer-term financing.

From the bank's point of view an overdraft is often unsecured, increasing its exposure. Even though a business pays interest on an overdraft only when it has one, interest rates are high to reflect the risk. Longer-term appropriately structured debt financing is much cheaper.

Loans against assets

When structuring debt, the most common way a bank can make sure that its position is protected is not through setting aggressive interest rates, but by securing its loan against assets in the business. If the business goes under, at least the bank can lay claim to and sell the asset against which it has secured the debt. Asset-rich businesses find it easier to borrow money. And assets are not just bricks, mortar and machinery; intangible assets can be used as well. Raising money against trade debtors, for example, is now well established and has the added advantage of growing as the business grows (assuming the debtor book grows with the business, which is usual). However, financiers will only lend money against quality debtors. Debtor finance is unlikely to be of much use to a new company unless it is buying an established business that has debt capacity on its balance sheet, or it has a guaranteed blue-chip order book.

Borrowing money against trade debtors (receivables in the US) is often called invoice discounting. In an alternative arrangement called factoring, a company sells its debtor book to a financier (a factor), which is likely to take over responsibility for debt collection and administration. Factoring is usually more expensive than invoice discounting.

Cash flow lending

An established business with a good track record may be able to take advantage of so-called cash flow lending. Rather than taking security against specific assets, a bank relies on the cash flow that the business expects to generate to give it the comfort it needs. The bank will seek safeguards in the form of warranties and covenants based on such measures as profitability, enterprise value and ratios comparing profit with interest. If the covenants are breached, the bank has the right to recall the loan. The bank usually puts measures in place that allow it to take control of the company's cash flows if it defaults on loan repayments. Enthusiasts for cash flow lending argue that it is more focused than asset-based lending on the ability of a business to repay its debts. Focusing on an assessment of future cash flows rather than assets that can be secured often increases the debt capacity of a business; it also increases the number of businesses able to raise debt finance. Cash flow lenders understandably are more enthusiastic about businesses that are not cyclical, although definitions of cyclicality change at various stages of the cycle. When times are good lenders are more likely to have a sympathetic view of cash flow lending than when times are bad, and banks may lend money to a company on the basis of business propositions that might otherwise be considered inappropriate for bank funding. Big, established businesses are a lot more likely to be able to access cash flow lending than small, young companies.

Corporate bonds and debentures

Big, established businesses have other debt options. A corporate bond or debenture is a longer-term debt instrument with a maturity date, a redemption value and a coupon (an interest rate, usually fixed). Corporate bonds are similar to the bonds issued by governments seeking to finance (or more often refinance) their debts, but they are issued by companies rather than countries. Like the shares of listed companies, corporate bonds are often traded on markets. The market's perception of the riskiness of the debt is reflected in its market price, which in turn affects the real interest rate earned by the acquirer of the bond.

Bond markets are regulated, and raising money this way can be expensive, not least in management time. It is a moot point whether from the perspective of the issuing company this sort of financing has all the disadvantages of raising money via the public equity markets with none of the advantages, or the other way around. But a corporate bond will enable a big company to access debt without the help of a bank. This may allow it to raise money for a lower interest rate. It may also allow it to put its debt out for a longer period than a bank might be prepared to countenance. Some bonds and debentures may also be convertible into shares, with the conversion triggered either by a particular event or after a fixed period of time. Convertibility usually makes the debt cheaper. Bonds and debentures that carry higher interest rates because they are considered to have a higher risk of default are often called junk bonds.

Guarantees

Even if a business has assets it can borrow against, or can secure other forms of lending, it will still need to repay the loan and to finance the interest. Companies cannot rely on interest rates going down when expected, as many have found in recent times when official interest rates have hovered around zero. Young, entrepreneurial businesses, even if they have debt capacity (that is, assets they can borrow against), are inherently risky propositions, and the interest rate a financier charges will reflect in part the risk inherent in the investment. The credit crunch made banks even less likely to be supportive and much more concerned with tidying up their own balance sheets than with providing finance to new businesses.

Small-business owners are often asked by banks for personal guarantees that put their own (as opposed to the company's) assets at risk if the company is unable to pay back the loan, notwithstanding the limited liability status of the company. Personal guarantee documents are long and complicated, and are designed to protect the bank's interests. But many of those asked to give personal guarantees pay insufficient attention to protecting their own positions before signing the documentation. A business owner should resist giving a personal guarantee and, if faced with no alternative, should take independent professional advice before agreeing to one. Wherever possible owners should spread the burden of the guarantee by involving joint guarantors, and limit the scope of the guarantee to a maximum amount. When the guarantee (or the debt) is no longer needed it should be legally withdrawn, otherwise it may be used in the future, possibly in relation to an entirely different piece of business.

Companies in the UK may be able to take advantage of government-backed debt-guarantee schemes such as the Enterprise Finance Guarantee Scheme. In the US the Small Business Administration provides guarantor services in a similar way.

Equity finance

The other principal source of finance, for businesses of all shapes and sizes, is equity, referred to as share ownership in the UK and stock ownership in the US. A shareholder owns a slice of the business. The share entitles its owner to a share of the future income distributed by the business in the form of dividends, or to a return of capital when the business is sold. There are different types of shares, and the nuances are spelled out in the small print of the documentation, but the most common are as follows:

- **Common stock or ordinary shares.** The basic type of share which entitles its holder to all income and capital after the holders of other classes of shareholder and debt holder have been satisfied. Ordinary shareholders typically are entitled to vote on key corporate matters.

- **Preferred or preference shares or stock.** Holders of these shares have preferential rights over the holders of ordinary shares. Typically, a preference shareholder is entitled to a dividend before an ordinary shareholder and is paid off first in the event of liquidation. Preference shareholders do not normally have a vote.

- **Preferred ordinary shares or stock.** Holders of these shares are entitled to the best features of ordinary and preferred shares. Typically, they have a vote, but they also have preferential rights when it comes to dividends or liquidation. Institutions usually invest in one or other type of preferred share so that they can benefit from the increased control provided by their preferential rights.

- **Cumulative shares or stock.** If dividends on these shares are earned but not distributed, the entitlement to the dividend may be aggregated cumulatively and paid out at a later date.

- **Convertible shares or stock.** These are convertible into another class of share. Typically, preferred shares can be converted into ordinary shares if the investment underperforms, thus allowing the holders of preferred shares to take control of the company. Institutional investors may also invest in convertible debt – debt instruments that can be converted into shares in certain circumstances.

- **Participating shares or stock.** The label refers to the right to participate in any dividend or distribution paid to the holders of ordinary shares. Otherwise, in many cases, preference shareholders are entitled to a fixed dividend only.

- **Any combination of the above.** Sophisticated institutional investors cook up share instruments that have the characteristics that best suit their interests in the investment. Cumulative convertible participating preferred ordinary shares are commonly used by institutions when investing in young companies.

Different types of shareholders will want to invest in different types of shares depending on their interest in the company. Founders usually hold ordinary shares, although external investors sometimes require the founders' shares to be qualified in some way, to ensure that they are motivated to stay in the business. In the UK, individual investors in private companies often prefer to have ordinary shares rather than any of the more complicated preferred shares, as this is often the only way they can benefit from tax breaks, such as the Enterprise Investment Scheme, designed to encourage investment in small companies. Institutions are not entitled to these tax breaks and usually prefer to take advantage of the additional safeguards and controls offered by preferred shares.

Friends and family: the first to turn to

Despite the advice from seasoned entrepreneurs that the best source of finance is other people's money or OPM, the first source of equity for a start-up is usually the founder. Would-be entrepreneurs will need to give up their day jobs so that they can focus on a new business idea – though few give up highly paid jobs immediately to become first-time entrepreneurs. Andrew Palmer, founder of New Covent Garden Soup, is an exception. He gave up a well-paid job in the City to work for nothing on his new chilled soup idea. Many entrepreneurs start when they have little; they then have little to lose. Increasingly, individuals use an MBA as the opportunity to resign from one job, formulate a business plan and then start a business when graduating. Even if entrepreneurs are not investing money, they are investing a kind of capital: intellectual and commercial capital, time and expertise. In return for their investment they own the business, have equity in it, or are shareholders – the terms are synonymous.

Once the entrepreneur's own funds have been exhausted, new businesses often call on what cynics refer to as the "three Fs" (friends, family and fools) for initial funding. One of the earliest investors in Body Shop was Ian McGlinn, a garage owner, whose initial investment of £4,000 ($6,600) in the new business ultimately turned into a 22.6% stake in a listed company worth £120 million ($198 million) when L'Oréal bought Body Shop in 2006. But "friends and family" often reflects the nature of the investment made in a fledgling business: emotional rather than rational, personal rather than commercial, instinctive rather than analytical. Investment in start-ups needs to be set in the context of how many of them fail. Numbers released by the American Small

Business Administration suggest that 30% of businesses last under two years. The failure rate for businesses based on new products, or seeking to develop new markets, is much higher.

Angels – and dragons and sharks

The first arm's-length equity investments are more likely to come from an individual – a "business angel" – than an institution. Angels (often, perhaps ironically, now known as "dragons" in the UK and "sharks" in the US, thanks to the TV programmes *Dragons' Den* and *Shark Tank* respectively) are usually successful business people who have changed from entrepreneurs to investors. They often take advantage of tax breaks giving exemption from capital gains when investing, in the US, in qualified small business stock. Angels in the UK can use the Enterprise Investment Scheme when investing, giving them significant income and capital gains tax benefits as long as they are qualifying individuals investing in ordinary shares in qualifying companies based in the UK. Angels often invest as members of syndicates. Their choice of investments is influenced by their personal experience; they therefore tend to invest close to home and in businesses they understand. It is important to remember that an angel will have more to offer than simply money and will be able to provide valuable experience, guidance and contacts. More often than not an angel will want to sit on the board. When considering whether to accept an angel's help, senior managers need to consider whether they want the sort of support that the angel is likely to bring, or whether the angel will just get in the way. An angel might be looking for a job as well as an investment opportunity; a company might need the money but might not have a vacancy.

At the heart of much equity investment is a paradox. Institutional equity investors, including venture capital firms, often find it difficult to invest in young ventures because the founders want too little money. Angel investors are usually prepared to invest less than institutions, and at earlier stages, and in part help plug the gap. But even angels interested in spending amounts small enough to satisfy the needs of many owner-managed businesses can be difficult to find. This partly reflects the characteristics of equity finance compared with debt finance. In theory debt finance is straightforward. Can the company offer security? Can the business afford the interest and the repayments? If the answer to both these questions is yes, debt is relatively easy to find. Equity financiers are not as comfortable with security; they look instead at the robustness of the proposition, the quality of the opportunity, the return it will generate and the business's ability to repay the investment, notwithstanding the lack of security. Such qualities are difficult to assess and the assessment process, called due diligence, takes time and costs money, which the investor must justify spending. Institutions, private equity houses and venture capitalists with sophisticated due diligence mechanisms to satisfy are therefore interested only in investing large sums. Business angels have cheaper assessment processes, but they have them nevertheless. Thus a new business often has to fall back on family, friends and contacts where business angels fear to tread.

Venture capital and private equity

Which institutions are likely to be interested in equity investment in growth companies? Venture capitalists and private equity houses at heart are the same. Both are run by management teams that seek to put together partnerships of investors interested in the high and risky returns that ambitious small or growing companies can provide. Both will try to raise a fund; they will then invest in a portfolio of companies for the life of the fund. By the end of the life of the fund both will have sought to have exited their investments and distributed handsome returns to their investing partners, while retaining a percentage for themselves (known as their carry) to complement the management fee they have charged throughout the life of the fund. Institutions that invest in early-stage companies are often called venture capitalists, and a typical venture-capital investment will be for a minority stake. When investments are made in established companies, or are used to fund the acquisition of a listed business (taking a company private), the investing institution usually talks about private equity, and the investment will more often be for a majority stake. When part-financed by a significant injection of debt finance, the deal will be called "leveraged".

Entrepreneurship is often associated with venture capital, but in reality such capital provides only a small proportion of the equity finance needed by entrepreneurial businesses. This is partly because of the particular qualities that a venture capitalist looks for in an investment: rapid growth prospects, an experienced team, a good fit with the venture capitalist's existing portfolio, a clear exit route and large enough returns to justify the costs of investment. Most entrepreneurial investment possibilities fail on one or more of these criteria.

The last criterion is perhaps the most important. Venture capitalists are interested only in opportunities that are likely to deliver a huge return, and their hunger for such a return can lead to conflict with a business's founder. For most entrepreneurs their venture is a once-in-a-career opportunity; but venture capitalists are protected to a certain extent by the portfolio effect created by investing in a pool of investments. When times are difficult they are inclined to pull in their horns, and the proportion of young businesses supported by private institutional investment shrinks further. And if they have funds available, they will be even more careful about how they allocate them.

Although it is only by investing in risky ventures that venture capitalists find the returns they are looking for, once the risky venture has been identified they work as hard as possible to "derisk" their investment, often by investing via a package of debt and equity instruments. As institutions they are less able to benefit from the tax breaks given to individuals investing in ordinary shares, so they are more likely to invest in types of preferred share, giving themselves advantages over ordinary shareholders when it comes to dividends or cash distributions resulting from sale. They also often take advantage of convertible instruments: preferred shares that can be turned into ordinary shares under certain conditions, or debt instruments that can be converted into equity, enabling the venture capitalist to seize control, particularly if things turn bad. Venture capitalists often ask for board representation so that they can keep a close eye on their investments from inside the boardroom. They might demand anti-dilution provisions, protecting them in the event of a refinancing at a lower value in the future, or various degrees of involvement in certain types of management decision. They will have a keen interest in the company's constitutional documentation, including its articles of association and shareholder agreements. Their cash might be invested stage-by-stage depending on the achievement of certain targets. They might insist that the equity stakes of the founders are also structured on the basis of some form of ratchet, giving the founders a bigger stake when certain milestones are achieved.

The realities involved

Even if the founders still own the majority of the shares in the business they have founded, they will have given up significant influence over their business as soon as they have said yes to external equity finance. Conflict is always possible, therefore, between founders and investors. For many the experience can be unpleasant. Andrew Palmer of New Covent Garden Soup told the *Financial Times* in 2004:

> *Any entrepreneur raising private equity should keep £100,000 in reserve in case you need to sue your backers. Otherwise you will be dead. They are experts in negotiating and tying up the small print. They will say [an advantageous] clause is needed "just to protect investors", but don't you believe it.*

Palmer felt he had reason to be bitter. After a successful launch, New Covent Garden Soup struggled with the management and organisational challenges that came with growth. Its venture-capitalist backers stepped in with the cash to turn it around, initially giving Palmer a second chance to sort things out, but then forcing his removal from the top role in the business and ultimately from the board.

Growth is hungry for finance, and business founders and owners have to recognise that in return for finance they will need to give away a stake in the business. That stake might earn for the investor the right to a dividend, though dividends are usually paid only by large businesses; many small businesses cannot afford dividends and even their investors would rather see the cash conserved and invested back in the business. The real payday for most equity investors comes when they exit: either by selling their stake, or by an overall sale or float of the business. If they are lucky, equity investors will earn much more from their investment than a bank will from its interest. But the risks are much higher too. Equity investors ride their luck and get rewarded for it. A bank lending money likes to make sure that luck has been eliminated, at least as far as the bank is concerned.

Many entrepreneurs are rightly nervous about bringing institutional equity finance into the business they have founded. They worry about the prospect of seeing an equity investor riding away with a sizeable sum of money made at their expense, and about the mismatch between their ambitions and those of the finance house. Most importantly, they recognise that giving shares to an outside investor always means that someone else is able, to a greater or lesser extent, to get involved in where the business is going and how it is run. Many entrepreneurs fight hard against the temptation to take institutional funding, and scrimp and save instead. Some argue that funding a business in its early stages by bootstrapping in many circumstances is healthier and is more likely to foster a business that focuses on building the top line and maintaining healthy margins. But owners and managers who believe that institutional equity finance is right for their businesses should make sure they think about more than just the money.

Business owners should look long and hard at the investors as well as the quality of their cash. Can you work with them? Do you like them as people? Do they understand your business? Are they flexible? Do they have something else to add other than money? If these questions are not answered satisfactorily, the owners should walk away; and even if the answers are satisfactory, they should look around for alternatives.

If new money is the difference between potentially growing the business, or not growing it at all, or even going under, there is every reason for equity investors to be welcomed, particularly when they bring ideas, experience and possibly customers (and can resist the temptation to meddle too much in operations). After all, a slice of a big cake is much more interesting than the whole of a cupcake, let alone no cake at all.

Exit

As suggested above, one inevitable consequence of taking third-party private equity finance, whether from an individual or an institution, is that it will usually focus attention on what financiers call "exit". The huge return that financial investors in early-stage companies want will not come from dividends – the founders will need to keep all the cash they can inside the business to fund its growth. The return to investors is most likely to come when the business is sold. Most commonly this will be a trade sale: in other words, the business will be sold to another business that has a strategic interest in the industry – a competitor perhaps, or a business looking to move into the market in which the younger business has established a position. Or another financial investor might provide an exit route, but this is less likely for early-stage investors than a trade sale. Financial investors in an early-stage business want to see their money put to work in the business, not used to fill the pockets of other investors.

Because financial investors are usually keenly interested in exit, the founders need to be too. This may mean a change of mindset on the part of the founding team. Most founders do not think of exit when they are setting up a business – it would be a bit like planning the funeral at a baptism. But investors will force them to focus on exit, not least because the investors will be depending on the founders to deliver the exit for them. The deal may be structured in a way that ensures the founders only benefit financially from the business once a successful exit has been achieved.

Exit is something entrepreneurs should think about anyway. Growth means change, and it is almost inevitable that the business will grow beyond the capability and interest of the original founders. It is healthy for founders to be continuously mindful of a future exit. Wise entrepreneurs worry more about when to sell their own business than when to buy someone else's. Those who do not think about exit are likely to leave it too late. It is better to exit too early than too late, thus leaving something on the table for the acquirer.

There can be times when entrepreneurs are looking for growth earlier than investors. Andy Phillipps, founder of Active Hotels, after five years of hard work establishing a successful business, says that he and his team were exhausted. Persuading the board that this was the time to sell was difficult; the investors knew their money was invested in an exciting growing business. Why sell now if you can sell in a few years' time for a lot more?

Another route to exit – but much rarer than a trade sale – is to secure a listing on a stockmarket.

Going public

When the shares of a company are available for the general public to buy on a regulated stockmarket, such as the London Stock Exchange or the New York Stock Exchange, the company is said to be listed. Obtaining a listing for the first time is known as a flotation or an initial public offering (IPO).

Entrepreneurs are often equivocal about going public. In 2010,

Mark Zuckerberg, founder of Facebook, outlined (on Facebook) arguments that many entrepreneurs will be familiar with:

> We aren't planning to go public anytime soon. As a company, I think we look at going public differently than many other companies do. For a lot of companies, going public is the end goal and they shoot for and optimise around it. For us, going public isn't a goal in itself; it's just something we'll do when it makes sense for us. Since we compensate people at Facebook with stock and we took investment, I view it as my responsibility to eventually make that stock liquid for people, but that doesn't have to happen in the short term and our primary responsibility is still just to make sure Facebook develops to its full potential.
>
> I tend to think that being private is better for us right now because of some of the big risks we want to take in developing new products ... The experience of managing the company through launching controversial services is tricky, but I can only imagine it would be even more difficult if we had a public stock price bouncing around. There are a lot more new things left to build like the examples I mentioned above, and I'd rather focus on building them than on going public right now.

Zuckerberg evidently decided that circumstances had changed sufficiently when Facebook was listed in May 2012.

For founders who stay around after the businesses they founded go public the experience can be traumatic. When promoting her book *Business as Unusual* in 2001, Anita Roddick, founder of Body Shop, said:

> Did flotation work? Well, it gave us money to build manufacturing plants ... Does it work now? I do not think so. [The Body Shop has] lost its soul since floating on the stockmarket ... it has no place as a cog in the international finance system ... [The Body Shop] is now really a dysfunctional coffin.

Roddick described attempting to take her business private again on at least two occasions, so that she could do business away from the glare of investor scrutiny. Richard Branson cheerfully floated Virgin on the stockmarket but bought it back again in 1998, stating, "Being an entrepreneur and the chairman of a public company just do not mix." Entrepreneurs in the US have been just as equivocal about taking their own companies public, as Zuckerberg's comments indicate.

Stelios Haji-Iannou's evolving relationship with easyJet is interesting in this regard. When resigning as chairman of easyJet in April 2002, he was quoted in the *Financial Times* as saying:

> *Starting a company requires a very different skill-set from those needed to chair a major plc, and I consider my strengths are in the former. The history of the City is littered with entrepreneurs who held on to their creations for too long, failing to recognise the changing needs of the company.*

It is not recorded whether Haji-Iannou remembered these words when, in a public row with management in November 2008, he argued that the company's growth strategy needed reining back, and a dividend needed paying by 2011. If he did not get his way, he threatened to exercise a right reserved to him: as long as he held more than 25% of the shares, he could appoint two non-executive directors. And as long as he held more than 10%, he retained the right to make himself chairman. The agreement could not be changed "unless approved by a resolution of the board, at which an independent non-executive is in the majority".

The source of Haji-Iannou's unusual power was a "relationship agreement" drafted at the time of easyJet's flotation. To be fair, the document stated that the company should have its own management, and that it should "make decisions for the benefit of shareholders as a whole and independently of the controlling shareholders at all times". But the clauses described above seem to have different implications for the role of the board. In the *Sunday Times* in November 2008 Haji-Iannou was quoted as saying: "I am merely applying my rights under the articles of incorporation of the company to protect my investment." The row continued to simmer through 2009, and in April 2009 easyJet's chairman, Colin Chandler, announced he was stepping down. He was reported in the *Guardian* as saying:

[I am] fed up with the situation of running a board, which is tough. You have got a recession, there are some strong characters on the board and public companies these days are very tough to run.

For his part, Haji-Iannou reportedly described the situation as "a debate, not a dispute". By July 2009, with the airline industry in crisis, the irony was that Haji-Iannou was seen to have won the argument; easyJet scaled back its plans. Some described it as a triumph of the entrepreneur over the moneymen.

In October 2010, however, Haji-Iannou agreed to give up the right to make boardroom appointments and allowed easyJet to keep its name. He signed a new licence agreement allowing the airline to enter branding agreements with other firms to sell things like insurance, hotels or car hire, even if this meant competing directly with easyGroup. The deal also made it easier for easyJet to lease planes from other firms to meet any extra demand, which had previously required easyGroup's consent. Other terms prohibited him from starting up a rival airline for five years and forced him to abide by "public communication protocols". In return, he received 0.25% of easyJet's turnover for up to 50 years, fixed at £3.9 million ($6.25 million) in the first year and £4.95 million ($7.9 million) the next, plus another £300,000 ($480,000) annually. The new chief executive, Carolyn McCall, said: "It gives us more freedom to operate and much greater clarity." Nonetheless, in January 2013 the *Sunday Times* was reporting once again the resignation of the chairman of easyJet, this time Sir Michael Rake, citing "three years of bruising battles" with Haji-Iannou.

That many founders find the experience of listing so uncomfortable shows just how big a transition it is. Indeed, a listing on a stockmarket is a crucial change in the history of a business, marking the separation of ownership from management. What should owner-managers think about when considering listing their businesses?

Positives

- It gives companies another important tool for financing business expansion and corporate acquisitions. Instead of paying cash to the shareholders of a target company, a company can offer its shares.

- Shares and options are more flexible when used as incentives for staff and management. If there is a ready market for the shares, individuals can convert their holdings into cash, subject to scheme rules. There is little that staff and management can do with shares and options in a private company other than wait until the business is sold – or listed.

- Listed companies and their directors are more highly respected than private businesses by the media, potential employees, customers and creditors.

Negatives

- Businesses that succeed on the markets must be confident that they can satisfy market expectations of stability and long-term growth; the markets, and the analysts that interpret and comment on them, do not like surprises. Usually businesses can be confident of such stability only once they have achieved a certain level of maturity; this partly explains why bigger companies often fare better on the markets than smaller ones.

- Financial markets are notoriously short-termist. They respond to the financial reporting cycles dictated by market regulation and company law, which for listed companies means not just the annual financial statements, but also interim and quarterly announcements. Owner-managers accustomed to taking a longer-term view often struggle with the short-term preoccupations of the markets. This was the case with Virgin. Richard Branson took the company private shortly after listing. Branson said that the business's long-term goals were being compromised.

- The listing process is time consuming and expensive, and will affect day-to-day business management.

- Maintaining a listing is expensive.

- There will be greater public scrutiny of directors' and management's actions and a more onerous set of regulations. Many have been lured by the glory an IPO is perceived to bestow on a company's directors, without appreciating the change of role that goes with it. Many former owner-managers/CEOs of newly listed businesses moan about how much time they have to invest in investor relations and answering analysts' questions. Notwithstanding the reasons Branson gave when taking Virgin back into private ownership (see above), it is often noted that the Virgin empire has always been opaque, despite the warm and ostensibly open personality of its founder. Opacity does not sit well with a listing on a regulated stockmarket.

- A listed company is no longer in control of its own destiny and can be subject to hostile takeover, particularly if its shares fail to perform.

- A listing provides the current owners with an opportunity to realise part of their investment, but it is not in itself an exit for the owners.

- A flotation is easier to achieve when the markets are doing well than when they are doing badly. In 2009, the world's stockmarkets virtually shut up shop for new entrants. Lastminute.com famously got its flotation away days before the dotcom bubble burst. Other arguably more robust business propositions missed the opportunity, and some wasted a lot of management time and cost preparing for a listing that had to be postponed or even cancelled.

■ A listed company is subject to the vagaries of the market. Share prices go down as well as up. The advisers of a company seeking to offer its shares on the market usually try to pitch the price at a level that allows the early investors a small increase in value. But the future for a share, particularly a new share, can be difficult to predict, and luck seems to have as much of an influence as the skills of management and their advisers. Unfortunately, many of the positives associated with having listed shares depend on the market perceiving those shares to be attractive. Of course, a company will pay the costs of maintaining a listing regardless.

A demanding process

Different markets in different jurisdictions have different rules and procedures for flotations and IPOs. The following briefly reflects what is typically involved.

A flotation takes time. The process itself is unlikely to take less than six months and could well take up to a year. And the business will need to be groomed for the market; if it wants to succeed, it will need to look the part before it gets there. In particular, its board, management team and governance processes need to be fit for purpose. As a minimum this will require replacing some individuals in key roles in the company and the recruitment of new non-executive directors; a new approach to public relations, brand management and customer care; and ensuring that internal accounting systems are able to cope with the new demands that will be made. Because private companies enjoy a less onerous regulatory environment, there may be skeletons that need shaking out of the cupboards. Senior managers and directors will have to accept and act in accordance with new standards of behaviour. Many find this hard. Grooming a company can easily add another year to the preparation process, if not longer.

As well as sorting out its own house, a company interested in floating will need to recruit new teams of advisers. It will need a sponsor to co-ordinate its entry to the market. It may also need a corporate broker, though sometimes this can be the same firm as the sponsor. It will need reporting accountants, lawyers and tax advisers, as well as experienced public-relations advisers. Long-standing corporate advisers may need to be replaced. Lawyers and accountants who have successfully guided the business through the entrepreneurial early years, venture capital and private equity, may not have the skills and experience required for listing. None of the replacements will come cheap.

There are different ways in which a company can go public. At one end of the scale is a (relatively) cheap and simple introduction to the market, raising no new money. A placing, in which shares are offered for sale to institutions selectively, might be in a company's best interests. At the other end of the scale is a public offer, in which both institutions and private individuals are invited to subscribe. A company's advisers will help identify the best route.

Whatever method of listing it chooses, the company and its advisers have to prepare a prospectus or listing particulars, as appropriate. This sets out all the information that has to be made public to investors under the listing rules. It also acts as an important piece of PR, providing a description of the business, its areas of activity and its prospects. The period from the preparation of the accountants' report on the company to the start of dealing on the main market is often around 24 weeks, although it can be less. The stages making up this period will depend on the route selected for flotation. Although a company looking for an introduction has to follow through the full due diligence and disclosure process, including the preparation of listing particulars, it probably will not need to conduct investor road shows. A flotation involving an offer for subscription to the public is a much bigger project. As well as full due diligence and disclosure, including the preparation of a prospectus, the company will probably have to participate in various marketing activities, including road shows, alongside the regulatory and disclosure duties.

While all this is going on, the company's directors will be having meetings with officials from the stock exchange to discuss the business and look at ways in which the stock exchange can help in developing an active trading market following admission. It is easy to forget that a listing is the start of something, not an end in itself. The company's lawyers will also be conducting the verification process, a painstaking task involving the confirmation of every statement or claim in each document. Precise valuations of the company's assets are produced. This often requires the involvement of yet more advisers and people such as actuaries and surveyors. Verification of directors' particulars often requires the directors to dig into their personal and professional records.

One of the most important decisions is the price put on the company's shares. The sponsor and broker will want a realistic price that the market will find attractive, whereas the company will naturally wish to raise as much money as possible. If underwriters are involved, their views must be taken into account too, as they will be exposed if the shares are not taken up. With good reason the final decision is left as late as possible, largely because market conditions can change overnight. Indeed, the price is often the last thing to go into the prospectus. In the worst-case scenario, a listing might have to be pulled in the event of a market collapse, which would leave the company with advisers' fees to pay and no listing to show for it.

People and growth

PEOPLE ARE THE MOST IMPORTANT resource in any business, the least understood and often the least well used. The problem is that people can be emotional, unpredictable and awkward. Furthermore, the right people can be difficult to hire and the wrong ones difficult to fire. However, a business that pays attention to people and manages them intelligently will find growth easier to achieve and sustain.

Recruitment

A business that is growing is a business that is recruiting. It is also one that needs in particular to be mindful of the skills that are needed in the next stage of the business's evolution, as well as those it needs now. It should also take care when recruiting the next generation of management not to overpromise and therefore disappoint.

Integrating new members of staff into a growing business can also be difficult, especially when they are replacing staff members who have been fired or were liked, or their appointment involves an adjustment to the roles of current staff, as is often the case when recruitment is being used as a catalyst for the change that growth demands. Existing employees tend to view changes of any kind with suspicion. (See Chapter 4.)

Recruiting staff from outside also has an inflationary impact on staff costs. Unless they happen to find themselves on the job market for reasons not of their own making, good recruits will need reasons to leave their current employers. Some will be prepared to move to secure better long-term opportunities, but in other instances a salary increase will be necessary to secure the move – and this may cause problems if and when their new colleagues find out how much the new recruit is being paid.

Recruitment is both a science and an art and requires a serious commitment of management time, thought and effort, even when a professional recruitment firm is being used. Businesses often find it difficult to justify the cost of using a third-party organisation to assist with recruitment. Indeed, for junior posts, it is often cost-effective for a business to do the work itself, particularly with the internet offering many low-cost advertising options. For senior posts, however, advisers can add value. Good advisers add a measure of objectivity. They can structure a selection process that gives the business the best chance of finding the right candidate, minimising the subjective elements in what will always remain a demanding exercise fraught with personal judgments. Advisers also provide a relatively objective point of contact for candidates. Many good candidates are wary of applying directly to a company but are willing to approach an intermediary, confident of being able to have exploratory discussions while retaining confidentiality. A company that seeks to recruit directly to senior positions without using advisers runs the risk of not attracting some candidates with real potential.

Getting the best from people

Growth demands change from the business and development on the part of key people within it. The systems necessary to do this effectively should provide personal goals and targets for employees in the context of career plans that are aligned with the plans for the business. Personal achievement should be assessed against these targets and actions recommended; these should be documented and reviewed later against a revised set of targets. In other words, a growing business needs effective staff appraisal and development systems that complement its growth plans.

Performance management and appraisal

Big businesses nowadays are comfortable with formal appraisal mechanisms for staff. Most small businesses deal with staff appraisal at best informally, at worst not at all. Far too many rely on a pay review (or lack of it) to pass on the good or bad news, leave the communication of detail to osmosis, assume that anyone who makes a mistake is not worth employing anyway, and trust the "X-factor" and "gut feeling" as substitutes for an objective analysis of competency and capability. But even the smallest businesses benefit from the formal appraisal of staff. The appraisal system need not be complicated; it should include space for a robust discussion about an individual's past and current performance, an opportunity to discuss the individual's future in the context of the organisation's future, an agreed action plan and some form of formal record of the process and the decisions reached.

As an organisation gets bigger and the points of contact for individual staff become more diverse, some form of feedback or comment from different parts of the organisation on an individual's performance can be useful. Some organisations invest in complicated, computer-based "360-degree" assessment systems – in which individuals score each other using pre-set competency questionnaires – which churn out sophisticated aggregate reports for the organisation and for each individual. Such systems can be expensive. They can also be inflexible and struggle to accommodate the changes that inevitably come with growth. Lastly, and most importantly, they depend for their effectiveness on participants submitting truthful feedback. If you put rubbish in, you get rubbish out.

If a solution is to work well in a growing, changing business it should be kept simple and therefore flexible. At the other end of the scale from sophisticated computer-based systems is a "three up, three down" system. A handful of individuals who know the appraisee well are required to identify and note three strengths and three development needs for the individual under review.

Information such as this, collected from two or three individuals with whom the appraisee has worked during the period under review, greatly enhances an appraisal discussion – and at little expense.

Performance management challenges in bigger businesses ambitious for growth are more difficult to assess. Increasingly performance management systems in such businesses are based on the balanced scorecard methodology developed by American academics and consultants Robert Kaplan and David Norton in the 1990s. This provides a mechanism for adding strategic non-financial performance measures to traditional financial measures when planning for and assessing the achievement of corporate strategic goals. The framework suggests how first departmental targets and measures, and then individuals' personal targets, might be drafted to reinforce corporate strategies. Corporate strategy is thus translated into detailed actions for individual members of staff. Kaplan and Norton describe their framework as follows:[1]

> *The balanced scorecard retains traditional financial measures. But financial measures tell the story of past events, an adequate story for industrial age companies for which investments in long-term capabilities and customer relationships were not critical for success. These financial measures are inadequate, however, for guiding and evaluating the journey that information age companies must make to create future value through investment in customers, suppliers, employees, processes, technology, and innovation.*

It is easy to see why this mechanism has been popular with large corporations interested in focusing the efforts of all staff on achieving growth.

Some individuals take the view that appraisals are processes only for junior staff. This is not true. Board directors of major corporations benefit as much from regular, formal appraisal as junior assistants. Indeed, the Corporate Governance Code for listed companies in the UK requires that the board should undertake a formal and rigorous annual valuation of its own performance and that of its committees and individual directors. The code also stipulates that the review of the boards of FTSE 350 companies should be externally facilitated every three years.

Training and development

As well as being appraised, individuals should be trained. The case for training staff is strong in any business. Business leaders who take the view that training is too expensive should consider the potential costs (in terms of failing to keep up with the times or the competition as well as the everyday needs of the business) of not training their staff. In a growing business the case is particularly strong because of the change that is integral to growth; anyone whose role is changing is likely to need assistance in acquiring the skills demanded by new challenges. One serial entrepreneur observes that senior managers newly recruited to fast-growth businesses should accept that their new roles will change between the time they accept the job and the day they start it.

The most senior individuals in the biggest businesses also need to refresh their skills and learn new ones. Corporate governance codes propose as good practice that the chairman should regularly review and agree with each director their training and development needs.

Training and development can only go so far. Senior managers in growing businesses should recognise the point when the needs of the business grow beyond the capabilities of its staff. New staff will be needed to tackle new challenges; old staff will need to move on. Again, what is true for junior staff is also true for senior directors. One experienced executive observed that a business needed to change its finance director when it reached a turnover of £7 million, £17 million and £70 million. The numbers may be wrong but the sentiment is correct. For many it is not so much capability that is the problem but appetite. Many managers want to work only in small or early-stage businesses. One price of success is that the individuals responsible for creating it may no longer want to be part of it. Another factor commonly forgotten in the context of business evolution is the age of members of the management team. Individuals change as they grow older, and so do their priorities, desires and expectations. Increasingly, retirement is not the issue, although it is important to acknowledge personal plans to withdraw from the business. What is more important is to ensure that an individual's changing priorities are acknowledged and reconciled with development and business plans.

To nurture, to retain, or to ...

Businesses with ambitions to grow often find themselves torn between two human resources strategies. The first is an "up-or-out" strategy. Staff are expected to look for and achieve promotion regularly. Failure to progress in an up-or-out organisation in effect means the end of an individual's career. Such organisations depend on senior posts being sufficiently attractive and rewarding to be coveted by junior staff. Those adopting this strategy inevitably foster aggressively competitive organisational cultures.

Large professional services organisations – lawyers, management consultancies and banks – typically adopt this type of strategy. It appears to be wasteful; in an up-or-out organisation there are bound to be capable individuals who leave because they feel they are unlikely to win the promotion that might have kept them. How can such a strategy be reconciled with the pressures of growth, one of the barriers to which is the capability and capacity – and thus availability – of talent? Organisations able to make such a strategy work are also those for which the availability of new talent is not a problem. Such organisations argue that the strategy makes for clean, efficient people-management, which looks after itself. In such organisations everyone is well paid. As the HR director at an international consulting firm observed:

> We do not need to pay bonuses here: if you're good enough to work for us you'll be well paid; if you're not good enough you will not get paid less, you will not work for us at all.

The alternative strategy is one in which an organisation works harder at retaining staff, trying to find the right level for everyone. Under up-or-out, middle-ranking positions are held by individuals who are on the way to the top or on the way out. Under the alternative strategy, middle-ranking positions may be held by individuals moving far more slowly through the organisation, or not moving at all. It is easier to reconcile such an approach with the inevitable shortage of capable senior staff in a growing organisation. However, such a strategy puts more pressure on performance management systems: there is not much difference between individuals finding their own level and the organisation tolerating lower standards. Remuneration systems under this strategy are also likely to have to be more complicated.

Regardless of the strategy adopted, when staff leave their departure should be handled as constructively as possible so that they are likely to represent the organisation well to the outside world. Organisations with up-or-out strategies can have just as effective alumni programmes as firms with softer approaches. Alumni from management consultancy McKinsey hold roles across industry, commerce and government. Most are pleased to acknowledge their time at McKinsey, even though many were in effect asked to leave. Former staff are among the most powerful and credible ambassadors any business can have. Big businesses often invest in sophisticated alumni management programmes. Small businesses cannot do this, but time, energy and money invested in ensuring that staff who are leaving are looked after, and kept in contact with, will pay dividends.

Remuneration

Staff remuneration is a difficult issue in any business. In a growing business or one ambitious for growth, it is often even more difficult. In growing businesses cash is often under pressure, so there is less available for paying staff. Smaller businesses have fewer resources than bigger ones anyway, but if they wish to grow they need to attract and retain people with the qualities and experience necessary to take the business to the next stage of its evolution. Again, they will not come cheap.

Bonus considerations

Unsurprisingly, many young and ambitious businesses incorporate some form of performance-related or deferred remuneration in their reward mechanisms. If a business cannot afford to pay good money now, it can at least guarantee that, if targets are met, the individuals responsible for the success will be rewarded in due course. Mechanisms for delivering performance-related or deferred rewards include bonus and equity schemes (including share options). They are powerful tools for motivating staff, but they come with health warnings:

- A good bonus scheme rewards employees for achieving predetermined targets. Defining such targets for a growing business can be difficult (see Chapter 5).

- Staff need to have faith in the fairness of the bonus scheme. But it can be difficult to determine which staff members have been responsible for what, and the allocation of bonuses at the end of a period can be divisive. Managers seeking to pick and choose between staff will have their judgments questioned. Conversely, managers who are insufficiently discriminatory may find that staff think some of their number have been unfairly rewarded for riding on the backs of others.

- It is difficult to identify and capture everything that matters in a set of performance measures tied to a bonus scheme. There is a trade-off between the wish to capture the complexity of reality and the need to design a scheme that is simple enough for staff to understand and that will influence change. If there are too many variables, staff will find it difficult to identify clearly what they need to do to achieve their bonuses, and therefore may not bother to make the effort the bonus scheme seeks to encourage. No more than three variables will ensure the clearest link between remuneration and performance. However, performance is rarely a matter of successfully delivering two or three variables, so such a system is likely to distort staff behaviour in some way. Simple systems that distort behaviour can be used to influence change; sophisticated systems that attempt to capture the complexity of a job will be better than simple ones at sharing the spoils fairly, but they will be less help as levers of change.

- Employees are always cleverer than the bonus schemes designed to motivate them, no matter how sophisticated the schemes. Bonus schemes should be thought of as short-term only. If they are left in place for too long, staff will find the loopholes, and the negative effects of the system will outweigh the positive.

- Staff do not react to bonus schemes in the same way. This can come as a surprise to managers. It may be attractive to managers to be able to link remuneration to future performance, but many staff would rather settle for a guaranteed higher income now than the prospect that it could, if all goes well, turn out to be much higher in the end. As one HR director observed: to some staff a bonus scheme is just an excuse for not paying people properly to start with.

- Bonuses are best at providing short-term reward for short-term performance. If the behaviours sought have long-term rather than short-term consequences, equity-based rewards may prove more effective.

Options and other equity-based incentives

Equity-based incentives, including share options, have several advantages for growing businesses. They defer the payout of cash and are thus easier to align with long-term growth plans. They can be used to tie employees to the business: if staff leave early, they may lose their rights to benefit from the scheme. Usually the source of the cash will be outside the business, coming from a future acquirer of the company's shares. The use of equity as a reward can also help engender a sense of ownership. However, such schemes also have drawbacks:

- Equity and option schemes can be complicated and expensive to establish in terms of advisers' fees in particular, as well as management time and effort – and these are costs that cannot be deferred. Businesses considering using such schemes should not cut corners. Professional advice should be taken to ensure documentation is in place to cover as many future eventualities as possible. This may include shareholder agreements and changes to employment terms and conditions. The costs of getting it wrong can be much more expensive than the set-up costs. Shareholder disputes can tear a company apart.

- In many jurisdictions equity and option schemes are viewed favourably by the authorities, particularly in the case of small companies, and are subject to advantageous tax schemes. Indeed, tax, for both the individuals and the company, is a specific and ever-changing complication that needs to be taken into account when introducing equity or option schemes. But tax should be thought of as the cart not the horse. Tax schemes can have the effect of encouraging management to focus on saving tax rather than more strategic business imperatives. What seemed like a good idea when the scheme was established can turn into a poisoned pill if it needs to be unwound for whatever unforeseen reason. Either the tax will need to be paid after all, or the scheme will prevent necessary change.

- In start-ups there are important issues to consider when deciding how much equity to give to whom. Many founding teams fudge the issue and give equal shares. Four friends with 25% each of the equity may seem fair in theory, but the result may be organisational stalemate after the four have fallen out and old friends start taking sides and vote accordingly. Besides, an equal allocation of equity presumes an equal contribution from everyone. This is rarely the case. When assessing contribution, team members should focus on capital contribution. Capital often takes the form of cash to finance the venture, but it can also take other forms – intellectual capital, for example.

■ Neither equity nor options mean much if the holder cannot see a way of turning them into cash. For public companies whose shares are quoted on the stockmarket there is no problem, but most growing businesses are not in this position. For private companies there is not a ready market for their shares, so schemes in such companies work best when there is a clear exit route that reinforces the overall business objectives. Classic exit routes include floating the business (quoting its shares on the stockmarket) or a trade sale (selling it to another business). In the absence of an exit route, equity and options are far less effective as incentives.

■ Scheme members in listed companies are more excited about equity or options when stockmarkets are doing well than when they are doing badly. When share prices are going down, their owners have reason for being doubly demoralised. A decision to "rebase" an option that is worthless because the share price has fallen below the exercise price on the option often results in ordinary stockholders crying foul.

■ Equity and option schemes are often implemented by entrepreneurs who are motivated by holding equity in the businesses they have founded. But many of the next generation of management may be much less interested in equity, though they may be reluctant to admit this if offered equity in a recruitment interview.

■ Equity is easier to give than it is to take away. Business founders should think carefully before giving equity to an untested member of the team, and should make sure it is not given on appointment but only after, say, the satisfactory completion of a probation period.

Making it a team effort

As with most other aspects of management, growing a business, whether it is new and small or large and established, is very much a team activity. "Without [Sinclair Beecham] it wouldn't work; without me it wouldn't be there," noted Julian Metcalfe of the joint contributions he and his fellow founder made to Pret a Manger. Research consistently shows that businesses founded by teams grow further and faster than businesses founded by individuals.

Team is perhaps too scientific a term for what, in a start-up, is often little more than a group of friends. Such teams need to ensure that their business is set up in such a way that it stands the best chance of surviving a failure in the friendship, so often the consequence of even a successful business venture between friends. John D. Rockefeller, according to a 1998 biography by Ronald Chernow, was fond of quoting his partner Henry Morrison Flagler's dictum that a friendship based on business is superior to a business based on friendship.

In their book, *The Wisdom of Teams*, Jon Katzenbach and Douglas Smith argue that, in businesses big and small, good teams do not just happen.[2] Without investment in team construction and management, the group will not even add up to the sum of its parts. But with such an investment, the parts may combine to become a high-performance team delivering far in excess of the sum of the individual contributions.

Out of the wealth of thinking that has gone into the management of teams, the following points are worth noting by a team with responsibility for growing the business.

Leadership

The role of team leader should be defined and allocated. In young businesses, particularly those founded by groups of friends, there is often a lack of clarity about the role of the leader. The leader of an established business is usually the CEO or managing director, who runs the business through the management team he or she is responsible for building and leading. In bigger businesses the role is often split between the chairman and the CEO, with the former responsible for the board and holding the CEO to account for the running of the business.

Complementary strengths and capabilities

Good teams include individuals with different strengths and capabilities; those who are similar often tread on each other's toes. Team-building methodologies give different labels to the different roles, often identifying the various personality types most likely to succeed in them. Meredith Belbin, an authority on teams, refers to:

- the plant (the creative problem solver);
- the resource investigator (the enthusiastic opportunity explorer);
- the co-ordinator (the chairperson);
- the shaper (thriving on pressure and focusing the team's attention on its goals);
- the monitor–evaluator (calmly reviewing and assessing options);
- the implementer (turning ideas into action);
- the completer (searches for errors and omissions);
- the teamworker (the doer who avoids friction and gets things done);
- the specialist (providing technical know-how for the task in hand).

None of these labels are used around real boardroom tables, but the notion that there are different types of activity within a team, and different types of people required to do them, is often ignored. Table 7.1 gives some more details of Belbin's role types.

TABLE 7.1 **Belbin's role types**

Team role type	Description and contribution	Allowable weaknesses
Resource investigator	Extrovert, enthusiastic, communicative Explores possibilities Develops contacts	Overoptimistic Loses interest once initial enthusiasm has passed
Co-ordinator	Mature, confident, a good chairperson Clarifies goals, promotes decision-making, delegates well	Can often be seen as manipulative Delegates personal work
Teamworker	Co-operative, mild, perceptive, diplomatic Listens, builds, averts friction, calms the waters	Indecisive in crunch situations Can be easily influenced
Plant	Creative, imaginative, unorthodox Solves difficult problems	Ignores details Too preoccupied to communicate effectively
Shaper	Challenging, dynamic, thrives on pressure Has the drive and courage to overcome obstacles	Can provoke others Tends to hurt people's feelings
Monitor–evaluator	Sober, strategic, discerning Sees all options Judges accurately	Lacks drive and ability to inspire others Overly critical
Implementer	Disciplined, reliable, conservative, efficient Turns ideas into practical actions	Somewhat inflexible Slow to respond to new possibilities
Completer	Painstaking, conscientious, anxious Searches out errors and omissions Delivers on time	Inclined to worry unduly Reluctant to delegate Can be a nit-picker

Team role type	Description and contribution	Allowable weaknesses
Specialist	Single-minded, self-starting, dedicated	Contributes only on a narrow front
	Provides knowledge and skills in rare supply	Dwells on technicalities
		Overlooks the "big picture"

Source: www.Belbin.com

In too many businesses the role of team members is to agree with the boss, and the best way of guaranteeing advancement is to take the boss as a role model. The finance director or chief financial officer is often the only person who likes to say no, but the CEO should be open to challenge from every member of the senior management team, executive and non-executive.

Clear objectives and a disciplined approach

A team will be more effective if it has clear objectives. For a team responsible for growing a business, this means drafting a long-term plan for the business, together with a shorter-term action plan and a budget aligned with the long-term plan (see Chapter 9).

Regular management meetings should be documented and agreed actions should be assigned to individuals and followed up. In short, meetings should be disciplined. A good chairman will make sure that all points of view are heard; that unresolved conflicts are identified and addressed; that, where appropriate, individuals are held accountable for their actions; and that team members do not fall into false consensus, with bullying or boredom taking the place of judgment and debate.

It is not just the main leadership roles that should be carefully defined. All members of a team responsible for managing growth should be aware of the scope of their authority and the nature of their expected contributions. Such definition, and the diversity it depends on, is easier for businesses with lots of staff. In small businesses individuals may have several jobs. Multi-tasking often extends outside the boardroom. In a family business, for example, an operations director might also be the finance director, as well as being a shareholder, the mother of another board director, the daughter of the company founder (who might also be a non-executive) and an influential individual in the local community. That individuals are required to play a variety of roles in many small businesses is often considered to be a strength; a team in which individuals share responsibilities is likely to be more flexible than one in which roles are clearly delineated. This is true, but lack of role definition can hinder accountability, particularly when the team is under pressure and the various bucks that are flying around need to be shared out or specifically allocated.

Discipline is not just about the conduct of individual meetings. Even small businesses can benefit from a business calendar, circulated in advance to the management team or board members, indicating when in the year various matters will be discussed. These may include strategy and business planning, budgeting, pay reviews, shareholder management and governance. In listed businesses, boardroom discipline is governed in great part by corporate governance codes. But smaller businesses need discipline too.

Decision-taking

The easiest decisions to take are those that everyone agrees on, though it is important that all sides of an issue are explored first. Where members of the team disagree a healthy debate should be easier to initiate, and opinions may change as a consequence. A CEO is likely to be more influential than other members of a management team, and ultimately, of course, a shareholder with a majority of the voting power can force decisions through, but decision-taking mechanisms that rely on an individual getting his or her own way all the time are unlikely to take advantage of the diversity of skills in the team as a whole. If consensus cannot be achieved following a debate, other mechanisms for taking decisions will be needed, and these should be agreed in advance. In a team where roles and responsibilities have been allocated and delegated, the responsibility for taking a decision when the team cannot reach consensus should be devolved to the individual responsible for the relevant area of the business. The rest of the team will have to accept that the wrong decision might therefore be taken. One of the rites of passage that a growing business will go through is the allocation of delegated responsibility. Such a change is difficult to implement, particularly for those used to being involved in every decision, but without delegated decision-taking many teams find it difficult to take decisions at all. If there is one thing worse than making the wrong decision, it is making no decision.

Measuring success

Defined mechanisms for acknowledging and measuring success help team performance. In the case of a senior management team, these include business performance indicators that attempt to capture all aspects of business performance (see Chapter 5), and a dashboard of key performance indicators (KPIs) that focus management's attention on the critical elements of business performance. In the case of a team responsible for implementing growth, the growth plan should include a framework for assessing progress along the way.

Intangible strengths and vulnerabilities

Building a business involves creating an entity with a distinctive identity separate from the founders. Internally, this identity is a composite of a particular organisational culture and set of values. The external manifestation of this identity in a successful organisation is seen most readily in the brand proposition. Where do these elements come from? The example below helps to explain how intangible elements such as brand and culture are often derived from the personality of the founders.

From personality to organisational culture

David Bruce built his pub business, Bruce's Breweries, the way he wanted, notwithstanding rational and well-meant advice to the contrary from advisers and financiers. Made redundant in 1979 by one of the big brewers several recessions ago, Bruce put his money into a rundown pub in London's Elephant and Castle district. But he did more than give the establishment a good refit. Out went the jukebox even though his bank manager advised him it would bring large amounts of much-needed cash every night; Bruce did not like turning up to a pub for a drink and having to shout at his friend over someone else's choice of music. He also put a microbrewery behind the bar and announced his intention to brew his own beer on site. He renamed the pub the Goose and Firkin. It was a great success. Within a few years Bruce was running a chain of pubs in south-east England, each of which brewed on site and none of which had jukeboxes. They all had "and Firkin" in their titles, thus giving rise to a slightly risqué advertising campaign playing on the mispronunciation of "firkin" after a pint or two, which appealed to Bruce's sense of humour.

After nine years Bruce surprised everyone by selling his business in 1988 to European Leisure, which in 1991 sold it to Allied Domecq, which in 1999 sold it to Punch Taverns. A couple of years later Punch sold over half of the pubs to Bass (now Mitchells & Butlers). After founder owner-manager Bruce had sold it, the business became the concern of a series of teams of professional managers, who worked successfully for a while growing the estate. But before long the character of the pubs changed significantly and the jukeboxes were back. In due course, the microbreweries went and were replaced with higher-margin bought-in real ale. Growth slowed, then stopped. In 2001 Punch announced that the Firkin brand was to be discontinued. Some of the pubs still keep the Firkin name, which has been used by chains in the US, Canada and elsewhere (with no connection to the original business), but most of the UK pubs have been renamed. Even the original Goose and Firkin is now the Duke of York.

It is easy to conclude that the Firkin story is just about brand building, or a brand that had run its course. Far more important for those interested in growing businesses is that many of the elements of the business Bruce built were derived from his personal preferences, his personality, even his sense of humour – rather than manufactured as a consequence of rational analysis. Indeed, if he had taken the advice of the rationalists at the start, his business might have looked very different. Once Bruce had sold the business it changed quite quickly.

Other companies in similar circumstances have tried to manage the transitions described above in a more considered manner. When Ben Cohen and Jerry Greenfield sold Ben and Jerry's, the ice cream business they had founded, to Unilever in 2000, many wondered whether the company's culture would change, particularly regarding its participation in global ecological and environmental campaigns. Unilever announced its determination to carry on with the campaigning, even though Cohen and Greenfield had stepped down from management involvement. Although Ben and Jerry's has undoubtedly changed in the years since 2000, Unilever has remained true to its word.

As Bruce's Breweries and Ben and Jerry's show, many of the important intangible elements of organisational cultures, values and brands are derived from the personalities of the founders. However, when a business has grown larger or the founder has sold out, it can be difficult to preserve these elements. At some stage a growing business will almost certainly lose some of the magic that made it special when it was founded. Managers wishing to recapture these elements need to find ways of recreating them. They cannot rely on rational performance management systems and processes. They need to invest in the irrational: in informal as well as formal communication mechanisms, in symbols, in who sits where, in the design of the office environment, in how things are done as well as what is done.

For many organisations a key to culture is organisational structure – including the size of each organisational unit and the autonomy given to it. Entrepreneurship is often identified as a quality that organisations wish to hang on to even as they get bigger and more institutional. In the context of bigger businesses, entrepreneurship is often labelled intrapreneurship, recognising its differences from as well as its similarities to entrepreneurship in smaller businesses. In addition to looking at structural solutions, big businesses wishing to rediscover their entrepreneurial roots might look at corporate venturing (investing in start-ups), joint ventures with other organisations, acquiring businesses further down the growth ladder, or new products and business lines. They might also consider breaking up into smaller businesses, recognising that parts of the business may be worth more to the shareholders than the big organisation it has become.

Informal structure is as important as official structure. Once they reach a certain size all businesses will have a formal structure (see Chapter 4), but they will also have an informal structure with communication channels and lines of influence that are unlikely to match those implied by the official structure. Wise managers do not try to force such structures into compliance, recognising that they will always exist and that they provide another set of tools for controlling the business. Research shows that informal, word-of-mouth communication from peer to peer is more likely to be believed than an official e-mail from the CEO. As Suzanne Crampton, John Hodge and Jitendra Mishra say in a 1998 article in *Public Personnel Management*, sophisticated communicators use these informal networks to their advantage, deciding which channels best suit which message.[3]

Other organisations see a connection between their culture and their organisational values. When defining their organisational culture they might start by inviting employees to identify the organisation's values and then compare and contrast these with their personal values. Attempts can then be made to explore the gaps between the two value sets, and adjust those of the organisation (if considered necessary) through training programmes, brand-awareness programmes and so on. Such exercises – which will be powerful as they are grounded in values that employees hold dear – can be used to influence all aspects of an organisation's behaviour.

Manufactured organisational cultures, compared with those organically derived from personality and belief, can be fragile and buckle under pressure – often the time the workforce needs them most.

Organisational identities can be sources of strength when businesses find themselves in difficulty. They can also become part of the problem. Culture can be difficult to change – not least because it is so difficult to talk about. But a failure to change culture is the reason the majority of change initiatives fail to change anything.

8

Different types of growth

THIS CHAPTER EXPLORES different types of growth, including organic growth and growth by association with another organisation through merger, acquisition or some form of joint venture or alliance. It also considers growth by replication, the pressures of different rates of growth and growth overseas.

Hypergrowth

Growth is what happens when the graph slopes upwards. But the gradient of the slope matters too. A business experiencing slow growth has different challenges from one experiencing rapid growth. The increasing use of the label "hypergrowth" for those whose growth graph slopes particularly steeply is an acknowledgement that fast-growing companies' experience of growth is qualitatively as well as quantitatively different.

Industries and markets can experience hypergrowth as a consequence of significant circumstantial change. The commercial exploitation of the internet has transformed many industries and created rapidly growing segments. Political change in China provides another example.

Managers experiencing hypergrowth need to do more than just hang on to their hats. They need to consider whether the growth they are experiencing is a consequence of internal or external drivers; externally driven growth is likely to hide internal weaknesses. Hypergrowth will probably be driven by the top line, but managers must remember to secure the bottom line. As discussed earlier, a business that grows too quickly will be unable to finance its own growth – it will be overtrading. A company boasting about hypergrowth must watch out for the danger signals of overtrading. It does not matter how fast the top line is growing as long as managers ensure that the business is generating enough profit to turn into sufficient cash flow, and that sufficient external sources of finance are lined up to support the growth.

Many of the characteristics of hypergrowth are those that successful early-stage companies experience all the time. Indeed, a hypergrowth company might be thought of as one whose experience of growth when small continues long after it might otherwise be expected to have slowed down. A hypergrowth company needs, therefore, both the qualities that enable a small company to grow fast and a big company to sustain the growth it has created. Such a company is in particular danger of failing to remember to grow up as well as grow, which superficially is fine until the factors that fostered the period of hypergrowth weaken, which they inevitably will.

Hypergrowth and delegation

In 2013 Fuhu, a US tablet-maker, reported three-year top-line growth of 158,957%. If anything counts as hypergrowth, this does. As reported in 2014 in *Inc. magazine*, the biggest growth problems were employee burnout and micro-management. The founders deliberately remained personally involved in key management decisions, worried about the implications of building a management bureaucracy, in particular the "entrenched silos" that they believed had hindered growth in other fast-growth, high-tech companies. Fuhu's approach to building an organisational structure fit for hypergrowth was unconventional: below the top two executives is a group of 27 managers called "the partnership", comprising fewer than 10% of staff but owning 18% of the company's equity. Employees were chosen for the partnership by demonstrating a belief "that we're a collective family that has decided to sacrifice for the business". On the one hand, members of the partnership carry walkie-talkies so that they can be contacted immediately; on the other hand, they receive personal mentoring from the top two executives – a management training experience that the partners value and that helps with staff retention.

Strategies for sustaining an organisation experiencing hypergrowth should seek to decentralise management fast while making sure that decisions continue to be co-ordinated and consistent. A rapidly growing company is likely otherwise to overinvest in an unnecessarily complicated and expensive central bureaucracy, thus becoming old before its time. Franchising (see later in this chapter) may provide a set of tools to help. Investment in internal communication methodology is also critical, ensuring the rapidly growing and decentralising organisation does not explode as centrifugal force gets the better of control systems. When people have more than enough to do to keep clients and customers happy, they need to be forced to communicate with each other. A company experiencing hypergrowth is one that can afford to think about the quality of its new business, and thus look to product or service differentiation as a way to increasing profit even if this is at the expense of slowing growth down.

Organic growth

Many of the issues, pressures and strategies discussed in this book so far have presumed linear, organic growth. Organic growth is generated from within or, to put it another way, it is growth that does not rely on an acquisition, merger, or other form of association between two or more organisations.

An examination of the ancestral trees of most of today's organisations shows that organic growth unadulterated by inorganic growth is rare. Indeed, big businesses without some history of acquisition somewhere are virtually non-existent. But even among big businesses there are undoubtedly some that are less acquisitive than others, and that have worked hard to develop opportunities and resources in-house rather than seeking to acquire them readymade. Apple is an example of such a business, making no acquisitions in the first 11 years of its existence. In recent years things have changed. Of the 69 acquisitions the company made between its first in 1988 and mid-2015, half have been made since 2011. But most of its acquisitions have been small companies that can be easily integrated into existing projects, in effect reinforcing an organic strategy.

A business relying on organic growth needs to be confident in its ability to grow its top line. Top-line growth cannot, of course, be left to its own devices. It needs proactive management and stimulation. Some factors are worth commenting on:

- **Market share.** A company opening up a new market with a new project will depend on market growth and its ability to achieve and maintain sufficient market share. If the new market grows rapidly, new competitors will be attracted – competitors that may benefit from the lessons the first company learned the hard way (so-called second-mover advantage) and may be bigger and better resourced than the first company. Companies that invent new markets should never congratulate themselves on having no competition. A company with no competition either is not worth competing with, or is a company that has failed to notice the competition it does have or identify where it will come from. A company might be able to make good money in a tightly defined niche the size of which deters effective competition, but it will not grow if it does not explore business outside the niche. Conversely, a new entrant to an established market can only capitalise on its growth opportunity if it can take market share from established competitors.

- **Geographical expansion.** A company with ambitions to grow will consider geographical expansion. Ambitious companies in some countries may be forced to consider this sooner than others. It has been observed that growth is easier in the US, as the domestic market is huge. Conversely, an ambitious Israeli company is obliged to look to export markets early, as the domestic market is small. Companies in other countries may be caught in the middle. A French entrepreneur observed that one of the many problems of growing a company in France is that the local economy is not as big as it seems, and comes with innate growth constraints – the French language, for example, which is not widely spoken outside France.

When expanding overseas it can be useful to work with business partners. Pret a Manger's attempt to enter the Japanese market was via a joint venture with its minority shareholder McDonald's. Although eventually unsuccessful, Pret could not have contemplated the venture without the knowledge and experience of McDonald's. Expansion into some territories is prohibited unless done in conjunction with a local partner, and even where it is permitted it is often advisable to work with locals. With regard to consumer propositions, every country in the world is different, and often there are significant differences within countries. In the UK, for example, it can be more expensive to find a high-quality retail location outside than inside London (even though the inexperienced might believe the contrary to be true as property is generally more expensive in London). This is because in cities outside London prime locations are in shorter supply and are more aggressively sought. Business-to-business practice also differs from country to country. Local businesses are often more inclined to trust and therefore do business with local businesses, but this is not always the case. It takes local knowledge to understand that some businesses in South-East Asia would rather take consulting advice from UK or US firms than from local ones, not because of perceptions of superior capability but because of fears about confidentiality.

■ **Follow the customer.** One of the least risky routes to organic growth is to follow the customer. Customers satisfied with a company's product or service might invite it to service their requirements in another country or industry segment. Following the customer is an effective way of establishing a bridgehead in a new market. A decision to turn down such an invitation might damage a profitable customer relationship, and stimulate unnecessary competition.

Companies that choose to pursue organic growth put a lot of faith in their ability to generate ideas, markets, businesses, people and other resources internally. They run the risk of becoming stale, and if they are ambitious for growth they need to find ways of replicating the stimulus and injection of fresh ideas from outside that an acquisition strategy almost always provides. Such companies need:

- corporate planning processes designed in such a way as to challenge existing thinking continuously;
- corporate radar that is tuned into changes in the market and industry, and new staff who are rigorously debriefed shortly after arrival for any insight they might have about changes outside;
- customer intelligence programmes that are sensitive to customer feedback.

Data collection alone is not enough. Managers should have the ability and willingness to interpret the data and adapt business strategy accordingly, which can be difficult if they were responsible for originating the strategy in the first place. One way big businesses keep their managers fresh is by rotating them regularly through different parts of the company – different business streams and job roles as well as different geographical locations. Businesses without the scale to rotate management internally may need to consider how they go about recruiting new staff from outside, adopting perhaps an up-or-out promotion strategy with regard to current staff.

Inorganic growth by acquisition

Growth by acquisition is often illusory. A simple acquisition for cash does not make an organisation bigger; it just converts the cash of one organisation into the assets of another. Even when new shares are issued, assuming the price paid is fair, an acquisition will result in two and two only equalling four. Given that an acquisition consumes management time and attention – both before the event to negotiate the deal and afterwards to make it work – in the short term at least the net result will show two and two making less than four. Growth by acquisition is only achieved if in a reasonable time frame the result is more than four. But acquisitions are notorious for their inability to deliver the value intended to shareholders. Many are funded partly by fresh injections of capital, in the form of either debt or equity from existing or new shareholders, but the availability of ready finance is no guarantee that growth will be secured. Indeed, research shows that over the longer term only 50% of acquisitions or mergers achieve the financial targets envisaged.

David Harding and Sam Rovit, partners at Bain & Co, have suggested that it can be misguided to think in terms of growth objectives when looking to acquire:[1]

The primary purpose of mergers and acquisitions is not to grow big fast, although that may be the result, but for companies to do what they do better.

Before exploring an acquisition or a merger, Harding and Rovit encourage management to focus on the source of each company's competitive advantage. A successful acquisition should be used either to strengthen that advantage or to transform a company's advantage, for example when the industry has changed and the company has struggled to catch up. Too many deals, they argue, fail because they attempt to transform fundamentally weak business models, or they are entered into in pursuit of growth for its own sake, or they are a consequence of hubris rather than strategy.

In what ways might an acquisition add up to more than the sum of its parts?

Undervalued companies

The most promising acquisition opportunities are those available cheaply. Acquisitions of undervalued companies are often driven by the circumstances of the vendor, which for various reasons may be obliged to sell. A compulsory sale, for whatever reason, is likely to put downward pressure on the sale price of a company, but it also often brings to the market a business that is otherwise strong. Thomas Cook Global Financial Services was put up for sale in 2000 when its majority shareholder, Preussag, acquired the UK's largest travel business, Thomson Travel. The reason for the sale was that Preussag knew that if it pursued its interest in Thomson Travel, the European competition authorities would force it to sell its interest in Thomas Cook's financial services business. Furthermore, one of Thomas Cook's other significant shareholders, Westdeutsche Landesbank, would also be obliged to sell its stake because of its close association with Preussag. Thus the disposal was in effect a forced sale and had little to do with the underlying quality of the business, which was eventually acquired by Travelex. In a similar case, it was reported in June 2015 that Ladbrokes could be forced to sell some 1,300 shops if it wanted to secure approval from the competition authorities for its £3.5 billion merger with Gala Coral. No doubt some of the businesses put up for sale would be underperforming; others might be good opportunities for investors.

Shareholders may be obliged to sell when a succeeding generation of a family-owned company is not interested in or capable of owning or running the business itself. Businesses funded by private equity may be sold as shareholders, particularly financial stakeholders, seek to realise some gain. Whether or not they are under pressure from external investors, successful entrepreneurs will sooner or later find they have created a business that has turned into something that demands skills they do not have or that no longer interests them. As already established, change is a price of successful growth, and thus the question for the entrepreneur is not whether to exit but when.

Businesses may be put up for sale quickly if the shareholders are under pressure to raise cash. Again, this may be a consequence of another transaction. The new owners of a group might finance their recent acquisition of the bits of the business they want by selling some of the others. A business that is performing badly might be put up for sale because its existing shareholders are unable to make the investment required to turn it around; a distressed sale such as this may present a good-value opportunity to a purchaser. The new CEO of a group might decide to sell parts of the business as part of a new strategy.

As these examples demonstrate, when seeking to make an acquisition, the first issue a potential purchaser should consider is the motivation of the vendor.

Of course, a business available only for its full value might still present opportunities for the purchaser if there are strategic benefits to be derived from the acquisition. A trade buyer from the same industry as the business for sale might be able to achieve "synergies" or cost savings by rationalising duplicate activities after making the acquisition. An acquisition target will be worth more to a purchaser able to make such savings. Trade buyers often offer the highest prices for a business for this reason, particularly if they can also take advantage of existing industry knowledge and expertise. However, such synergistic benefits are easier to identify in theory than they are to realise in practice. Too often an excited acquirer will use synergies to rationalise overpayment for an acquisition. Besides, if you pay the vendor for the synergies you are planning to achieve, you are paying for something that has not yet been achieved and are eating into your own profits. Synergies should influence the price you sell a company for, not the price you pay for it.

Injecting new ideas and talent

The strategic benefits of acquisition can be derived from differences as well as similarities between acquirers and their targets. As noted in Chapter 3, Larry Greiner suggests when commenting on his own growth model that in the later stages of a company's evolution in particular further growth might well be dependent on what he calls "extra-organisational solutions". An acquisition is often used as a way of injecting new ideas and talent. A recruitment campaign might succeed in recruiting a handful of new managers, but an acquisition might bring in hundreds or thousands, as well as new ways of doing business, business systems, brands, patents, and research and development capabilities. Exposure to such a sudden dose of high-voltage intellectual capital might have a transformative effect on the business of the acquirer, assuming that the businesses can be integrated and the differences between the two turned to positive advantage. An acquisition might also provide a shortcut to new markets, or new customers or geographical areas. An acquisition might be seen as a route to achieving critical mass more quickly than would be the case otherwise, bringing the stability, security and credibility of being bigger.

A study published in 2004 by Anthony Mitchell and Simon Hill of Ashridge Management College seeks to understand perceptions of the differences between successful and unsuccessful mergers and acquisitions in the marketing communications sector.[2] Figure 8.1 shows that the most significant difference between successful and unsuccessful deals is perceived to be related to the ability to execute change after the acquisition has been completed. An acquisition strategy based on recruiting difference is particularly dependent on post-merger integration, and the greater the differences the more difficult the integration. Furthermore, too many acquirers pay little attention to post-acquisition integration. Pursuing the deal has always been perceived as more exciting than managing its implications. Integration always springs surprises because, notwithstanding good intentions, acquirers only get to

FIG 8.1 **Process drivers: the best and worst transactions**

	Strongly disagree/ poor	Neutral		Strongly agree/ excellent
	1	2	3	4	5
Negotiation – positive tone?					■
Pre-acquisition planning – adequate?					■
Due diligence – adequate?					■
Enhanced due diligence – carried out?					■
Price – correct?					■
Acquired employees – positive reaction?					■
Acquired employees – expectations managed?					■
Post-acquisition changes – well executed?					■
Acquisition process – effective?					■
Communication (senior management) – effective?					■
Communication (fee earners) – effective?					■
Communication (others) – effective?					■

‑‑‑‑ *Worst*
‑‑‑‑ *Average*
‑‑‑‑ *Best*

Source: A. Mitchell & S. Hill, "The Great Mergers and Acquisitions Gamble", *The Ashridge Journal 360°*, autumn 2004

see what they have bought after the deal has been completed. Successful integration requires a focus on systems, policies, terms of business, client and customer relationships – there will be differences of approach everywhere. Above all, it requires careful management of people. Members of both acquired and acquiring teams will be suspicious of each other; earning trust will take time. There are bound to be casualties, not all of them looked for.

Some acquirers do not intend to get involved in the management of their new acquisitions, preferring to run them in a hands-off way. An acquirer buying a company for its difference may worry that too active an involvement in the acquisition's activities might do more harm than good. Such an attitude is commonly seen when a large, established company acquires a smaller, entrepreneurial one: the acquirer is often worried about damaging the "entrepreneurial culture" that made the target attractive in the first place. However, the terms "hands-off" and "hands-on" imply a black-and-white distinction that does not reflect reality. When one company buys another some form of management involvement should be taken for granted, otherwise there is little reason for acquiring the company in the first place. The shareholders of a listed company might complain that if they had wanted to make an investment in the acquired company, they would not have needed the management of the acquiring company to take the decision for them, and perhaps better use could have been made of the acquiring company's resources. Similarly, "business as usual" claims made by the managers of the acquired company should be taken with a pinch of salt. At the very least the managers will have new owners to answer to; if the managers themselves were also among the shareholders who sold out, they may have a reasonable amount of cash, in which case they may find their motivation for day-to-day management of the business under new ownership changing.

In some situations an "earn-out" will be agreed, under which some or all of the consideration is either deferred pending the acquired business achieving targets or based on a variable performance formula negotiated as part of the deal. In theory, such arrangements allow acquirers to mitigate some of the risks associated with the acquisition. However, earn-outs are also sources of potential conflict, especially when the old owner-managers are still involved in the management of the newly acquired subsidiary. It is difficult, for example, for the new owners to step in and influence the direction of their new business; the old owners (if still the current managers) may claim that such interference will prevent them from delivering the numbers they believe are possible and on which some of the consideration is determined.

Management buy-outs

A management buy-out (MBO) is a particular type of acquisition that can provide a platform for future growth for a company. In an MBO, the shareholders sell the company to the existing managers. Typically, the managers will need external finance to finance the transaction, so an MBO will share the characteristics of a venture-capital investment (see Chapter 6): rapid growth potential; the potential to get very big; and a definable exit for the financial investors within a time frame that is consistent with the objectives of the fund. An MBO will also share many of the same tensions, in particular between the financial investors and the managers. However, it should mark a significant improvement in the growth prospects of a business or it should not happen in the first place. An MBO should signify the transfer of control of a business to a team with a greater appetite for growth, driven in no small part by the need to satisfy the demands of the financiers. Managers involved in an MBO do not always recognise what they have chosen to take on – particularly the implications of taking on external finance.

It is common for a management team buying a company to need additional management as well as financial resources. A company bought by a combination of current and new management is sometimes called a BIMBO (buy-in management buy-out). Financiers and advisers with a penchant for acronyms have come up with other variants on the MBO label that reflect the nuances of particular situations.

Only a minority of businesses are suitable for an MBO (or its variants), and an MBO will not be possible in all of those that are suitable. Companies often prohibit MBOs for parts or the whole of the business, with good reason. Managers who are contemplating buying the company they are working for have significant conflicts of interest that might lead them to act against the interests of the current shareholders. For example, they might be tempted to run the business down so as to benefit from a cheaper purchase price when it is time to buy. Furthermore, an MBO, just like any other transaction, demands a huge amount of time and effort, which might be considered by the current shareholders to be better directed at managing the business. So managers dreaming of an MBO need to tread carefully.

Inorganic growth by merger

A merger is when two businesses are dissolved into each other. In legal terms, a merger suggests the creation of a new, third business, into which the assets of the two merging businesses are transferred. But, in reality, even when a merger is intended, the transaction is often effected by way of an acquisition, with one organisation paying the shareholders of another for its assets. It is hardly surprising that mergers and acquisitions are often confused with each other, especially when many deals are presented as mergers even though the parties involved intend one partner to be dominant. Indeed, cynics argue that one partner in a merger is always dominant even when the intention is otherwise. A merger in the true sense, however, is a process in which the end result is an organisation that takes the best of the combining companies and creates something that can generate more than the two could produce separately. Unfortunately, relatively few mergers do.

Big, multi-stakeholder businesses such as listed companies or large professional partnerships are most likely to attempt mergers. Organisations in which individuals or small groups of individuals are dominant find mergers difficult to pull off, despite good intentions, as it is difficult to reconcile the personal aspirations of powerful individuals with the aggregate interests of the newly merged organisation. Even for big businesses a true merger is more difficult to pull off than a successful acquisition. Corus was the product of the merger between Hoogovens, a Dutch company, and British Steel in 1999, aimed at achieving critical mass in the international metals market. It did not deliver. By 2003 Corus's stockmarket valuation had dropped to $230 million from $6 billion at the time of the merger. Various reasons were given, including the cultural differences between the merged two organisations and the lack of attention to HR matters on integration; downsizing and cost-cutting led to significant labour unrest, which seriously hindered the success of the newly merged company. Corus was bought by Tata, an Indian company, in 2007.

The $182 billion merger of Time Warner and AOL, announced in January 2000, was the largest deal to date and is commonly regarded as the most unsuccessful. Technically this merger was effected by an acquisition – AOL bought Time Warner using stock and debt – but in terms of strategic intent was a merger. Strategically this particular deal made sense as a merger, and so it should have, bearing in mind the amount of brainpower from both boardrooms applied to developing the business case. The union of the old media world and the new – the creation of a new media organisation with extraordinary reach – had much to commend it. Nonetheless, the deal was falling apart even before it was approved by the regulators, by which time the dotcom bubble had burst and the AOL side of the business, the acquiring company, was worth a lot less than it had been when the deal was announced. Economic troubles exacerbated cultural and attitudinal differences between the two sides, and the post-deal integration on which every merger or acquisition depends never took off. By 2010, the combined market value of the two now separated companies was only one-seventh of that of the newly merged firm in 2000.

Sprint's acquisition of Nextel in 2005 was described as a "merger of equals", but by 2012 *Forbes Magazine* was asking whether this was one of the worst deals of all time, "not as bad as AOL and Time Warner for capital destruction, but definitely right up there as an example of M&A gone wrong".

Since Sears and Kmart's first reported income for their newly merged entity in 2005, in-group earnings have plunged by 84%. Eddie Lampert, CEO of Sears and architect of the deal, earned himself the title of worst CEO of the year in 2007. But at least the deal looked good at the time. Many observers doubted the wisdom of Microsoft's acquisition of Nokia's mobile phone business when the deal was done in 2014; little over a year later Microsoft wrote off its investment, and many of the 25,000 ex-Nokia staff lost their jobs.

At the other extreme, ExxonMobil is often cited as an example of one of the most successful mergers – albeit one that joined together companies that, ironically, had originally been created when J. D. Rockefeller senior's Standard Oil was broken up in 1911. The merger successfully achieved cost savings and the integration of two different cultures, though even this transaction was technically a takeover, with, in most instances, Exxon executives appointed to positions senior to their Mobil equivalents.

Other types of inorganic growth

Mergers and acquisitions are not the only ways in which two or more companies can be associated, nor are they the only inorganic platforms for growth.

Minority investments

A minority investment by one company in another can be part of an arrangement intended to provide an impetus to the growth of both. In 2001, McDonald's, a fast-food business, bought 33% of the equity of Pret a Manger, a sandwich retail chain. McDonald's was interested in exploring new avenues for value creation outside its core business. Its investment in Pret a Manger was one among several it made in successful, up-and-coming fast-food businesses. From Pret's point of view, the investment was accompanied by strategic advice and financial and tactical support for its international expansion plans, facilitating its opening in Japan, in particular. As it turned out, Pret's growth strategy proved to be misjudged; international expansion was more difficult than anticipated and the infrastructure needed to support the scale of investment planned was too expensive. Insufficient attention was paid to the company's core business in the UK, which, in the face of increasingly difficult circumstances, began to lose money. Under new management Pret retrenched, pulling out of Tokyo, cutting back in New York and Hong Kong, and focusing on sorting out the core operation. McDonald's stuck with Pret through the turnaround, only exiting when Pret was sold to Bridgepoint, a private equity firm, for £345 million ($552 million) in February 2008, by which time the business was growing well in the UK and prospects were looking good in the US.

Joint ventures

Companies interested in what they might do with and for each other need not buy or exchange each other's shares; they can put together some form of joint venture, both as an end in itself and as a means of exploring whether a more formal union between the two companies might be appropriate in due course. Joint ventures range from the very formal to the very informal. There are few legal frameworks to worry about, other than those preventing participants in the same market from colluding in anti-competitive practices. It is down to the parties concerned to determine the nature of the venture and to agree which parts of the arrangement need to be governed by contract, but they are usually built around a contractual arrangement to share in the profits or losses from an arrangement.

A joint venture is normally a vehicle for the delivery of a particular project, resulting in the creation of a venture that has an existence independent of its founders for a predetermined period of time. Unlike a merger or an acquisition, there is no intention on the part of either party to interfere in the management or strategy of the other, except in relation to the joint venture itself. Companies interested in a joint venture should be aware that there are three sets of objectives to be satisfied: those of the joint venture itself and those of each of the joint-venture partners. In other words, joint-venture partners will almost certainly have objectives that they choose not to share with each other. To claim otherwise is to risk underestimating the full value to be derived from a joint venture. For example, it might not achieve the financial targets both parties planned for, but it might provide other benefits, such as giving managers experience that they might not otherwise have had, or enabling the partners to develop intellectual capital that might have taken them much longer on their own, or, indeed, preventing a merger or acquisition that might have proven disastrous to both parties.

Strategic alliances

Joint ventures are generally associated with single, time-specific projects. Strategic alliances are longer-term, more general arrangements between companies interested in helping each other create value, thus mitigating the risks associated with an organisation's pursuing a particular course of action on its own. Rosabeth Moss Kanter, a professor at Harvard Business School, likens strategic alliances to modern marriages:[3]

Separate careers, individual cheque books, sometimes different names, but the need to work out the operational overlap around household and offspring.

The formation of a strategic alliance does not necessarily mean the creation of a separate entity to conduct the alliance, though this might happen. Indeed, an alliance is about a relationship, not about legal agreements. A strategic alliance will stand a better chance of success if the partners have complementary interests (which does not rule out alliances between potential competitors) and respect each other. But as with joint ventures, parties to an alliance need to be big enough to acknowledge that each party will have its own reasons for being interested in the alliance which the other party cannot necessarily be expected to share in or even agree with.

Replication: franchising and licensing

Replication is when a business idea or system is copied and rolled out elsewhere, in another location or maybe another industry. Replication is a strategy that a company might follow in pursuit of its own organic growth. It might choose to replicate in partnership with other organisations, via a joint venture, a franchise arrangement or licensing. Replication is a strategy that new market entrants might follow too. Rather than establish and grow a new concept, an entrepreneur might copy another company's idea, with or without the support or consent of that company.

Franchising

Franchising and licensing are often considered by organisations that are looking to grow by replicating what they do overseas. Under a franchise arrangement a business develops a business system that in effect it sells to others, who then run their own small businesses using the franchisor's tried-and-tested model. The fast-food industry has many franchise businesses, McDonald's perhaps being the best-known example. Under most franchise arrangements, the franchisee pays for the right to use the name, logo and merchandising, as well as essential elements of the business process. The franchisor provides training in the use of the business methodology and support. The arrangement is governed by a franchise agreement between the franchisor and its franchisees.

Franchising is one way in which businesses have sought scale without sacrificing the owner-managed qualities often associated with smaller businesses. For many would-be owner-managers, a franchise arrangement is one way of founding a business in which many of the usual risks of entrepreneurship are significantly reduced. For the franchisor, it allows rapid growth and access to capital. In terms of growth, the model enables franchisors to have their cake and eat it; business units stay relatively small, but the business as a whole can grow rapidly. Franchisees, however, need to be aware of the barriers to their own growth: the growth of each outlet will be constrained by its location. A franchisee that wishes to grow will need to acquire more franchises, perhaps becoming a master-franchise within a wider franchise network.

Not every business that has tried to franchise has been satisfied with the results. A business that chooses to franchise itself and replace subsidiary businesses, directly run outlets and so forth with franchise income has to work harder at controlling important elements of the brand proposition such as quality and culture. In effect, direct supervision has to be replaced by careful selection of franchisees and by the controls set out in a carefully worded franchise agreement. Pret a Manger tried franchising in its early years, but the experiment petered out after a few stores. Starbucks has an ambivalent relationship with the concept. In some parts of the world, such as the Middle East, it is run in effect as one franchise, though even here it should be noted that stores tend to be owned by the regional partner rather than franchised. In the US, where the business started, most Starbucks outlets are owned and operated by the company. Howard Schultz was interviewed shortly after his return to Starbucks as CEO in 2009 when growth was faltering. His comments, quoted in *Harvard Business Review* in July 2010, highlight the problems facing many successful CEOs when considering franchising:

> *You have to have 100% belief in your core reason for being. There was tremendous pressure in the first three of months after my return to dramatically change the strategy and the business model of the company. The marketplace was saying, "Starbucks needs to undo all these company-owned stores and franchise the system." That would have given us a war chest of cash and significantly increased return on capital. It is a good argument economically. It is a good argument for shareholder value. But it would have fractured the culture of the company. You cannot get out of this by trying to navigate with a different road map, one that is not true to yourself. You have to be authentic, you have to be true, and you have to believe in your heart that this is going to work.*

There are, however, many businesses that have made franchising work well. McDonald's has already been mentioned. Body Shop's early growth was through franchising, and it succeeded through not just the originality and appeal of the concept but also the robustness of the franchise arrangement and its ability to recruit franchise owners who shared the enthusiasms and vision of the founder.

Timing is important when franchising. A franchisor can attract franchisees only if the proposition it wants to franchise has a successful track record, which will take time to establish. Potential franchisees who are wooed too early might take the view that insufficient risks are mitigated and they might as well take all the risks themselves and set up on their own from first principles. Conversely, a franchisee who joins a franchise at the beginning might be able to negotiate to keep more of the value than one hoping to join a well-established franchise. Owners who have set up a successful business but are still wrestling with the fire-fighting that growth brings may be susceptible to an approach from a potential franchisee offering to open up a new territory, thus providing a route to expansion beyond their current management capacity and capability. As well as worrying about expanding their own business, successful business founders need to think about copycats. A franchise arrangement might provide a satisfactory compromise for a business looking to replicate.

Licensing

Licensing is a smaller-scale arrangement than franchising. A franchise is in effect a multi-dimensional licence governing many aspects of the business: brand, product, uniform, pricing, and so on. A licence usually gives the right to provide one or other of these elements. It therefore typically gives its user the legal right to use something that might otherwise be protected by, for example, a patent or trademark. It is another vehicle for facilitating the replication of a business.

Organic *and* inorganic growth

Organic growth and inorganic growth are often seen as mutually exclusive strategies. As with much in business, this view is too black and white. A company in its earliest stages will inevitably focus on organic growth. But once it has reached sustainability even a young company will often find that some form of partnership arrangement with another organisation with complementary capabilities will fast-forward growth. The commonest exit for a young venture is via a sale of the business to another company – inorganic growth for the acquirer at least.

However, companies are often reluctant to explore different types of growth. Laurence Capron, a professor at INSEAD in France, and Will Mitchell, a professor at Rotman School of Management, University of Toronto, show in their ten-year study of 162 telecommunications companies that only one-third actively use all the growth options available to them. Some companies choose to develop almost all resources in-house; others focus on licensing or joint ventures; others favour mergers and acquisitions. Capron and Mitchell argue that their study:[4]

> ... demonstrates conclusively that firms using all the resource acquisition methods outperform those with a narrow approach. Specifically, firms acquiring resources in multiple ways are 46% more likely to survive over a five-year period than those relying mainly on alliances, 26% more likely than those focusing on M&A, and 12% more likely than those sticking with internal development.

A company ambitious for growth should consider all routes to growth. A company that fails to consider an option merely because it has no experience of it is yet again falling into the oldest growth trap of all: not understanding that what worked last time probably will not work next time. Growth is about change.

Planning for growth

NONE OF THE OBSERVATIONS and insights we have discussed in this book will have much impact unless they change what managers and directors acutally do. In a well-run business the best way of initiating action is through business planning. In this chapter we consider how growth should influence business planning.

Accounting for growth drivers and barriers

Companies should identify their growth drivers and barriers and make sure that the implications of both are accounted for in their business plans, specifying where a business is now and how it plans to grow in the future. The simplest way of evaluating growth drivers and barriers is through a SWOT analysis (strengths, weaknesses, opportunities and threats). Strengths and opportunities are both growth drivers. A strength is an internal capability in the business that might lead to growth if properly managed and an opportunity is a quality of the external commercial environment offering potential for growth if the business exploits it properly; management can choose to take advantage of both when planning for growth, or focus on one rather than the other. Unlike a strength, an opportunity for one business is an opportunity for other businesses as well. Weaknesses and threats, conversely, are types of growth barrier. Mirroring strengths and opportunities, a weakness is an internal characteristic of the business and a threat is a characteristic of the external commercial environment.

Opportunities and threats, both characteristics of the external environment, can be identified through brainstorming, benchmarking the competition and monitoring customer feedback (see Chapter 3). The mnemonic LEPEST (or PESTLE) is often used to remind managers to consider legal, economic, political, environmental, sociological and technological influences on the commercial environment of the business, all of which might present opportunities or threats, or encourage management to invest in new capabilities.

Strengths and weaknesses, both characteristics of the internal organisation, are much more under the control of management than opportunities and threats and reflect management's choices as much as its capabilities. Bearing in mind the issues discussed in this chapter, a list of strengths and weaknesses can be assembled through an honest internal assessment of organisational capabilities, reinforced by competitor analysis and benchmarking. Analysis using the growth models in Chapter 2 will help tease out hidden weaknesses, particularly weaknesses exacerbated by the changes generated by growth and the recent evolution of the business.

Many business managers are familiar with SWOT analysis. Surprisingly few, however, go on to the next stage and ask "So what?" about their SWOTs.

One way of exploring the implications of lists of internal and external strengths and weaknesses and opportunities and threats is to match them against each other using a simple matrix (see Figure 9.1). Each strength is matched against each opportunity. If a strength helps you take advantage of the opportunity, it is marked with a tick; if it has nothing to do with the opportunity, it is marked with a zero. A strength might go some way towards ameliorating a threat, in which case it is marked with a tick. In rare circumstances, a quality that managers consider to be a strength might become a weakness when a particular opportunity is considered; in this case the appropriate box is marked with a cross. Similarly, if a strength does nothing to ameliorate a weakness, it is marked with a zero; but if it makes things worse, it is marked with a cross.

FIG 9.1 **Internal strengths and weaknesses matrix**

		Opportunity			Threat			Extent of strengths and weaknesses
✓ positive situation		1	2		1	2		
✗ negative situation								
O neutral situation								
Strength	1	✓	✓		✓	✗		2
	2	✓	0		0	✓		2
Weakness	1	✗	0		✗	✗		−3
	2	0	✗		✓	0		0
	Extent of opportunities and threats	1	0		1	0		

Source: Author

A similar exercise can be undertaken for weaknesses. The existence of a weakness might prevent an organisation from taking advantage of a particular opportunity, in which case it is marked with a cross. A cross is also used to indicate when a weakness exacerbates a threat. If a weakness is irrelevant as far as any particular opportunity or threat is concerned, it is marked with a zero. As with strengths, there might be rare circumstances in which a quality normally perceived as a weakness turns into a strength when considered in the context of a particular opportunity or threat. Generally, however, strengths should be scored with lots of ticks and a few zeros, and weaknesses with crosses and zeros.

Adding across the row will give managers an indication of the importance of a strength or weakness, given the opportunities or threats confronting an organisation. This may help them decide where to prioritise resources. Many management teams take comfort in, boast about and waste investment in nurturing a strength that has little relevance to the circumstances in which the business finds itself. Businesses in markets that are subject to disruptive innovation are particularly susceptible to this tendency, failing to invest in the competencies that the changing market now values. Adding down the column will give an indication of the importance of an opportunity or a threat given the current portfolio of strengths and weaknesses at the organisation's disposal.

Accentuate the positive; eliminate the negative

Taking SWOT analysis to this second stage is not the only way in which management teams can identify the implications of their growth drivers and barriers. As an alternative, or indeed a complement, to working on specific opportunities and threats, they may focus on an overall strategic goal using a version of a technique first developed in the social sciences called force-field analysis (see Figure 9.2).

There are three things management teams need to do:

- Have a clear vision of what the organisation is trying to achieve. There should be a robust analysis of where the organisation is now and the extent to which organisational reality falls short of the target.

- Identify what is holding back the organisation from the achievement of its targets, and what positive qualities it possesses. In the model such forces are often labelled driving forces and restraining forces, but they might just as easily be called growth drivers and barriers. This work can be delegated to middle- or junior-level staff, who often

FIG 9.2 **Force-field analysis**

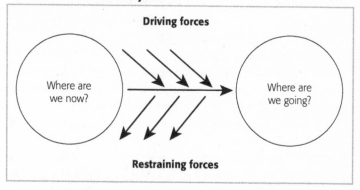

Source: Author

have a clearer picture of organisational reality than senior management.

■ Identify actions that will accentuate and foster the growth drivers, and reduce if not eliminate the barriers. Again, such an exercise can usefully be delegated. If staff are allowed a role in the identification of actions, they are more likely to be committed to implementing them.

Identifying and implementing actions is ultimately the only way of effecting change in any organisation. Talk of targets and workshops that lead to the identification of strengths and weaknesses, driving and restraining forces, growth drivers and barriers is all very well, and will give managers plenty of excuse for arguments, but it is actions that can be implemented in the real world that will ultimately make the difference. If an organisation succeeds in implementing just a proportion of the actions it has identified, it will succeed in moving towards its targets and realising its growth ambitions.

The growth plan itself: principal contents

Before the D-Day landings General Eisenhower, observed, "In preparing for battle I have always found that plans are useless, but planning is indispensable." It is certainly the case that the only thing that can be guaranteed about any business plan is that reality will not turn out that way. Even so, planning is still a useful exercise as it will help identify and focus attention on specific growth levers and barriers and avoid unnecessary dilution of management attention.

Business plans are drafted for many reasons, at the request of both internal and external stakeholders. Many big businesses have a regular long-term planning cycle, which is the starting-point for annual planning and budget processes and an essential mechanism co-ordinating resource. Start-ups might draft a business plan at the request of a potential financier. Regardless of their purpose, most business plans have elements in common, as outlined in Table 9.1.

A business plan for growth – a growth plan – might also include many if not all the items listed in Table 9.1, as well as addressing the growth levers and barriers identified in Chapters 3 and 4. Managers planning for growth should also pay particular attention to the following:

- Focus. Planning for growth is often not so much about identifying growth levers and barriers as picking which ones to focus on.

- Changes in the competitive environment. Much business analysis focuses on current rather than future competition. The competitive environment for a growing business changes all the time. Success will bring new competition, which should be anticipated and a response planned.

- The ambitions of owners and senior managers. Plans for growth should consider the key individuals involved in the business. Such individuals' aspirations will change and they may not share the same ambitions, so a growth plan should consider their ambitions and capabilities, and how differences between them can be reconciled with the plans for the business.

■ The management bottleneck. Plans for growth should pay particular attention to alleviating the barrier to growth created by the capacity and capability of management.

■ Organisational change. Growth is about change, and planning processes for growth need to anticipate the changes that growth will bring. Managers should be suspicious of "more of the same" plans. Careful use of one or other of the growth models discussed in Chapter 2 can help.

■ Cash costs of growth. Growth consumes cash at a rate that can take management by surprise. Planning is all about anticipating surprises, and there are few more important than this one. It merits a separate chapter (see Chapter 6).

■ A framework for monitoring and measuring growth (see Chapter 5).

TABLE 9.1 **Business plan contents**

1 Executive summary
■ Summary of customer needs and how to address them
■ Financial consequences of plan
■ Finance required

2 The business and the opportunity
■ Customer needs addressed
■ Product descriptions and applications
■ How business operations convert custom into cash
■ Manufacturing process
■ Make or buy considerations
■ Sources of supply and security
■ Plant needed
■ Proprietary position/barriers to entry
■ Guarantees and warranties
■ Reliance on third parties
■ New product development plans
■ Corporate structure
■ SWOT analysis

3 Industry, market and competitors
■ PESTLE analysis
■ Market and segment size and growth

- Industry structure: five-forces analysis
- Current and potential competitors
- Customer decision criteria
- Target market segments (showing differentiation from competition)
- Marketing strategy

- Pricing policy
- Choice of location and premises
- Distribution channels
- Competitor response
- Market share projection
- Sales forecast

4 Selling

- Current selling method
- Proposed selling methods

- Sales channels
- Sales resources

5 Management and staffing

- The management team
- Other principal human resources
- Specific management roles for existing and planned staff and general organisation of the business

- Planned recruitment and selection
- Reward packages and their relationship to the required business performance
- Training and development plan

6 Mergers & acquisitions, joint ventures, divestments

- Logic for acquisition
- Target profile

- Plans for search

7 Actions

- Principal actions, showing responsibilities, costs, deadlines, dependencies, priorities

- Milestones
- First-year actions outlined in more detail

8 Financial data and forecasts

- Summary of financial performance ratios: return on investment, etc
- Summary forecasts: profit and loss, cash flow

- Assumptions underpinning financial forecasts
- Key performance indicators
- Sensitivity analysis
- Risk mitigation

9 Financing requirements

- Current shareholders, loans outstanding
- Funds required and timing, including leasing
- Use of proceeds

- The deal on offer
- Anticipated gearing and interest cover
- Exit routes for investors
- Appendices

Appendices

- Biographies

- Names and details of advisers

- Technical data and drawings
- Patents, copyrights, etc
- Audited accounts
- Consultants' reports
- Published data on product, market, etc

- Orders in hand and enquiry status
- Detailed market research methods and findings
- Organisation charts
- Sources of data

10

The future of growth

IN THE 19TH and much of the 20th century, businesses got bigger and bigger. The 21st century started with globalisation increasingly taken for granted, with implications for the optimum size of the world's most powerful and influential businesses. In their book, *The Alchemy of Growth*, Merhdad Baghai, Steve Coley and David White wrote:[1]

> *Growth is a noble pursuit. It creates new jobs for the community and wealth for shareholders. It can turn ordinary companies into stimulating environments where employees find a sense of purpose in their work ... Growth's transformative power is akin to the alchemy of old.*

However, in the wake of the financial crisis that started in 2008, public opinion has hardened against the influence exercised by some of the biggest organisations merely because of their size. Even the desirability of globalisation has been questioned. But size is not just a question of fashion or sentiment. As discussed in Chapter 4, the optimum size of businesses in some industries will always be smaller than in others. And some more general trends – particularly technological – have influenced the optimum size of organisations and therefore affected growth. This chapter discusses some trends in these general influences on organisational size and on growth and considers their implications.

Bigger is better

Other things being equal, bigger companies generally have the following advantages over smaller ones.

Economies of scale

The bigger an organisation the more it is able to make efficient use of its assets and resources. It can make better use of fixed-cost inputs; sales and output are likely to be more evenly distributed over time; and the use of internal resources can be planned more efficiently. It can achieve greater economies by buying materials and services in bulk. It is also more likely to be able to afford internal professional expertise: an HR department to deal with the increasing mountain of employment legislation; a marketing department to establish brand propositions; an IT department to build and maintain tailor-made systems infrastructures. But economies of scale are not endless. An organisation will reach a size where the management costs of holding it together outweigh the cost savings derived from scale; this is the point when diminishing returns to scale will set in.

Ronald Coase, a Nobel prize-winning economist, expounded his theory about the role and size of the organisation as a function of the optimum trade-off between costs and benefits in a classic article, "The Nature of the Firm", published in 1937.[2] He compares what he calls transaction costs (the costs of doing a transaction in the open market) with organisation costs (the costs of an organisation performing the same task itself). The fact that organisation costs tend to be lower than the equivalent transaction costs helps explain why business organisations come into existence in the first place. But Coase's thinking has been extended to help determine the optimum size of an organisation. Using the transactional cost theory, a business will tend to be larger if:

■ the costs of managing the business are lower and rise more slowly with the size of the business;

- the entrepreneur is less likely to make mistakes and the increase in mistakes decreases in proportion to the increase in size of the business;
- there are economies of scale with regard to costs of supplies and resources.

The first two costs will increase with the geographical distribution of the business's products and services and the increase in the range of products and services provided. Coase's theory helps explain why companies tend either to be in different geographic locations or to focus on particular types of business. It has also helped explain why some businesses have managed to grow so large: in effect their organisational costs are lower than their transactional costs, despite their exceptional size (examples are Standard Oil, General Motors and General Electric).

Market power

A bigger organisation will have a bigger market share, so it is more likely to be able to dictate terms to the market, particularly on prices. Smaller businesses have to accept the prices set by bigger organisations unless they can undercut them, which for many is unlikely as they will not be able to take advantage of economies of scale in the cost structure.

Credibility

A big organisation is often more credible than a smaller competitor. For example, small companies have long complained that the odds are stacked against them when they apply for government contracts. The huge amount of paperwork involved favours big organisations with the administrative resources to deal with it – but this is another economy of scale. Just as important is the IBM syndrome – that is, "no one ever got fired for buying from IBM" – even though the products of smaller, newer companies may be demonstrably superior or better suited to the customer's purpose. Buying from a big, well-established company is not as risky for a manager as buying from a less well-known company.

Credibility affects small companies in other ways, in particular their ability to receive favourable credit terms, to attract capable, ambitious staff, and to secure leases on premises.

Technology and the size of the firm

An implication of Coase's theory of the firm is that organisations such as General Motors or General Electric grew so big because they were more efficient at managing and implementing transactions internally than through the external market. Some have argued that modern developments in information technology, the internet in particular, have changed this. In their book, *Unleashing the Killer App*, Larry Downes and Chunka Mui argue that the internet has dramatically reduced many transaction costs, particular those associated with the flow of information and payment.[3] Big businesses have less of a comparative advantage than has been the case historically and small firms less of a disadvantage. Indeed, Downes and Mui predict a shift of influence from the large firms that have dominated the commercial landscape in the past two centuries to smaller firms. The "law of diminishing firms" has usurped the influential role previously occupied by the law of diminishing returns.

Not everyone agrees with Downes and Mui's thesis. Some, arguing from a theoretical standpoint, have noted that the internet has the effect of reducing organisational costs as well as transactional costs (as defined by Coase), and that organisational size is not necessarily affected. In practice, there is no doubt that in some ways modern technology does improve the relative lot of small firms. Using the criteria outlined above, a small firm can take advantage of the internet to win positions of influence in the market quickly in ways not previously possible. It can be difficult to appreciate the true scale of an organisation behind a good website, thus problems of credibility that smaller firms have historically struggled with are mitigated. In the post-internet age, small firms have access to a breadth of information at a unit cost previously allowed only to big organisations with the ability to invest in their own networks.

At the same time, a networked world enhances the prospects of much more flexible organisational entities and eases the relationships between them. Internet technologies and structures have conspired to make previously omnipotent, giant companies seem weak and inflexible, and exposed them to attacks from organisations of a size that would previously have posed no threat. Regulators continue to struggle to keep pace with change in the music and publishing industries, for example.

However, although technology has empowered smaller organisations, the spectacular growth of organisations such as Microsoft, Apple, Google and Facebook shows that technology can provide an environment in which organisations can grow extremely large. Perhaps it is the pace of change that technology has influenced even more than the optimum size of organisations. Facebook was founded only in 2004; by 2015 the now listed company was reporting 1.4 billion users and a market capitalisation of well over $200 billion. The converse is also true: in some instances technology exacerbates the speed of an organisation's decline. The well-publicised struggle of *Encyclopaedia Britannica* when confronted with the rise of the internet is one example of a business model whose very existence has been threatened by technology, not helped by it. There will certainly be many more.

Small is beautiful

Technological change is just one force that continues to provoke questions about the optimal size for organisations. There have been others and there will be more.

British economist E. F. Schumacher's book, *Small is Beautiful*, was published in 1973 when the world was reeling from an oil crisis.[4] It has been in print ever since, a testament to the fact that its thesis has found supporters in different economic circumstances responding to different economic crises. Schumacher argues that focusing on output and technology is dehumanising, and that greater priority should be given to the meaning and dignity of economic activity and its use (or abuse) of natural resources than to efficiency and the thirst for profit. His conclusions cannot be reduced to a simplistic notion that small is good and big is bad; more characteristic of his thinking is the notion of "smallness within bigness", which takes him towards organisations that have worked hard to preserve the culture of the small as they grow bigger, looking to decentralisation and different types of organisational structure for help. Schumacher was also one of the earliest thinkers to express concerns about the relevance of gross national product when assessing economic success, arguing that a better objective was to "obtain the maximum amount of well-being with the minimum amount of consumption". In some ways, therefore, Schumacher also heralds the "gross national happiness" movement (see Chapter 5).

Schumacher developed his thesis during the oil crises of the early 1970s. But economic crises have a habit of fostering supporters of small businesses. Conversely, big businesses are often held accountable for the crisis itself. Big banks, big car corporations and other big companies have been considered too big to fail as a consequence of the credit crunch of 2008, while smaller companies have gone to the wall. As economists and regulators embark on an inevitably futile search for ways of ensuring that an economic crisis never happens again, big businesses and the practices and cultures they stand for are once more in the firing line. New visions are being developed for the next generation of managers – with implications for growth and growth plans. In February 2009 Gary Hamel, a management guru, in an article published in *Harvard Business Review*, proposed a new programme of enquiry for business thinkers and a new set of challenges for managers.[5] Many of his challenges touch on themes that Schumacher would have championed: "Eliminate the pathologies of formal hierarchy", "Reduce fear and increase trust",

"Redefine the work of leadership", "Develop holistic performance measures". Others take careful aim at some of the traditional growth levers and measures:

> *Ensure that the work of management serves a higher purpose. Most companies strive to maximise shareholder wealth – a goal that is inadequate in many respects. As an emotional catalyst, wealth maximisation lacks the power to fully mobilise human energies. It is an insufficient defence when people question the legitimacy of corporate power. And it is not specific or compelling enough to spur renewal. For these reasons, tomorrow's management practices must focus on the achievement of socially significant and noble goals.*

Hamel's propositions, like Schumacher's before him, are not new. Adam Smith's first book was not *The Wealth of Nations*, often cited as the bible of free-market economics, but *The Theory of Moral Sentiments*, in which he argues that while "prudence" is "of all virtues that which is most helpful to the individual", it is "humanity, justice, generosity, and public spirit" that are "the qualities most useful to others".[6] Smith does not mention the "noble pursuit" of growth, at least not in this context. Hamel's exhortation that we should reconsider our commercial and economic priorities suggests that debates about the role and value of growth will have a long future as well as a long history.

Glossary: an A–Z of growth

Accounts

In their published form in both the UK and the US these are often called financial statements, but the two terms are used interchangeably. Typically, these comprise a **profit and loss account** (income statement) for the year under review, a balance sheet of the business at the year end, a statement of cash flows, and some notes giving more detail and setting out assumptions and accounting policies.

The problem with accounts is that they look backwards and businesses with ambition to grow are interested in looking forwards. Audited accounts are even more problematic in that they look backwards from a point that is itself likely to be several months old.

It takes years to qualify as an accountant but not so long to be able to get a good enough grip on accounting principles for commercial purposes. Here are a few tips for the general user of accounts in growing businesses:

- Accounting is an art not a science.
- With regard to published financial statements, different countries and jurisdictions have developed over the years different sets of accounting standards. Financial statements of different companies within the same country are therefore easier to compare than the financial statements of companies from different countries. The development of International

Financial Reporting Standards (IFRS) has made some progress towards international standardisation, but it is only a start.

■ Accounts are just ways of telling the story about a business. There are always two stories – the story that the directors are trying to tell and the story that they are trying to hide.

■ The devil is in the detail. The notes at the back of sets of accounts often provide the only clues as to what is hidden in the more frequently read pages at the front.

■ **Cash flow** is as important if not more so than profit in a growing business, so check the funds statements, or statement of cash flows, as well as the income statements and **balance sheets**.

■ In a relatively young business, management accounts (or whatever passes for internal management information) are often a more useful source of information for an outsider than the published financial statements. These are the documents that the managers use to take decisions – they are likely to be more up to date and less likely to have been shoe-horned by the demands of accounting regulation into an unnatural shape.

Accounts payable

See **creditors**.

Accounts receivable

See **debtors**.

Accruals accounting and cash accounting

Under the accruals concept, accounting revenue and costs are recognised as they are earned or incurred and not as the money is received or paid. Under cash accounting the reverse is true. Standard accounting practice follows the accruals rather than the cash approach, as this ensures that actual business performance is reported rather than just cash movements. But it is the cause of much confusion in the minds of those not used to reading **accounts**. It is possible for a business to show a profit but go bust for lack of cash. The distinction is of particular importance to smaller growing businesses where cash is always under pressure.

Acquisitions

See **mergers and acquisitions**.

Additional paid-in capital

See **share capital and share premium account**.

Alternative Investment Market

London's junior stockmarket. Rather than list on the main market, companies might choose to list on the Alternative Investment Market (AIM). It costs less and there are fewer rules. But it is also less prestigious, is less liquid and provides less access to funds. There are no real equivalents to the AIM in the US, which is why it also attracts US companies. Not right for venture capital and too small for NASDAQ, these companies find the AIM the most appropriate source of finance.

There have been attempts to set up junior markets elsewhere in the world, including Alternext (part of Euronext in Paris and Amsterdam) and the Growth Enterprise Market (GEM) in Hong Kong. However, neither of these has so far replicated the AIM's success.
See Chapter 6.

Amortisation

See **depreciation**.

Ansoff matrix

Commonly used when analysing growth options, particularly new products and markets. This two-by-two matrix (see Figure 3.3) is designed to reduce to manageable proportions the numerous strategic alternatives open to a business. The model provides a useful way of evaluating the risk inherent in a new initiative. Selling a new product to a new market is much more risky than selling a new product to an existing market or an existing product to a new market. Though many would argue that doing nothing is probably the riskiest of all.

See Chapter 3.

Arm's length

An arm's-length transaction is one conducted according to normal business rules between third parties. The term is often used for deals between two parties who have a relationship with each other to indicate that the relationship has not prejudiced the deal. **Entrepreneurs** notoriously have difficulty with the concept.

Articles of association

Known as articles of incorporation in the US. In effect the constitution of the company governing internal affairs such as share issues, directors' elections, **dividend** policies. Most business owners pay too little attention to the articles when the business is founded; many subsequently regret such casualness, particularly if members of the founding team fall out and start fighting for control. Well-advised business owners with growth ambitions read the small print carefully and work out the implications for the business under different scenarios.

Articles of incorporation

See **articles of association**.

Asset-based finance

See **factoring**.

Asset turnover

A commonly used ratio in financial analysis is turnover/total assets. It indicates how efficient a company is at using the resources tied up in the business to generate activity. In practice, many figures on the **balance sheet** (notably the long-term assets and liabilities) are notoriously unreliable, particularly as measures of the amount of resources tied up, when used for analysis and decision-making. This is because the numbers cited are influenced far more by accounting policy and convention than by any realisable notion of market worth.

Audit report

A report by independent auditors, indicating their opinion as to whether the financial statements are free from material error. A "clean" report is what most companies aim for. A "qualified" report states why a clean report cannot be given. Many smaller companies in the UK and the EU are exempt from what is otherwise a statutory requirement to have an audit. The only US incorporated companies required to have an audit are publicly traded ones or where it is specified in a debt or equity agreement (as in the UK and the EU, where a bank loan agreement may require an audit regardless of the size of the company). There are no size-related audit exemptions in the US.

Bad debt

Not all **debtors** pay what they owe. Such debts are either doubtful or bad. A bad debt is removed from the **balance sheet** and written off to the **profit and loss account** (income statement). Debt management is a critical part of cash management in any business, but particularly a growing business, in which cash is often under pressure. Many growing businesses do not give it the attention it deserves.

Balance sheet

A statement at a specific date of the assets and liabilities of a business, prepared using certain assumptions. It is one of the key components of the financial statements or **accounts**. It shows where the money came from originally and in which parts of the business it is invested at the balance-sheet date. It is a poor indicator of the value of a business, particularly a rapidly growing one, because of the conventions used in its construction. Nonetheless, a comparison of the balance sheet from one year to the next provides one measure of the growth of the business

Benchmarking

Businesses often like to compare themselves with other businesses. When formalised the process is called benchmarking. Some consultants have earned good money selling benchmarking services. Critics argue that it fosters a "me-too" mentality. However, many growing businesses do not know much about their competitors or their offerings and benchmarking can help. It can equally well be used as a basis for a differentiation **strategy** as for a me-too strategy. Companies can usefully benchmark all sorts of things. In many instances certification programmes help to provide benchmarking standards, such as the ISO 9001 quality standard which is increasingly recognised around the world. Many companies attempt to benchmark salary levels against key competitors.

Board of directors

The group of individuals with statutory responsibility for running the business of an incorporated company. Directors are appointed by **shareholders**. If you have the majority of the shares you can control the composition of the board, but you cannot control the management of the business unless you sit on the board. The majority of board members in big businesses are now commonly **non-executive** or outside directors so the day-to-day task of running the business is delegated to an executive or **management team.**

Book value

The amount at which an item (usually an asset) is recorded in the **accounts.** Usually items are recorded at the lower of their cost or net realisable value – and as the former is likely to be lower, book value often has little relationship with any notion of current or market value. In the UK, however, there are also provisions in accounting practice for revaluing some types of asset. Consequently, in any set of accounts some items might appear at cost, some at what a business expects to get for them if sold, and some at what an independent valuer thinks they might be worth. In the US, the Financial Standards Accounting Board does not allow the upward revaluation of fixed assets.

Boston matrix

Another of those two-by-two boxes on which business analysis seems so dependent (see Figure 3.1). This one was invented by the Boston Consulting Group. At its simplest the matrix helps identify future product-development options and rationalise expectations. It usefully illustrates how the most exciting areas of the business often make little money, and why the most cash-generative areas of the business are seen as boring. If initiatives are unlikely to become cash cows in the future, they are not worth focusing on. If they are likely to become cash cows, it may be worth taking a loss on them now.
See Chapter 3.

Break-even analysis

Determines how much bigger a business needs to be to generate a profit (or how much smaller before it starts making a loss). It is based on the assumption that some costs are fixed and some are variable; if the business grows, it will earn enough to cover the

fixed costs and will become cash-positive. Break-even analysis is also used when assessing individual projects. It is an important tool for the managers of growing businesses.
See Chapter 5.

Business angel

A name given to a wealthy individual interested in investing in private (often start-up) businesses – often one of the few sources of funds for companies in the notorious funding gap – when they are too big to rely on the founders' pockets, not big enough to interest the institutional sources of equity financing (such as **venture capital** or **private equity**) and insufficiently creditworthy to be able to raise debt from banks. Angels invest their own money, unlike venture capitalists, who invest money raised from other investors. Angels' investment decisions are therefore influenced by their personal preferences.
See Chapter 5.

Business plan

Some businesses think they need to prepare a business plan only because a bank will demand one before considering a loan. Some also argue that time spent planning is futile as what is planned and what happens bear little relation to each other. Time spent planning, however, usually pays rewards – even if reality turns out differently – if only because it makes businesses think about the future. Indeed, the act of planning is more valuable than the plan that results. Nonetheless, the document provides a business with something to monitor progress against.
See Chapter 9.

Capital

A word with many meanings. Some of the most common are as follows:

- At the bottom of the **balance sheet** it refers to the **shareholders'** financial interest in the business.

- It is used more loosely to describe all long-term financial stakes in the business, including loans (long-term **creditors**).

- When associated with expenditure, it refers to the purchase of **fixed assets** or long-term investment; in contrast, revenue expenditure is written off each year against the **profit and loss account** (income statement).

Capital expenditure

Expenditure on an item the benefits of which it is hoped will be derived over a long period – certainly one stretching over several years of financial statements. Rather than being written off entirely against profit in the year of acquisition, a capital item will be depreciated or amortised in instalments over its useful life. (See **depreciation** and **revenue expenditure**.)

Capital surplus

US term for share premium account. (See **share capital and share premium account**.)

Cash

For accountants, not just coins and notes in the cash box, but bank balances and other investments that are exceptionally secure and readily converted into cash. Nothing is more important to a business than cash, and few things are less well understood. Cash management is about understanding the nature of the cash cycle: how long it takes to convert cash tied up on the **balance sheet** in stock and debt into cash in the bank, and the extent to which the drain represented by that cash cycle widens as the order book grows and the business expands. It is possible for a profitable company to go bust because it grows faster than can be sustained by the cash-generative capabilities of the business. That gap must

be plugged somehow, either with external finance or by changing the dynamics of the cash cycle.
See Chapter 6.

Cash flow, cash flow forecast

Money coming in (or going out) in the form of cash. If the net flow is inwards, cash flow is called positive; if the net flow is outwards, it is called negative. A cash flow forecast gives the expected dates of cash flows in and out of the business. Cash flow is an important concept in **discounted cash flow** calculations. It is also important in staying alive – cash is the blood of a business.
See Chapter 5.

Cash flow statement

This indicates the cash generated by the business (as opposed to the profit). It helps readers assess the **liquidity** of a business.

Change

A manager of a business ambitious for growth who is not involved in change will not be a manager for long. Change and growth are inextricably linked. A big business is not a larger version of a smaller one. A business has to evolve as well as grow if its growth is to be sustainable. In other words, a business has to grow up as well as grow.
See Chapters 2 and 4.

Common stock

US term for ordinary shares (see **share capital** and **shareholders**).

Consolidated statement

Companies are often interconnected under the same ownership. Consolidated statements are statements or **accounts** that give figures for the various parts of a group added together. It is often difficult to get accounts or statements for the individual businesses themselves.

Control

A crucial decision for an **entrepreneur** is when, or if, to give up control of a business. Control is often confused with ownership. You do not have to own all the shares in a company to control it. Many entrepreneurs are reluctant to allow others to have a slice of the equity, and this can constrain the growth of the business. It is possible to allow others in on the action without giving up control. For example, all other things being equal, shareholders, though they might otherwise have to concede some rights to minority shareholders, give up control over a company only if they lose control over the majority of the shares. However, majority shareholders need to be careful when they take in financial investors. In some cases, clauses in the documentation governing an investment in the business by an institutional equity investor (such as a venture capitalist) compromise the control of the majority shareholder regardless of the size of the latter's shareholding.

Convertible

A convertible bond or loan stock is a debt instrument that has the potential to be converted into equity in the future if certain conditions are (or are not) fulfilled. A convertible preferred or preference share is one that has the potential for conversion into an ordinary share. Convertible debt is often used by venture capitalists as part of a funding package. If business targets are not met, the debt is converted to equity, often reallocating control of the business from the owner to the financier in the process.
See Chapter 5.

Core competence

A term often used by those interested in corporate **strategy**. Early strategists were mostly concerned with analysing the market and the competition. Core competence advocates, including Gary Hamel and C. K. Pralahad, authors of *Competing for the Future*, argue that

businesses should first look inwards at what they are best at and what makes them different.[1] Businesses that understand their own core competences are rare. Typically, younger businesses trust gut feelings rather than analysis. They are good at making assertions about the nature of their products, services and competition, but have little evidence to back them up. Identifying core competences is the first step towards developing critical success factors, which can be measured by **key performance indicators**.
See Chapters 3 and 6.

Corporate bond

A type of long-term debt finance whereby a company quotes its long-term debt on a stockmarket.
See Chapter 6.

Cost of capital

The amount that needs to be paid to **shareholders** and long-term lenders to keep them happy. This is a simple definition of a complex concept. In essence, cost of capital has two main components: cost of equity (what needs to be paid to shareholders) and cost of debt (the interest that is paid to long-term **debt holders** or **debenture** holders, who are among a company's **creditors**).

Creditors

Those to whom a business owes money, usually split between short-term creditors (sometimes called **current liabilities**) and long-term creditors. In the US, creditors are called accounts payable. They could include amounts owed to banks, suppliers, tax authorities, and so on. Managing short-term creditors, particularly trade creditors, is another important part of **cash management** in a growing business.
See Chapter 5.

Culture

All those undocumented and informal things that distinguish one business from another, often best understood by identifying what is "not done around here" or "not talked about" – things that are so obvious that no one questions them. Culture is difficult to change (not least because it is so difficult to talk about). But a failure to adapt or change the organisational culture is often the reason change initiatives fail to change anything. Small organisations arguably do not have cultures; they have personalities, reflecting usually that of the founder. As the business grows, the founder's personality has less influence – a matter of simple mathematics, of course. In many ways, defining and influencing organisational culture are simply attempts to compensate for the waning influence of the founder. Awareness of a business's culture and its implications gives management an important additional set of levers and controls.
See Chapter 7.

Cumulative

Often used as part of a long label to describe a funding mechanism, such as cumulative, convertible participating preferred share (or stock). In this sense, cumulative usually refers to the **dividend** on the share, which is probably fixed on a preferred share. If it is not paid in a year, the right to the dividend is not lost, but is rolled forward.

Current assets

A component of **working capital** comprising stock, cash and **debtors**; the short-term assets of a business that are held as cash or that may be converted into cash within one year.

Current liabilities

Commonly used to describe those **creditors** that are payable in the short term – that is, payable within one year.

Current ratio

A ratio used in analysing the financial statements, usually defined as current assets/current liabilities. This gives an indication of **liquidity**, that is, the extent to which the business is able to pay its short-term **creditors** with cash and assets easily convertible to cash. It is an important ratio for any business in which cash is an issue, as it often is for growing businesses. Ideally, the figure should be more than 1. In other words, the business is demonstrably able to meet its short-term liabilities with cash, quasi-cash or soon-to-be cash on the **balance sheet**. (See **quick ratio**.)

Debenture

A form of long-term **debt finance** (a **creditor**). In the UK, the term usually refers to debt secured on an asset of a business. In the US, it usually refers to an unsecured **corporate bond**.
See Chapter 6.

Debt factoring

See **factoring**.

Debt finance

Also known as loan capital. Long-term loans offered to a business, sometimes in the form of a **debenture** or **corporate bond**.

Debt holder

A long-term debt holder (sometimes called a bond holder) is different from a **shareholder**. Confusingly, a debt holder is a **creditor** of the business not a **debtor**, and typically receives a fixed amount of interest at regular intervals. A shareholder owns the business, and may be entitled to a **dividend** but has no guarantee of receiving one. If the business goes bankrupt, a shareholder will rank behind a debt holder in terms of who gets paid. (See **equity finance**.)
See Chapter 6.

Debtors

Those who owe money to a business. In the US, debtors are called accounts receivable. A debtor is an asset of a business whereas a **creditor** is a liability. **Debt finance**, however, is all about a business owing money to someone else.

Depreciation

A way of allocating the cost of a tangible fixed asset to the **profit and loss account** (income statement) bit by bit over the life of the asset rather than writing it off in the period in which it is bought. It may also be considered a measure of wear and tear. **Intangible assets** do not depreciate, they amortise, but it is in effect the same thing. They are both non-cash adjustments to the **accounts**, and are subject to the judgment exercised by accountants.

Discounted cash flow

A complicated mechanism frequently used as part of investment appraisal, or in deciding whether to pursue a long-term project. Essentially, discounted cash flow (DCF) attempts to measure and compare all the positive and negative **cash flows** projected to arise from a project, discounting by a predetermined amount cash flows that occur in the future using a figure known as the discount factor. The logic behind DCF is complicated, but is best summarised by accepting that $10 received today is worth more than a promise today of receiving $10 next year, so to make the comparison fair next year's $10 needs to be valued at less than $10 today. The size of the discount depends on how big the risk is that you will never see the money.

DCF is much used by financiers as part of their evaluation of investment opportunities. It is fraught with difficulty, however. First, the cash flows are future cash flows and are estimates. Second, slight changes in the discount factor can have enormous effects on the calculation. That some big corporations have worked out their discount factor to four decimal places suggests that determining discount factors is more important than it should be. Unfortunately for scientists, the biggest component of risk (and therefore determinant of the discount factor) is the unpredictability of future events.

Diversification

When a business seeks to involve itself in activities that are essentially different from its current activities. Some years ago a well-diversified conglomerate was often thought of as a desirable business structure to aim for. Now that **core competence** has become fashionable, diversification as a business **strategy** has fallen out of favour. Managers are now encouraged to stick to their knitting. Diversifying is something that investors are encouraged to do instead – advice that investors in young businesses are particularly encouraged to heed.

Dividend

A formal payment made to a **shareholder** from time to time out of profits. The concept is simple. A business makes money (profit). Some of this is kept in the business for investment; some is needed to pay **creditors** and the tax authorities; the rest might be distributed to the owners of the business (the shareholders) in the form of a dividend. Technically, dividends are not an expense or a cost, they are a mechanism for distributing profit – so it is rarely possible to distribute a dividend unless a business has distributable reserves (essentially retained profits) on the **balance sheet**.

Those involved in growing businesses often wear several hats. As owner-managers, for example, they can pay themselves as employees with wages and bonuses, and as owners with dividends. The tax implications of doing one rather than the other differ – and doing something for tax reasons often confuses other more important issues, such as understanding the difference between management and ownership. Either all the shareholders with shares of the same class get a dividend or none of them do. A company cannot pick and choose.

Due diligence

Investigations carried out by parties interested in doing a deal. A company seeking to acquire another might appoint a firm of accountants to do due diligence on the target, examining its financial statements, projections, and so on. An investor or a bank seeking to finance such an acquisition might perform its own due diligence (or appoint a firm of accountants to do it). Due diligence usually starts with the financial statements and the stories they are trying to tell, or not tell, but then wanders far wider into all aspects of commercial activity, the market, the strength of the **management team**, and so on.

Earnings per share

Often abbreviated to EPS, usually defined as the amount of profit after tax and interest that has been earned by each ordinary share.

EBIT, EBITDA

Earnings before interest and tax (EBIT) measures the **net profit** of a business ignoring the costs of financing it – that is, interest costs on debt and tax, as well as payments (**dividends**) to **shareholders**. Earnings before interest and tax, **depreciation** and **amortisation** (EBITDA) is similar, but it also ignores (adds back) depreciation and amortisation – which are accounting adjustments, not cash costs to the business. By adding them back EBITDA gives a useful shorthand approximation of the cash generated by the business operations, ignoring **capital expenditure**. Like all approximations, particularly accounting approximations, it should be handled with care.

Empowerment

Management-speak for the useful concept of giving staff the authority and wherewithal to take decisions for themselves. Intelligently managed empowerment can lead to better, quicker decisions and therefore help a business to grow. But the concept can be difficult to introduce, partly because some managers confuse empowerment with abdication or passing the blame, and many staff – when push comes to shove – quite like being told what to do.

See Chapters 2, 4 and 7.

Entrepreneur

In essence, the individual behind an organisation who gets it from the drawing board into profitable existence, in contrast to the inventor who merely gets the idea onto the drawing board – though, of course, some inventors are also entrepreneurs. At the heart of the entrepreneurial urge is the desire to do your own thing, a yearning for independence, a determination that something can be done better by you than by someone else. In entrepreneurship, therefore, qualities of personality are perhaps more important than qualities of ability, or a yearning for riches.

Entrepreneurs are committed, enthusiastic, energetic motivators with a willingness to accept risk. Although motivated by the desire for independence, entrepreneurs are not necessarily loners (many are two or more person teams), nor are they reckless gamblers – the risk is usually calculated. But they are people who do not like being told no. They ask "why not?" rather than "why?" and a sophisticated view is that they are perhaps best at marshalling **intangible assets** to make up for an absence of tangible assets to achieve a particular goal. At the heart of entrepreneurship therefore is a paradox. On the one hand it is all about making concrete the abstract. On the other hand it is all about not losing heart when the only thing you have on your side is the abstract. (See **team**.)

See Chapters 6 and 7.

Equity finance

Finance for a business provided by ordinary **shareholders** in return for a slice of ownership of the business. (See **debt finance**.) See Chapter 6.

Factoring

Once thought of as the corporate equivalent of a visit to the pawnbroker, debt factoring and other forms of asset-based finance are increasingly seen as important additions to the financial armoury of growing businesses. And, bearing in mind that small businesses in particular have few sources of finance on which to draw, a change of attitude towards factoring can only be a good thing. Factoring or invoice discounting comes in several forms. The basic principle involves raising money from a bank or specialist finance house either by selling your trade **debtors** (factoring) or by using them as security for a loan (invoice discounting). Critics argue that asset-based finance is expensive. But enthusiasts note that most small businesses fund themselves with nothing cheaper than an overdraft, which can have hidden costs given that it is repayable on demand and banks usually want their money back when it is most needed. Another advantage for a growing business is that its capacity for raising asset-based finance increases as it grows. See Chapter 6.

Family business

The majority of businesses worldwide are family businesses, but only a small proportion of these survive to the third generation, suggesting that family and business are not natural bedfellows. This has important implications for businesses with ambitions to grow. Successful family businesses spend a lot of time and money establishing mechanisms to ensure the successful survival of the business as one generation hands over the reins to another, designed to ensure the interests of business and family are met. See Chapter 4.

Fixed assets

Assets that have been acquired not for resale but for use by the business in the longer term. They may be tangible (physical objects) or intangible (such as goodwill or patents).

Flotation

See **initial public offering**.

Games

Much recent thinking on business **strategy** has sought inspiration in other disciplines. Modern maths has proved fertile territory – with chaos theory and game theory providing lateral lines of thought – particularly for those interested in the subtleties of relationships between competitors and customers and suppliers. Try thinking of competitors as fellow players in a game for a change rather than enemies from some evil empire. To what extent are all players in a market useful to each other? Adam Brandenburger and Barry Nalebuff, in their book *Co-Opetition*, invent and consider new roles in the game of business.[2] For example, there are "complementors", whose activity in the market adds value to your own. Video film is a well-known example, first seen by the cinema industry as a threat and then welcomed for the additional revenue it provided once the period of a film's general release had effectively ended. The evolution of the DVD and the increasing popularity of downloadable films are reminders that markets never stay still. Businesses that are keen to grow need to understand the subtleties of their markets, and this type of thinking adds some useful insight.

See Chapter 3.

Gearing

Commonly used in the UK to refer to the level of long-term debt in a business (that is, the proportion of long-term **creditors** to **shareholders' funds** or owners' equity). In the US the more common term is leverage. A highly geared or leveraged company is one whose **balance sheet** shows a large amount owing to long-term creditors proportional to shareholder funding. Such companies are often thought to be financially risky as debt carries an interest charge that must be paid whether business is good or bad. A lowly geared company, however, with a high proportion of shareholder or **equity finance**, can choose not to pay a **dividend** when cash is short. However, in the longer term **debt finance** is usually thought of as less expensive than equity finance, not just because it carries less risk for the investor but also because interest is tax-deductible.

See Chapter 6.

Gross profit

The amount of profit derived from a business's operations, ignoring overheads and other fixed costs (see **net profit**). For retailing businesses, therefore, gross profit is simply sales less the cost of goods sold. In manufacturing businesses, gross profit is sales less the costs directly attributable to manufacturing. In businesses such as professional services, gross profit is a less meaningful concept.

See Chapter 5.

Gross profit margin

Gross profit as a percentage of revenue or **turnover**.
See Chapter 5.

Hypergrowth

Exceptionally fast growth.
See Chapter 8.

Incentives

Staff incentives take many forms. Cash bonuses are the simplest way of encouraging short-term performance, but those who implement bonus schemes are often surprised by how little impact they seem to have on the conduct of some employees. Management performance is often rewarded with forms of equity or quasi-equity in the belief they are more likely to encourage long-term thinking. But as well as being much more expensive to implement, equity-based mechanisms run the risk of confusing management with ownership – a rock and a hard place with which **family businesses** in particular are only too familiar. See Chapter 7.

Income

See **turnover**.

Income statement

See **profit and loss account**.

Incorporation

The act of turning an organisation into a limited company (or limited liability **partnership**), thus offering those who invest their money (**shareholders** in the case of a company) the benefit of limited liability with respect to the company's **creditors**. If a company goes bust, the shareholders risk losing only the money they have invested and possibly some pride. If an unincorporated business goes bust, the business's owners are personally liable for any debts. With the protection of limited liability comes the requirement to publish **accounts** and in many circumstances to have them audited, though smaller businesses, and in some jurisdictions all private businesses, are often exempt from the full force of the regulations. Furthermore, the protection from creditors offered to shareholders by incorporation does not apply if they have given personal guarantees or, depending on the circumstances, if as directors they allow the business to trade while insolvent.

Initial public offering

When a company's shares are offered for sale to the public for the first time, often abbreviated to IPO. The process is also known as flotation.
See Chapter 6.

Insolvency

Not necessarily the end of the road. Insolvency loosely applies to several states of precarious existence either side of the terminal line, from some of which – administration, Chapter 11, and so on – there is often a route back.

Intangible assets

Long-term assets of a business that have no physical existence, such as goodwill, patents, brands.

Interest

There are several meanings. The commonest are as follows:

- The amount charged by and paid to **creditors**.
- A financial investment in something.
- A non-financial involvement in something.

Interest cover

The ability of a business to pay its long-term **creditors** the interest they demand. Often expressed as a ratio (profit before interest and tax / interest) used in determining a business's **liquidity**.

Internal rate of return

A term associated with **discounted cash flow**. The internal rate of return (IRR) is the discount factor at which all the present and future positive and negative **cash flows** associated with a project added together total zero. Businesses often have target IRR figures below which they reject any proposed investment or **capital expenditure**. Institutional investors have a target IRR from their investments.

Intrapreneur

A senior manager given the task of setting up a new business within the context of a large organisation. An intrapreneur has some of the characteristics of an **entrepreneur**. But in terms of access to corporate resources and accountability to corporate management, intrapreneurship is quite different.

Inventory

US term for **stock**.

Invoice discounting

See **factoring**.

Key performance indicator

The measure that matters most in a business. Key performance indicators (KPIs) are closely connected to a business's **strategy**, and the board should pay attention to them.

The KISS principle

Short for "keep it simple, stupid", a fundamental principle for much management. It is often ignored in growing a business when the temptation to complicate unnecessarily can be significant. Complexity adds costs that damage margin, which is under enough pressure already in a growing business. Einstein refined the principle: "Keep things as simple as possible – but no simpler." See Chapter 7.

Leader

Much has been written about leadership and the distinction between leadership and management. Both are critical to a successful organisation, but if management is mostly about effectively delivering the present, leadership is increasingly identified with **change**. Leadership, of course, can be collective, although in Anglo-American business **culture** the cult of the business leader as individual hero (and villain) is strong.

Successful start-ups are often rich in leadership but poor in management, which does not matter until they reach a size when the "suits" need to be brought in to ensure that the bundle of resources that makes up the business does what it has to do effectively and efficiently. Conversely, there are many established businesses that are rich in management and poor in leadership, as a consequence of having let the suits take over and squeeze the life, personality and spirit out of the business.
See Chapters 2 and 7.

Learning organisation

A fashionable management buzzword in the early 1990s. A learning organisation is one that learns as an organisation through a co-ordinated approach to the learning of its individual members. Growing businesses need to change as they grow. Therefore they need to be learning organisations.

Leverage

See **gearing**.

Limited liability company

See **incorporation**.

Limited liability partnership

See **partnership**.

Liquidation

The end of the road for a business: what remains is broken up, converted to cash and distributed first to the **creditors** then, if there is anything left, to the **shareholders**. (See **insolvency**.)

Liquidity

How easily a business's assets may be converted into cash.

Listed company

A company whose shares are publicly quoted on a stockmarket. See Chapter 6.

Loan capital

See **debt finance**.

Losses

Bad news if maintained in the long term, of course, but for tax purposes losses can often be offset against **profits** in another period or part of the business.

Management buy-in

Or MBI. When outsiders buy a business and put themselves or another **management team** in as management.

Management buy-out

When the managers of a business buy it from the owners. The managers are often seen as sensible people to sell the business to: they know the business well, and they may believe that without the current owners breathing down their necks they can do a better job. Good business opportunities do not come cheap, however, and management buy-outs (MBOs) are often encumbered with a lot of external finance provided by, typically, venture capitalists, which may insist on having a **non-executive**

director on the board as well as owning shares in the business. Besides, managers with their eyes on an MBO are managers with an inherent conflict of interest. If they run the business badly, they might be able to buy it cheaply, and they certainly might be distracted from the day-to-day task of management. Because of this, many large companies have a policy of not countenancing any MBOs, so managers know it is not worth thinking about it.

Management team

The group responsible for managing the business; not necessarily the same as the **board of directors**.
See Chapter 7.

Market capitalisation

The market value of each share in a **listed company** multiplied by the number of shares issued. This gives the market's view of what the business is worth. Market capitalisation has little to do with any figure quoted on the face of the **balance sheet**, which is prepared under historical cost conventions and reflects the amount of money originally paid for shares when they were issued, not the price at which they change hands in the market.

Mergers and acquisitions

There are no such things as mergers, only takeovers, argue cynics. The sad thing about mergers and acquisitions is that, as research shows, the majority of them fail to deliver the planned and promised benefits. The good thing is that the chance of failure does not seem to stem the flood of **management teams** willing to give it a go.

Technically, a merger involves the creation of a new company from the union of two independent companies. It involves batteries of advisers: financiers to provide the wherewithal; lawyers to create the documentation; and accountants to conduct **due diligence** on each of the parties on the part of the various interested parties. And then there are the people issues: regulations to be complied with, and the concerns and worries of employees, customers and suppliers affected by the deal but not party to it.

An acquisition is when one business organisation buys another, or buys enough of the shares of another to gain control of it. The majority of acquisitions fail to meet their objectives. What makes sense on paper often makes less sense in reality. Consolidating financial statements is much easier than integrating a new business. It is common for the acquiring company to focus on getting the numbers right and not put enough time or resources into sorting out the softer issues, such as **culture**, systems, processes, "the way things are done around here". It is what happens after the acquisition that will determine if it works, not what happens before. Some argue that business owners should focus more on when to sell their business than when to buy someone else's. (See **control**.)

See Chapter 8.

Mezzanine finance

Finance provided "in the middle", between debt and equity, and sharing some of the characteristics of both. Often a feature of **venture capital** and **private equity** deals.

See Chapter 6.

MIFROG

The maximum internally financed rate of growth – a way of determining how quickly a business might grow without overtrading or resorting to external finance.

See Chapter 5.

Net current assets

Current assets minus current liabilities.

Net present value

Or NPV, used in **discounted cash flow** calculations to describe the aggregate value of all the present and future **cash flows** arising from an investment after applying the discount factor to adjust future cash flows to be comparable with present cash flows.

Net profit

Gross profit minus expenses, overheads, and so on, but before **dividends** and tax.
See Chapter 5.

Non-executive director

An executive director has a day-to-day management role in a business; a non-executive director does not. An executive director probably has an employment contract, and all the duties and worries of employment and management as well as those imposed by statute and by the company's articles on the director. Non-executive directors have to focus on the duties of a director. This can leave them with responsibilities and duties but no hands-on control or real-time access to information.

Non-executive directors can provide input to **strategy**. They can also help boards when conflicts of interest arise, such as directors' remuneration and dealing with auditors. Many boards have a non-executive chairman. In young businesses, non-executive directors can lend credibility to the **management team** (important when seeking business or finance). They can also bring valuable experience of the problems likely at the next stages of a company's evolution, and help prepare the growing business for them.
See Chapter 7.

Notes to the accounts

An important component of a set of **accounts** or financial statements is the notes that follow them. They are a source of further information, and are often where the important information is buried.

Operating cash cycle

All businesses in effect process cash. A manufacturer buys materials and labour that are paid for after an interval. The raw materials are used to make products that sit as stock until sold, with payment made after another period of time. The passage of cash from a business's customers to the business itself and from the business to its suppliers is the operating cash cycle. Understanding the components of the operating cash cycle, and how they relate to the long-term financing needs of the business, is a critical part of managing the business.

See Chapter 6.

Operating lease

A mechanism for acquiring the right to use an asset without the intention to purchase it outright or under hire purchase, and so on.

Operating profit

Profit derived from operations. Sometimes used synonymously with **net profit** (net income).

Ordinary share

The US term is common stock. See **shareholders**.

Overtrading

When a profitable business runs short of cash because it is growing too quickly and cannot finance its growth. Growing businesses need to finance their growth. The faster they grow the more cash they need to oil the wheels, and that cash has to come from somewhere. The most obvious sources are **profits** (internal finance), debt or more equity.

See Chapter 6.

Partnership

A form of unincorporated enterprise in which a group of individuals work together in a business and share the **profits** and **losses**. In most forms of partnership the partners do not have the benefit of limited liability, so they are personally liable for the debts of the business. So why would anyone bother? Sometimes there is no choice and individuals are obliged to form partnerships either by law or by industry regulation (for example, accounting and law). Others choose to remain partnerships and benefit from administrative economies (for example, they do not need an audit) and a degree of secrecy not permitted in limited companies (for example, partnerships do not have to publish **accounts**).

In recent years partnerships have been allowed to become limited liability partnerships (LLPs). This offers some of the tax advantages of being in a partnership and some limits to the liability of the partners for each other's actions, along with an obligation to publish accounts. Many have been prepared to pay the price, and this form of incorporation has proved popular for start-ups.

Personal agenda

In addressing the personal issues at the heart of a growing business it is imperative to recognise any conflicting roles. Each role – whether director, **shareholder**, manager, employee, spouse, friend or parent – involves a set of potentially conflicting tasks and objectives. **Entrepreneurs** need to know what hat to wear and when. When times get tough (which they will) they need to know which set of objectives takes priority or they will be in a weak position compared with other stakeholders, who either have a simpler set of objectives or have simply worked out where their priorities lie.

Preferred or preference shares

The US term is preferred or preference stock. See **shareholders**. See Chapter 6.

Price/earnings ratio

The market price of a share divided by the **earnings per share**. Applied backwards, the price/earnings (P/E) ratio is often used to value a business that is to be sold: a company looking to estimate its own value finds the P/E ratio of a similar business that has either been sold recently or is listed on a stock market and applies it to its own profits. Although less scientific than other valuation techniques (such as **discounted cash flow**), the P/E ratio is simple to apply and is commonly used. When private companies take the P/E ratio of a **listed company** in the same industry and apply it to themselves they need to apply a discount to account for the fact that privately held shares are less valuable than listed shares because they are less liquid.

Private equity

Investment in the equity of a private company (as opposed to a **listed company**, unless the effect is to take the company private), made by an investment fund or institution. Private equity investment by an investment fund or institution in early-stage businesses is commonly called **venture capital**. (See **Business angel**.)
See Chapter 6.

Product life cycle

Organisations have life cycles (see growth models in Chapter 2) and industries have life cycles (see Chapter 3). Products do too.

Profit

Often called income in the US. Profit is one of the most important, yet most misunderstood, concepts in business. At its simplest, it is what is left over from sales (revenue) after costs have been deducted:

■ **net profit** is what is left over after all costs (except tax) have been deducted;

■ **gross profit** is calculated by deducting only those costs directly related to the sale, that is, not deducting overheads or back-office costs.

Other common labels include:

■ net profit before tax (PBT);
■ earnings before income tax depreciation and amortisation (**EBITDA**).

See Chapter 5.

Profit and loss account

Or income statement. One of the most important components of a set of **accounts**. The profit and loss account summarises the financial performance of the business during the period of time under review (usually a year), showing the revenue earned from sales, the costs of goods sold, other expenses and continuing costs, and the resulting profit or loss made during the period.

Quick ratio

Another popular measure of **liquidity**. It is similar to the **current ratio**, but ignores stock, thus giving a clearer picture of a business's ability to meet its **current liabilities**.
See Chapter 5.

Retained profits

An entry on the **balance sheet** indicating the **cumulative** profit retained in the business (that is, the aggregate of profits minus **dividends** paid each year).

Retirement

The least noticed of the big three Rs: recruitment, redundancy and retirement. The concept of retirement is at last being rethought. In Europe it is often assumed that this is because of age-discrimination legislation, but in reality it is because of fundamental economic and demographic changes that affect all Western economies, including the US, which has not been subject to the same regulatory pressure. For many people retirement is not financially attractive; they are also living longer than earlier generations. Businesses with ambitions for growth are beginning to find roles for older employees, taking advantage of their experience and contacts. Employees beyond the traditional age of retirement know more and need less and are thus a potentially valuable resource.

Return on capital employed (ROCE)

Or return on invested capital (ROIC). A commonly used ratio in financial analysis that gives some indication of the relative profitability of a business from the business's point of view. Usually calculated as profit before tax and interest/total assets minus current liabilities. Note that there are many other definitions.

Return on equity (ROE)

Or return on shareholders' funds (ROSF). A commonly used ratio in financial analysis that gives some indication of the relative profitability of a business from the shareholders' point of view. Usually calculated as profit after tax and interest/shareholders funds. Note that there are many other definitions. (See **return on capital employed.**)

Revenue

US accounting term for sales, **turnover** or income.

Revenue expenditure

Short-term expenditure that is written off to the **profit and loss account** (income statement) each year. It has nothing to do with **revenue.** (See **capital expenditure.**)

Share capital and share premium account

In the **balance sheet**, share capital (common stock) represents the nominal value of the shares in the business purchased by the original **shareholders** (stockholders). If they paid a premium on the nominal value of their shares, the difference appears in the share premium account (capital surplus or additional paid-in capital in the US).

Shareholders

Often, though not always, called stockholders in the US. In theory they are the owners of a business – though in big **listed companies** they tend to behave more like the owners of **capital**, as if the share is what they own rather than the business. There are two main types of shareholders:

- Ordinary shareholders share in the **profits** and **losses** and have voting rights. They may receive income in the form of **dividends**, but not until interest has been paid to **debt holders** and only if the business can afford to distribute cash, which in a rapidly growing business is often not the case.

- Preferred or preference shareholders come in many forms depending on the business, but essentially they have rights not available to ordinary shareholders, including the right to receive dividends and capital distributions before the ordinary shareholders. They generally do not have voting rights, though preferred ordinary shareholders may do. Preferred shares are often used as part of financing mechanisms provided by venture capitalists. ("Preferred" and "preference" are usually used interchangeably, though sometimes preference is used to describe a share or stock that is junior in terms of rights to a preferred one.)

See Chapter 6.

Shareholders' equity

See **shareholders' funds**.

Shareholders' funds

Sometimes shareholders' equity or equity account in the US. The shareholders' financial interest in a business (this is not the same as the value of the business). The amount can be calculated either by working out the business's net assets, or by adding together the **share capital, share premium account, retained profits** and other distributable reserves.

Share or stock options

The right to buy shares (stocks in the US) in a company at a predetermined price regardless of the actual value of the shares at the time the options are exercised. Incentive schemes for directors often include options.
See Chapter 7.

SME

Short for small and medium-sized enterprise, variously defined by different agencies.

Sole trader

Where many businesses start – as unincorporated entities in which it is impossible to distinguish the business from its owner.

Staff promotion

One of the most misunderstood and mishandled resourcing processes. People who are good at their current job may not be good at a job higher up; and people who are bad at their current job may do well at a higher level (though, of course, they will not get the opportunity to show this).

Stock

There are many meanings. Some are as follows:

■ On the **balance sheet** in the UK, it refers to goods bought for resale or components bought for assembly. In a manufacturing business, it can also refer to the amount of work in progress and finished goods waiting for sale, and thus includes direct labour costs and other direct costs as well as materials. In the US this is called inventory.

■ In the US it is a common term for shares.

■ In the UK it can mean the same as bond, a tradable form of debt as opposed to a share.

Strategy

A word used by those purporting to know a lot about businesses but who might struggle to define it clearly. For some, business strategy is almost synonymous with management and gets confused with tactics. For others, it is all about formal ways of thinking about the big picture and putting together grand plans to get there. Businesses ambitious about growth stand a better chance of achieving it if they take business strategy, however defined, seriously. Perhaps the most succinct definition is given by Gerry Johnson and Kevan Scholes:[3]

> *Strategy is the direction and scope of an organisation over the long term: which achieves advantage for the organisation through its configuration of resources within a challenging environment, to meet the needs of markets and to fulfil stakeholder expectations.*

See Chapters 3 and 4.

Subsidiary company

When one business owns the whole of another business, or has effective control of it, the latter business is a subsidiary of the former. (See **consolidated statement**.)

Succession

One of those processes that most businesses give little thought to until it is too late. In **family businesses**, for example, it is easy to see that succession (or rather transfer from one generation to another) is a matter of corporate life or death (the majority of family businesses do not survive to the third generation). But for any owner-manager the issues can be just as serious. In a business that is dependent on its owner, succession planning is essential if the owner wants to hand it on or sell it and extract some sort of value.

See Chapter 7.

Sustainable growth

Many profitable businesses get into trouble because they grow too quickly, or rather because their managers worry too much about getting in new business and not enough about generating cash quickly enough to pay the bills. A growing business consumes a lot more cash than is often anticipated, and that cash has to come from somewhere. If the business does not generate the cash, it will have to come from outside.

See Chapter 6.

Tax

Whatever your views about tax, two principles are worth keeping in mind:

- Saving tax is rarely the prime objective of a business, so sensible managers determine what the business objectives are and then establish the most tax-effective way of delivering them, not the other way round.

- The tax authorities will be ever watchful. Once lost, their trust is hard to regain.

Team

Simply putting a group of people together and telling them they are a team is likely to result in the sum of the efforts of the individual members being less than if you had left them alone in the first place. Without attention to the team itself, a group of people – particularly ambitious managers – are likely to tread on each other's toes. Team construction and management takes time, effort and money. What is important is that there is a good reason for forming a team in the first place, that it is put together intelligently and managed well.

The enormous range of tasks that need to be done in a growing business means many **entrepreneurs** are in effect teams rather than individuals. Indeed, there is evidence to suggest that businesses founded by teams of individuals grow faster than those founded by individuals. (See **management team**.)
See Chapter 7.

Trade sale

When a business is sold to another business rather than to a group of financial investors. A business for sale is usually worth more to a trade buyer in the same industry than to anyone else because such a buyer is likely to be able to achieve savings by eliminating double costs, and because it is likely to understand the industry well.

Turnover

Sales revenue. The top line in the **profit and loss account** (income statement) in the financial statements. Also called income or revenue.

Valuation

In theory, the value of a **listed company** is the price its shares sell for on the stockmarket, although a potential buyer of the whole company will usually have to pay more to persuade sufficient numbers of **shareholders** to sell. Valuing a private company is more difficult. Where a value needs to be determined other than through negotiation, the process should be conducted by an agreed specialist who will, in the case of a sale of a minority shareholding, put a lower value on the share price than if the whole company is sold. This can result in unhappiness on the part of those wanting to untangle their involvement in a business. Otherwise, it is generally worth remembering that something is worth what someone else is prepared to pay for it – no more, no less.

Venture capital

Private equity firms that specialise in investing in high-growth early-stage companies are called venture capitalists. They look for high returns and are prepared to take high risks. They invest money they raise from investors in a portfolio of businesses that they hope will grow rapidly. Venture capitalists aim to realise their investments in a short time (around five years), usually by selling the investments on or refinancing them in some way, keeping some of the gains themselves and distributing the rest among the investing partners.

See Chapter 6.

Weighted average cost of capital

Or WACC, the average return required by investors in a business. If a business is to succeed, in the long run its profits must exceed the cost of capital. Working out WACC involves calculating the cost of the equity and taking the actual average interest rate on the debt; these two elements are then weighted according to the proportion of equity and debt in the total capital.

Working capital

The financial resources tied up in the day-to-day operation of a business, or the money tied up in goods and services that have been, or are waiting to be, made or sold. The bigger the business the more money needs to be tied up in working capital. The need to finance working capital often puts unexpected financial pressure on a growing business.

See Chapter 6.

Acknowledgements

AS IS EVIDENT on every page of this book, a huge debt is owed to a wide range of previous thinkers and writers. Where possible acknowledgements have been made directly in the text or in the endnotes. If any have been missed, I apologise.

Particular thanks are owed to my fellow faculty members at London Business School from whom I have learned an enormous amount – particularly Keith Willey, with whom I have taught a course called Managing the Growing Business for over 15 years, Andy Phillipps, with whom I have taught entrepreneurship, and John Bates, without whom I would not have been at LBS at all.

I would also like to acknowledge the contributions of former colleagues at BDO, particularly Iain Henderson and Don Williams in London and Maria Karalis in New York.

Lastly, I would like to thank my wife, with whom I have shared this book on too many family holidays.

Notes and further reading

Notes

2 Stages of growth

1   Kotter, J., *Leading Change*, Harvard Business School Press, 1996.
2   Newman, J., "Leadership and Management", *Journal of Business Growth and Profitability*, 1997.
3   Greiner, L., "Evolution and Revolution as Organisations Grow", *Harvard Business Review*, 1972.
4   Churchill, N. and V. Lewis, *Five Stages of Small Business Growth*, Harvard Business School Press, 1983.
5   Adizes, I., *Managing Corporate Lifecycles*, revised edition, Prentice Hall Press, 1999.
6   Flamholtz, G. and Y. Randle, *Growing Pains: Transitioning from an Entrepreneurship to a Professionally Managed Firm*, Jossey Bass, 2000.
7   Baghai, M., S. Coley and D. White, *The Alchemy of Growth: Practical Insights for Building the Enduring Enterprise*, Basic Books, 2000.
8   Levie, J. and B. Lichtenstein, "A Terminal Assessment of Stages Theory: Introducing a Dynamic States Approach to Entrepreneurship", *Entrepreneurship Theory and Practice*, 2010.
9   Phelps, R., R. Adams and J. Bessant, "Life Cycles of Growing Organisations: A Review with Implications for Knowledge and Learning", *International Journal of Management Reviews*, 2007.
10 Sull, D., *The Upside of Turbulence: Seizing Opportunity in an Uncertain World*, Collins Business, 2009.

3 Growth enablers and drivers

1   Bhidé, A., "The Questions Every Entrepreneur Must Answer", *Harvard Business Review*, 1996.

2   Champion, D. and N. Carr, "Starting Up in High Gear: An Interview with Venture Capitalist Vinod Khosla", *Harvard Business Review*, July 2000.

3   Mulcahy, D., "Six Myths About Venture Capitalists", *Harvard Business Review*, May 2013.

4   Barker, E., "Start With Nothing", *Inc. Magazine*, February 2002.

5   Ulwick, A., "Turn Customer Input into Innovation", *Harvard Business Review*, January 2002.

6   Steinbeck, J., *East of Eden*, Heinemann, 1952.

7   Quoted in Bhidé, A., *The Origin and Evolution of New Businesses*, Oxford University Press, 2000.

8   Moore, G., *Crossing the Chasm: Marketing and Selling Technology Products to Mainstream Customers*, HarperBusiness, 1991. There have been various editions and revisions.

9   Prahalad, C. K. and G. Hamel, "The Core Competence of the Organisation", *Harvard Business Review*, 1990.

10   Zook, C. and J. Allen, *Profit from the Core: Growth Strategy in an Era of Turbulence*, Harvard Business School Press, 2001.

11   Zook, C., *Beyond the Core: Expand Your Market Without Abandoning Your Roots*, Harvard Business School Press, 2003.

12   Ansoff, I., "Strategies for Diversification", *Harvard Business Review*, September 1957.

13   Porter, M. E., *Competitive Strategy: Techniques for Analyzing Industries and Competitors*, The Free Press, 1980.

14   Brandenburger, A. and B. Nalebuff, *Co-Opetition*, Currency Doubleday, 1996.

15   Stangler, D., "The Economic Future Just Happened", Ewing Marion Kauffman Foundation, June 2009.

16   Quoted by Handy, C., in *The New Alchemists*, Hutchinson, 1999.

17   Stangler, op. cit.

18   Field, A., "The Most Technologically Progressive Decade of the Century", *American Economic Review*, 2003.

19   Drofial, A. and E. Garnsey, *The Cambridge High Tech Cluster*, Institute for Manufacturing, Cambridge University, 2009.

20   Quelch, J. and K. Jocz, "How to Market in a Downturn", *Harvard Business Review*, April 2009.

21   Quelch, J. and K. Jocz, "Managing in a Downturn", in a supplement "Keeping a Keen Eye on Consumer Behaviour", *Financial Times*, February 2009.

4 Growth barriers

1 Packard, D., *The HP Way: How Bill Hewlett and I Built Our Company*, HarperBusiness, 1995.
2 Newlands, M., "Shocker! Entrepreneurs Often Are Not CEO Material", *Entrepreneur*, May 2015.
3 Tobak, S., "Why Entrepreneurs Make Terrible CEOs", *Inc. Magazine*, 2013.
4 Hamm, J., "Why Entrepreneurs Don't Scale", *Harvard Business Review*, December 2002.
5 Galbraith, J. K., *The New Industrial State*, Hamish Hamilton, 1967.
6 Wasserman, N., "The Founder's Dilemma", *Harvard Business Review*, February 2008.
7 Katzenbach, J. R. and D. K. Smith, *The Wisdom of Teams: Creating the High-Performance Organization*, HarperBusiness, 1994.
8 Vermeulen, F., P. Puranam and R. Gulati, "Change for Change's Sake", *Harvard Business Review*, June 2010.
9 Porter, M. E., "What Is Strategy?", *Harvard Business Review*, November 1996.

5 Measuring and describing growth

1 Simons, R., "How Risky Is Your Company?", *Harvard Business Review*, May 1999.

6 Financing growth

1 "The Walmart You Don't Know", *Fast Company*, December 2003.
2 Churchill, N. and J. Mullins, "How Fast Can your Company Afford to Grow?", *Harvard Business Review*, May 2001.

7 People and growth

1 Kaplan, R. and D. Norton, "Using the Balanced Scorecard as a Strategic Management System", *Harvard Business Review*, January 1996; and *The Balanced Scorecard: translating strategy into action*, Harvard Business School Press, 1996.
2 Katzenbach and Smith, *The Wisdom of Teams*, op. cit.
3 Crampton, S., J. Hodge and J. Mishra, "The Informal Communication Network: Factors Influencing Grapevine Activity", *Public Personnel Management*, 1998.

8 Different types of growth

1   Harding, D. and S. Rovit, "Building Deals on Bedrock", *Harvard Business Review*, January 2004.
2   Mitchell, A. and S. Hill, "The Great Mergers and Acquisitions Gamble", *The Ashridge Journal 360°*, autumn 2004.
3   Rosabeth Moss Kanter blog, June 1st 2010.
4   Capron, L. and W. Mitchell, "Finding the Right Path", *Harvard Business Review*, July 2010.

9 The future of growth

1   Baghai, Coley and White, *The Alchemy of Growth*, op. cit.
2   Coase, R., "The Nature of the Firm", *Economica*, Vol. 4, Issue 16, Blackwell Publishing, 1937.
3   Downes, L. and C. Mui, *Unleashing the Killer App: Digital Strategies for Market Dominance*, Harvard Business School Press, 1998.
4   Schumacher, E. F., *Small is Beautiful: a study of economics as if people mattered*, Blond & Briggs, 1973.
5   Hamel, G., "Moon Shots For Management", *Harvard Business Review*, February 2009.
6   Adam Smith (1759), *The Theory of Moral Sentiments*, Knud Haakonssen (ed.), Cambridge University Press, 2002.

Glossary

1   Hamel, G. and C. K. Prahalad, *Competing for the Future*, Harvard Business School Press, 1994.
2   Brandenburger and Nalebuff, *Co-Opetition*, op. cit.
3   Johnson, G. and K. Scholes, *Exploring Corporate Strategy*, 7th edition, Financial Times/Prentice Hall, 2006.

Further reading

Barrow, G., L. Burke, D. Clarke and P. Molian, *Growing Your Business: A Handbook for Ambitious Owner-managers*, Routledge, 2008.

Drucker, P., *Innovation and Entrepreneurship*, revised edition, Butterworth-Heinemann, 1994.

Grundy, T., *Breakthrough Strategies for Growth*, Financial Times/Prentice Hall, 1995.

Komisar, R., *The Monk and the Riddle: The Art of Creating a Life While Making a Living*, Harvard Business School Press, 2001.

Merson, R., *Rules are Not Enough: The art of governance in the real world*, Profile Books, 2010.

Mullins, J. and R. Komisar, *Getting to Plan B: Breaking Through to a Better Business Model*, Harvard Business School Press, 2009.

Porter, M. E., *On Competition*, updated edition, Harvard Business School Press, 2008.

Timmons, J. A. and S. Spinelli, *New Venture Creation: Entrepreneurship for the 21st Century*, 8th edition, McGraw-Hill Higher Education, 2008.

Index

Page numbers in *italics* indicate figures; those in **bold** indicate tables.

80:20 rule 119
360-degree assessment 158

A
accountancy firms
  horizons of growth 27–9
  industry consolidation
    116–18
  see also partnerships
accounting policies 103–4, 109,
  122–3
accounts 103, 215–16
  consolidated 224
  notes to 104, 243–4
accounts payable (creditors) 226
accounts receivable (debtors)
  229
accruals accounting 216–17
acquisitions 183
  earn-outs 188
  of new ideas and talent 186–8
  as part of organic growth
    strategies 179–80
  undervalued businesses 184–5

see also management buy-
  outs (MBOs); mergers and
  acquisitions
Active Hotels 147
active inertia 32
Adams, Richard 31
additional paid-in capital 249
Adizes growth model 19–21,
  20
Adizes, Ichak 19
agency businesses 65
airline industry 108
  see also easyJet
Aldi 77
Allen, James 56–7
alliances, strategic 194
Allied Domecq 173
Alternative Investment Market
  217
Alternext 217
amortisation *see* depreciation
angel funding 43, 46, 141–2
angels 222
Ansoff, Igor 57

Ansoff's two-by-two matrix
57–8, 58, 217–18
AOL 191
Apple 84–5, 180
appraisal systems (staff) 158–60
arm's-length transactions 218
articles of association
(incorporation) 218
asset-based finance 131, 135, 233
asset turnover 219
asset values 71
assets
depreciation 107, 229
as security for loans 135
valuation 109, 221
audit report 219
automotive industry 66, 99–101
see also Ford Motor Company

B
bad debt 219
Baghai, Merhdad 27–8, 208
balance sheet 220
balanced scorecard 159
Ballmer, Steve 50
banks 134
see also debt finance
Barker, Emily 46
barriers to growth
external 97–101
internal 80–97
Bass 173
Baylis, Trevor 50
BCG matrix 51–3, 52
BDO Stoy Hayward (now BDO
LLP) 21

Beecham, Sinclair 84
Belbin's team role types 168–70
Ben and Jerry's 174
benchmarking 70, 220
Bentley 100
Bessant, John 31
Bhidé 3D growth model 30–31
Bhidé, Amar 30, 42
Bhutan, Kingdom of 120
BIMBO (buy-in management
buy-out) 189
board of directors 90, 159–60,
220–21
Body Shop 140, 148, 197
bond holders 228
bonds, corporate 136–7, 226
bonus schemes 163–4, 235–6
see also equity-based
incentives (staff)
book value 221
bootstrapping 46, 145
borrowings see debt finance
Boston Consulting Group 51, 221
Boston matrix 221
bottom line 105
Brandenburger, Adam 66, 234
brands and brand management
59
founder personality 32–3,
173–4
franchised businesses 196
premium 75, 99–101
Branson, Richard 149, 152
break-even analysis 110, 221–2
Brown, Gordon 71
Bruce, David 173

Bruce's Breweries 173–4
Bugatti 100
business angel funding 43, 46,
    141–2
business angels 222
business planning 70, 222
    force-field analysis 202–3
    plan contents 204–7
    SWOT analysis 199–202
business risk exposure
    calculator 125–6
business-to-business sector
    international 181
    in a recession 77–8
    working capital finance 128,
    131
business valuations 112–18,
    253–4
Butlins 75–6
buy-in management buy-out
    (BIMBO) 189

C
capital 222–3
capital expenditure 223
capital surplus (US) 249
Capron, Laurence 198
car industry 66, 99–101
    see also Ford Motor Company
cash 223–4
cash accounting 216–17
cash cycle, operating 244
cash flow
    business variations 127–8
    forecasts 224
cash flow lending 135–6

cash flow statement 224
cash management 127–32
CEOs (chief executives)
    and entrepreneurs 82
    role of 90, 168
chairman (of the board) 90
Chandler, Colin 150
change
    and accounting policies 122–3
    business plans 205
    and growth 2–3, 32, 88, 224
    management of 96–7
Chernow, Ronald 167
Chrysler 101
Churchill growth model 15–19,
    38–9
    UK clearing bank application
    24–5
Churchill, Neil 15, 131
co-ordination, central 12
Coase, Ronald 209
Coca-Cola 62
Cohen, Ben 174
Coley, Steve 27–8, 208
collaborative working 12–13
common stock (US) 138, 249
    see also shareholders
communication 158, 175
compensation see remuneration
competitive environment 60–61,
    66, 204
complementors 66
conflict
    founders and venture
    capitalists 143
    management teams 8, 170–71

in young growing business
245
conflicts of interest
managers 119, 189, 241
use of non-executive directors
243
consolidated accounts or
statements 224
consolidator phenomenon
116–18
consumers
recessionary behaviour,
75–7
see also customers
controlling interest 225
convertible debt 137, 139, 225
convertible shares/stock 139
core competence 55, 225–6,
230
see also focus based strategies
corporate bonds 136–7, 226
corporate cholesterol 97
Corporate Governance Code
159–60
corporate life cycle 19–21
corporate structure *see*
organisational structure
corporate venturing 175
Corus 190–91
cost of capital 226
costs
control 108, 129–30
fixed and variable 122–3
transactional 211
Crampton, Suzanne 175
creativity 11, 23

creditors 226
culture 32–3, 174–6, 227
business size 82–3, 213
risk exposure 125–6
cumulative dividends 227
cumulative shares/stock 139
current assets 227
current liabilities 227
current ratio 133, 228
customers
following to new markets
181–2
identifying needs and
opportunities 47–51, 53–4
recession generated consumer
segments 75–7
and suppliers 65–6
CVC Capital Partners 63

D

Daimler–Chrysler merger 101
debentures 136–7, 228
debt factoring 135, 233
debt finance 134–8, 228, 235
debt holders 228
debt management 219
debtors 229
decentralised structures 11, 92–3,
179
decision taking 171–2, 179
delegation 11, 91–2, 172
demographic changes 78
depreciation 107, 229
DIAMOND growth model 21–6,
22, 24, **34–6**
differentiation 99–100

directors 220–21
    appraisal 159–60
    board 90
    incentive schemes 250
    non-executive 243
discounted cash flow (DCF)
    229–30
diversification 23, 55–8, 100, 230
dividends 130, 230–31
Donnellan, Declan 73
Dorfman, Lloyd 63
dotcom boom 72
Downes, Larry 211
Drofiak, Alex 74
due diligence 142, 231
Dyson, James 50

E
e-commerce 79
early adopters 53–4
earnings per share (EPS) 231
easyJet 149–50
EBIT (earnings before interest
    and tax) 231
EBITDA (earnings before
    interest and tax, depreciation
    and amortisation) 107, 231
economic environment 69–78
economies of scale 98–9, 209–11
Edison, Thomas 74
education 78
Eisenhower, Dwight D. 204
employee–dollar ratios 111
employee turnover 112
employees
    appraisal systems 158–60

headcount 30, 110–12
    US businesses 4
    job rotation 182
    overseas business 68
    performance management
        157–62
    promotion 250
    recruitment 65, 156–7
    remuneration and incentives
        151, 161, 162–3, 235–6
            benchmarking 220
            bonus schemes 163–4
            equity-based incentives
                164–7
            management tensions 87
    staff costs 108, 111–12, 156
    surveys and measurement
        120
    training and development
        160–61
empowerment 232
Encyclopaedia Britannica 212
Enterprise Finance Guarantee
    Scheme (UK) 138
entrepreneurs 74, 232
    as managers 8
    and public companies 148–9
    qualities 50
    see also founders
equity-based incentives (staff)
    119, 164–7, 250
equity finance 138–46, 233
estate agencies 65
evolution–revolution cycle of
    change *see* Greiner's five-
    phase growth model

exit routes 62, 146–7, 198
  equity-based incentives (staff)
    166
ExxonMobil 192

F
Facebook 148, 212
factoring 135, 233
family businesses 8, 91, 95–6,
    233
Farmer, Sir Tom 62
FedEx 73–4
Ferrari 99–100
Field, Alexander 73
film industry 28, 234
financial analysis indicators 72
financial statements 103, 215–16
  notes to 104, 243–4
financiers
  angels 141–2, 222
  banks 134
  expectations 43–6
first-mover advantage 60–61
five-forces analysis 63–5, 64, 66
fixed assets 234
Flamholtz, Eric 26
flotation *see* initial public
  offerings (IPO)
focus based strategies 55–8
  see also core competence
force-field analysis 202–3
Ford Motor Company 47–8,
    62–3, 100
founders
  ambitions and motivation
    38–9, 42–3, 204–5

changing roles 81–5
  exit routes 62, 146–7, 198
  personality 173–4
  see also entrepreneurs
franchising 69, 195–7
friends and family 140
Fuhu 178–9

G
Gala Coral 184
Galbraith, J. K. 83, 102
Garnsey, Elisabeth 74
Garson II, Frank 129
Gates, Bill 50
gearing 234–5
General Electric (GE) 13, 74, 77
Germany, governance structures
    90
Gianforte, Greg 46
Gillette 106
globalisation 208
goodwill 118
governance structures 89–90
government support 138
Grant Thornton 9
Greenfield, Jerry 174
Greiner, Larry E. 10, 185
Greiner's five-phase growth
    model 10–15, 12
gross profit 106–7, 235, 247
gross (profit) margin 106, 235
growth
  Adizes model 19–21
  Bhidé model 30–31
  Churchill model 15–19, 38–9
  DIAMOND model 21–6, **34–6**

Greiner model 10–15
horizons of 27–9
hypergrowth 177–9, 235
inorganic 183–94, 198
leadership and management
6–10
management worries 41–2
measurement 16, 29–30, 102–
12, 119–23, 172
organic 179–82, 198
pace of 29, 123–6, 132–3
re-creation 26–9
replication 195–7
shareholder perspectives
112–19
sustainable 26–7, 33, 252
use of models 23–6, 31–3
Growth Enterprise Market
(GEM) 217
growth imperative 37–40
guarantees 137–8
Gulati, Ranjay 97

H
Häagen-Dazs 75
Haji-Ioannou, Stelios 149–50
Hamel, Gary 55, 213–14, 225–6
Hamm, John 82
hand-made products 98–9
happiness 120, 213
Harding, David 183
Hewlett-Packard Development
Company 74
Hill, Simon 186
Hodge, John 175
Hoover, Herbert 71

Hoover, W. H. 50–51
horizons of growth 27–9
human resources strategies
161–2
hypergrowth 177–9, 235

I
IBM 78–9, 210
ideas 48–51
incentives (staff) 151, 163–7,
235–6, 250
income statement 247
incorporation 236
industry life cycles 60–65
inflation 103
information management 125–6
initial public offerings (IPO) 237
advantages and disadvantages
151–3
Body Shop 148–9
easyJet 149–50
Facebook 148
process 153–5
Virgin 149
Innocent Smoothies 62
innovation 25
inorganic growth 183–94, 198
insolvency 237
institutional investors 43–4
intangible assets 58–9, 229, 234,
237
see also brands and brand
management
Intel 66
intellectual property 58–9
interest 237

interest cover 237
interest payments 107
internal growth *see* organic
    growth
internal rate of return (IRR)
    237–8
international expansion 67–9,
    123, 180–81, 210
International Financial
    Reporting Standards (IFRS)
    215–16
internet and business size 211
intrapreneurs 175, 238
inventory (US) 251
invoice discounting 135, 233
ISO 9001 quality standard 220

J
Jabil 94–5
Jobs, Steve 84–5
Jocz, Katherine 76
Johnson, Gerry 251
joint ventures 69, 193–4
junk bonds 137

K
Kanter, Rosabeth Moss 194
Kaplan, Robert 159
Katzenbach, Jon 86, 167
Kellogg 77
key performance indicators
    (KPIs) 172, 238
Khosla, Vinod 45
Kiam, Victor 74
KISS principle 238
Kotter, John 6

Kwik-Fit 62–3

L
Ladbrokes 184
Lampert, Eddie 191
Lastminute.com 152
leadership 168, 239
leadership/management matrix
    6–8, 7
learning organisations 239
LEPEST (PESTLE) analysis 200
leverage (US) 234–5
leveraged investment deals 143
Levie, Jonathan 31
Levy Gee 116
Lewis, Virginia 15
licensing 197
Lichtenstein, Benyamin 31
Lidl 77
limited liability 236
limited liability partnerships
    (LLPs) 245
liquidation 240
liquidity 228, 240
listed companies 240
    equity based incentives (staff)
        166
    founders' experience 147–50
loan capital *see* debt finance
loans, secured bank 135
long-termers (consumer
    segment) 76
losses 240
Loveable Company, The 129
luxury goods 75, 99–101

M

Machiavelli 96

management 7–10
  Greiner's guidelines 14
  systems and processes 11

management accounts 103–4,
  120–21, 216

management buy-ins (MBIs)
  240

management buy-outs (MBOs)
  189–90, 240–41

management hierarchies 91–2

management structure 88

management teams 8, 167,
  241
  conflicts of interest 189, 241
  delegated responsibility
    171–2
  importance of to private
    equity firms and venture
    capitalists 97
  individual priorities 160–61
  meetings 170
  recruitment to 32, 85–7
  roles 168–71
  short-termism 119

market capitalisation 241

market life cycles 60–65

market share 104–5, 180, 210

market size 100

Match.com 76

matrix structures 13, 93–4

McCall, Carolyn 150

McDonald's 181, 192–3, 195

McGlinn, Ian 140

McKinsey 162

measuring growth 16, 29–30,
  102, 119–23, 172
  headcount 110–12
  market share 104–5
  profit 105–10, 246–7
  sales revenue 80–81, 102–4

Mercedes-Benz 101

mergers and acquisitions 123,
  190–92, 241–2
  post-merger integration
    186–8
  see also acquisitions;
    management buy-outs
    (MBOs)

Metcalfe, Julian 84, 167

mezzanine finance 242

Microsoft 66, 78–9, 192

MIFROG (maximum internally
  financed rate of growth) 242

migration 78

minority investments 192–3

Mishra, Jitendra 175

Mitchell, Anthony 186

Mitchell, Will 198

Mitchells & Butlers 173

Moore, Geoffrey 53

Morrisons 104

motivations of founders 38–9,
  42–3, 204–5

Mui, Chunka 211

Mulcahy, Diane 45

Mullins, John 131

N

Nalebuff, Barry 66, 234

Nasser, Jacques 62

naysayers (consumer segment)
76
net current assets 242
net present value (NPV) 243
net profit 107–8, 243, 246
networks 94
new businesses
assessment 120–21
cash management 129–30
equity distribution 165–6
survival rates of 141
New Covent Garden Soup 140,
144–5
Newman, Jeremy 7, 9
NeXT 84
Nextel 191
Nokia 192
non-executive directors 220–21,
243
Norton, David 159
Numerica 116–17
Nypro 94–5

O
operating cash cycle 244
operating leases 244
operating profit 244
opportunities 48–50
optimism 72
ordinary shares 138, 249
see also shareholders
organic growth 179–82, 198
organisational culture 32–3,
174–6, 227
business size 82–3, 213
risk exposure 125–6

organisational structure
as barrier to growth 88–9
and culture 174–5
decentralised structures 92–3
evolution 87
management multilayer
hierarchies 91–2
matrix structures 93–4
networks 94
other people's money (OPM) 140
overdrafts 134–5
overseas expansion 67–9, 123,
180–81, 210
overtrading 131, 132–3, 178, 244
Owlstone 69

P
Packard, David 80
Palmer, Andrew 140, 144
participating shares/stock 139
partnerships 114–18, 245
patents 59
people management 87
performance management
157–62
permabulls (consumer segment)
77
personal agendas 245
see also conflicts of interest
personal guarantees 137–8
personal-service businesses
98–9
personal touch requirement
98–9
PESTLE (LEPEST) analysis 200
pharmaceutical industry 58–9

Phelps, Robert 31
Phillipps, Andy 147
planning cycles 70
political changes 79
Porsche 122
Porter, Michael 63, 99
Pralahad, C. K. 55, 225-6
preferred/preference shares/
    stock 138-9, 249
    see also shareholders
premium brands 75, 99-101
Pret a Manger 68, 84, 98-9, 167,
    181, 192-3, 196
Preussag 184
price/earnings ratio (P/E) 246
pricing strategies 108, 130
private companies
    equity based incentives (staff)
      166
    valuation 113-14
private equity 246
    see also debt finance; venture
      capital
Procter & Gamble (P&G) 77
product life cycles 51-4, 246
product range 53, 119
professional services industry
    114-18, 161
profit 105-10, 246-7
profit and loss account 247
public (listed) companies 240
    equity based incentives (staff)
      166
    founders' experience 147-50
Punch Taverns 173
Puranam, Phanish 97

purchasing power 128-9

Q
quality certification 120, 220
Quelch, John 76
quick ratio 247

R
R&D 61
Rake, Sir Michael 150
Randle, Yvonne 26
re-creation of businesses 26-9
recessions
    business size 69-70
    consumer behaviour 75-7
    entrepreneurship 73-4
    opportunities 75-8
recruitment 156-7
    agencies and advisers 65, 157
remuneration 161, 162-3, 235-6
    benchmarking 220
    bonus schemes 163-4
    equity-based incentives 151,
      164-7
    management tensions 87
replication 195-7
responsibility, delegated 11,
    91-2, 171-2
retained profits 247
retirement 247-8
return on capital employed
    (ROCE) 248
return on equity (ROE) 248
return on invested capital
    (ROIC) *see* return on capital
    employed (ROCE)

return on shareholders' funds (ROSF) *see* return on equity (ROE)
revenue expenditure 248
revenue recognition 103, 104
revenue (US) 80–81, 102–4, 253
revolution *see* Greiner's five-phase growth model
RightNow 46
risks 31, 230
  business risk exposure calculator 125–6
  business valuations 114
  debt fuelled investments 71, 235
  interest rates and debt 134–5, 137
  overseas business 67
  venture capitalists 44–5, 143–4
Rockefeller, John D. 167
Roddick, Anita 148–9
Rogers, Everett 53
Rolfe, Andrew 68, 84
Rovit, Sam 183

S
Safeway 104
Sahlman, William 74
sales revenue 80–81, 102–4, 253
Schlee, Clive 84
Scholes, Kevan 251
Schultz, Howard 196
Schumacher, E. F. 212–13
Sears 191
second-mover advantage 180

service industry 107
  see also professional services industry
share capital 249
share premium account 249
share prices 37, 112–13
share (stock) options 119, 164–7, 250
shareholders 228, 249
  ambitions 47
  classes 138–40
  emphasis on 118–19
shareholders' funds 250
short-termers (consumer segment) 76
Shoval, Nadav 82
Simons, Robert 112, 125–6
simplifiers (consumer segment) 76–7
size, business 61
  big businesses 209–11
  headcount as measurement of 30, 111
  optimum 208
  recessionary effects 69–70
  small businesses 212–14
  technology impact 211–12
Skandia 120
Small Business Administration (US) 138
Smith, Adam 214
Smith, Douglas 86, 167
sociological changes 78
Sock Shop 124–5
sole traders 250
Southwest Airlines 108

Sprint 191
staff *see* employees
staff costs 108, 111–12, 156
stakeholder value 118–19
Stangler, Dane 73
Starbucks 196
start-ups
  assessment 120–21
  cash management 129–30
  equity distribution 165–6
  survival rates of 141
Steinbeck, John 48
stock 251
stockholders (US) *see*
  shareholders
strategic alliances 194
strategic positioning 99–101
strategy 251
structure, organisational
  as barrier to growth 88–9
  and culture 174–5
  decentralised structures
    92–3
  evolution 87
  management multilayer
    hierarchies 91–2
  matrix structures 93–4
  networks 94
subsidiary companies 251
succession planning 9, 252
  growth imperative 40–41
  human resources strategies
    161–2
Sull, Donald 32
supermarkets 67, 77, 104
SWOT analysis 199–202

sympathisers (consumer
  segment) 77
systems and processes,
  introduction of 11

T
tax 107, 252
  equity based incentives (staff)
    165
  interest payments 134
  investment incentives 140, 141
teams 13, 253
  see also management teams
Tech Tour Growth 50 105–6
technological advances 29, 78–9,
  211–12
technology industry 59, 74
telecommunications sector 198
Tesco 104, 128–9
Thomas Cook Global Financial
  Services 129, 184
three up, three down appraisal
  system 158–9
Time Warner 191
timescales 29
Title Research 61, 89, 109
Tobak, Steve 82
too big to fail 213
top-line growth 102
Toyoda, Akio 123
Toyota 123
trade (business) sales 253
training and development
  160–61
transactional costs 211
Travelex 63, 129, 184

turnover 80–81, 102–4, 253

U
Ulwick, Anthony 47
Unilever 174

V
vacuum cleaners 50–51, 60
valuations, business 112–18,
  253–4
values, cultural and individual
  175–6
Vantis 117
venture capital 142–4, 246, 254
  see also debt finance; private
    equity
venture capitalists 44–6
Vermeulen, Freek 97

Village Roadshow 28
Virgin 149, 152
Volkswagen 100

W
Wall Street crash (1929) 71
Walmart 129
Wasserman, Noam 83
weaknesses 72
weighted average cost of capital
  (WACC) 254
White, David 27–8, 208
working capital 131, 254–5

Z
Zaleznik, Abraham 6
Zook, Chris 56–7, 121
Zuckerberg, Mark 148

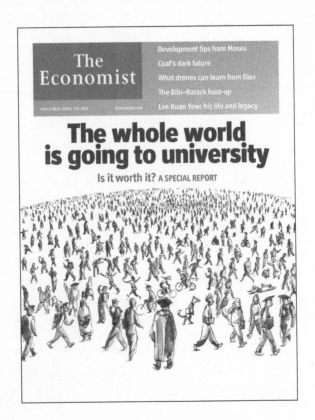

The Economist

Development tips from Moses
Coal's dark future
What drones can learn from flies
The Bibi–Barack bust-up
Lee Kuan Yew: his life and legacy

MARCH 28TH–APRIL 3RD 2015   economist.com

The whole world is going to university

Is it worth it? A SPECIAL REPORT

You've seen the news.
Now discover the story.